"This thoughtful, perceptive book **reminds us that silent places—modest buildings and simple statues as well as noble memorials—often speak loudest in linking us with our past.** These embodiments of our shared national memory are worthy of our deepest respect and our most determined preservation efforts."—Richard Moe, President, National Trust for Historic Preservation

"Join a master teacher on his pilgrimage throughout the Lincoln landscape. . . . Percoco ponders the ongoing meaning of Lincoln with his thoughtful meditations on public sculptures."—Thomas F. Schwartz, Illinois State Historian, Abraham Lincoln Presidential Library and Museum

"Lincoln monuments have become traditional. Tradition is something permanent that reminds the public of something notable. The Lincoln sculptures covered in this book give meaning to life by providing our communities a way to communicate their traditions and beliefs from generation to generation. **James Percoco tells us how these statues represent Lincoln's lasting ideas that commemorate those principles we preserve, honor and cherish.**"—Frank J. Williams, Chief Justice of the Supreme Court of Rhode Island and founding chair of The Lincoln Forum.

"A **uniquely engaging and informative** contribution to our understanding of Lincoln and his memory."—Jean Baker, Goucher College, author of *Mary Todd Lincoln: A Biography*

"Jim Percoco is a wonderful teacher, a fine writer, and **just the right person to take readers with him during his *Summers with Lincoln*"**—Ed Linenthal, Indiana University, author of *Sacred Ground: Americans and Their Battlefields*

"Reminds us how artistic interpretations—even of dated, monumental sculptures of one imperfect, though persevering and empathetic, man—**can enrich and inspire us** to realize our own human potential."—Michael Fowler, University of South Carolina, Aiken

"Readers of James Percoco's **breezy, informative, and entertaining** examination of seven prominent Lincoln monuments may feel an irresistible urge to leap from their chairs and rush to Washington, Chicago, Cincinnati, Newark, and Fort Wayne."—Michael Burlingame, Connecticut College, author of *The Inner World of Abraham Lincoln*

"Percoco's colorful narrative brings alive monuments of Lincoln and . . . **unravels Lincoln the myth, reconciling it with Lincoln the man.**"—Thayer Tolles, Metropolitan Museum of Art

Summers with Lincoln

Summers with Lincoln

LOOKING FOR THE MAN
IN THE MONUMENTS

JAMES A. PERCOCO

FORDHAM UNIVERSITY PRESS
New York   2008

Library of Congress Cataloging-in-Publication Data

Percoco, James A.
  Summers with Lincoln : looking for the man in the monuments / James A. Percoco.—1st ed.
      p.   cm.
  Includes bibliographical references and index.
  ISBN 978-0-8232-2895-9 (cloth)
  1. Lincoln, Abraham, 1809–1865—Monuments.   2. Lincoln, Abraham, 1809–1865—Influence.   3. Lincoln, Abraham, 1809–1865—Anecdotes.   4. Monuments—United States.   5. Historic sites—United States.   6. Sculptors—United States—History.   7. Percoco, James A.—Travel—United States.   8. United States—Description and travel. 9. United States—History, Local.   I. Title.
  E457.6.P47   2008
  973.7092—dc22

                                                          2007048569

Printed in the United States of America
10   09   08   5   4   3   2   1
First edition

Gina, this one is for you

Would I might rouse the Lincoln in you all.

—Vachel Lindsay

For myths are realities, and they themselves open into deeper realms.

—Thomas Merton

CONTENTS

FOREWORD

Harold Holzer

IN JULY 1871, a large crowd gathered inside Oak Ridge Cemetery in Springfield, Illinois, to witness the unveiling of the Lincoln Tomb, at whose base had risen Larkin Goldsmith Mead's newly cast bronze sculpture of Abraham Lincoln as the Emancipator.

As the throng watched in hushed silence, the president's remains, stored for six years in a receiving vault down the hill from the soaring new monument, were solemnly transferred into the tomb. Then the tiny coffins bearing the bodies of Lincoln's late sons, Eddie and Willie, were borne up the slope and placed alongside that of their father. For the many onlookers who had personally known the three Lincolns, all of whose lives had been so tragically cut short, it was a deeply moving experience to watch them being transferred to their final resting place.

But when Lincoln's old friend Richard J. Oglesby, now head of the National Lincoln Monument Association, took the platform to deliver the main address that day, he focused not on the building he had helped erect to protect Lincoln's remains. Instead, he stressed the statue being unveiled at its base to celebrate the sixteenth president for his central role in eradicating American slavery. Here, notably, was an image not of the clean-shaven lawyer-politician who had lived in this city for a quarter of a century, but of the bearded statesman who had made history far away in the nation's, not the state's, capital.

Oglesby no doubt spoke for both Lincoln's local neighbors and his national admirers when he observed of the martyred leader and this latest sculptural tribute, "He has gone to the firmament of Washington, and a new light shines down upon his beloved countrymen from the American constellation. 'Behold the image of the man.'"

For the next six decades, Americans beheld images of the man: bronze and marble tributes, majestic artistic achievements and well-meaning duds alike, erected to adorn public squares, historic sites,

government buildings, museums, schools, and bucolic parks throughout the country. By author James Percoco's own estimate, no fewer
than 106 of them rose from coast to coast. Forty-two of them were
in Illinois alone, thirteen in Pennsylvania, twelve in New York,
eleven in Iowa, ten in California, and nine each in Wisconsin and
Massachusetts.

The political and artistic culture that embraced—and paid for—
these heroic images thrived virtually until the Great Depression.
Public clamor to celebrate Lincoln in public statuary grew so fe-
vered that commissions and unveilings grew likely to stir intense
scrutiny and the occasional public outcry. When Congress authorized $10,000 to hire a young sculptor named Vinnie Ream to create
a heroic marble Lincoln for the Capitol Rotunda, her detractors,
including the president's widow Mary, denounced the choice and
predicted a disastrous result. (The resulting statue, unveiled like
Springfield's in 1871, was not universally acclaimed, but it has remained a Capitol fixture ever since.) Daring experimental efforts—
like George Gray Barnard's impressionistic, irreverent 1917 slab for
Cincinnati—unleashed even more controversy.

Nevertheless, the public demand for these heroic tributes continued insatiably, reaching its apex with the dedication of the Lincoln
Memorial in 1922. The opening of this majestic Washington temple,
with the nineteen-foot-high seated marble statue by Daniel Chester
French that dominates its interior, was attended not only by President Warren G. Harding but also by Lincoln's sole surviving son, former Secretary of War Robert T. Lincoln. The Memorial has remained
a major capital tourist attraction ever since.

In a modern culture whose images are growing ever smaller and
yet more ubiquitous, reduced to the size of postage stamps inside
iPhones and BlackBerries, it is difficult to imagine an era in which
monumental statues captured the attention—and reverence—of
large numbers of Americans. But in the first few generations after
Abraham Lincoln's assassination, cities and states rushed to commission leading sculptors to produce monumental outdoor portrait
sculptures to adorn public parks and other central spaces. Their dedication ceremonies often attracted large throngs of reverential admirers and lured major orators who typically recalled Lincoln's heroism
and called on their contemporaries almost to worship at these newly
installed public shrines. No fewer than fifty thousand Philadelphians

massed in Fairmount on the ninth anniversary of the preliminary Emancipation Proclamation in 1871 to witness the unveiling of Randolph Rogers's ten-foot-high bronze, dedicated "with gratitude for the services of Abraham Lincoln."

Many of these early heroic statues were paid for by private subscription, and in the case of Thomas Ball's now-controversial Emancipation Group in Washington, by funds collected exclusively from the African American community (Congress appropriated $3,000 to erect the base). The dedication of that particular sculpture in 1876 proved one of the central occasions in the entire history of Lincoln memory. President Ulysses S. Grant himself pulled the cord that revealed the bronze showing a kneeling slave rising to freedom beneath Lincoln's benevolent gaze. And the great black leader Frederick Douglass intoned the unforgettable dedication address. To Douglass, the Ball statue would ideally be the first of many such tributes. In honoring Lincoln that day, he exhorted the crowd to "build high his monuments; let them be of the most costly material, of the most cunning workmanship; let their forms be symmetrical, beautiful, and perfect; let their bases be upon solid rocks, and their summits lean against the unchanging blue, overhanging sky, and let them endure forever."

As it turned out, nearly all of these once-revered public statues long endured. But not without encountering some bumpy spots along the road to preservation, restoration, and new appreciation.

Years after its dedication, for example, Ball's statue began, understandably, to embarrass many African Americans. Its depiction of a kneeling slave was humiliating enough; but to show him dressed in rags seemed too much. Not too far away, on the other side of the U.S. Capitol, Lot Flannery's neglected bronze, one of the first ever erected in Lincoln's honor, turned a sickening shade of green, a silent victim of public indifference and neighborhood decline. The story was the same throughout the country: statues oxidizing, passersby doing nothing but passing by, the sculptures' admiring constituencies confined mainly to happily roosting pigeons. In Newark, where Gutzon Borglum had designed a seated Lincoln on a copious bench that long beckoned modern admirers to plant themselves down beside the Great Emancipator for commiseration and photo opportunities, the statue ceased to attract visitors. The park had become too dangerous. Besides, with graffiti littering the sculpture, tourists could no longer take decent pictures. Even the Lincoln Memorial began to show signs of neglect. Its archaic illumination system revealed the statue in less-than-ideal light after sunset, and the black stenciling of Lincoln's greatest words, etched on either side of the statue, began to fade.

The nadir was painfully chronicled in 1984, when photographer George Tice marked the 175th anniversary of Lincoln's birth by publishing a portfolio of depressing pictures of Lincoln's neglected public sculpture. Here were images of a standing bronze in Bunker Hill, Illinois, framed by a nearby gas station; an ill-advised, eroding statue of a top-hatted Lincoln comforting two naked children in Bennington, Vermont; Boston's version of Thomas Ball's Emancipation Group now surrounded by a pizzeria, dry cleaner, and screaming billboards advertising soft-rock radio and Avis rental cars; and worst of all, the site of a once-revered Lincoln statue in Wilkinsburg, Pennsylvania, where nothing but an abandoned granite base was left amidst overgrown weeds. The statue itself had been uprooted.

Then the tide turned again. It is difficult to pinpoint when and why, but in our modern electronic culture, it is surely no surprise that some of the credit belongs to television. In 1993, C-SPAN announced plans to broadcast re-creations of all seven Lincoln-Douglas debates in the very Illinois villages where the Republican and Democratic Senate candidates had battled publicly back in 1858. The decision triggered a sudden avalanche of urban renewal, and in the effort to clean up these sites before their TV debuts, communities in Freeport, Ottawa, and Alton commissioned new Lincoln-Douglas sculptures to adorn each location. Soon, Illinois was installing new Lincoln statuary on all manner of hitherto ignored sites: to mark Lincoln's service in the Black Hawk War, for example, and more recently, to adorn two spots in downtown Springfield.

Gettysburg soon erected a statue of Lincoln, too, planting it on the sidewalk outside the home where the president had slept the night before delivering his most famous speech in 1863—this particular bronze showing Lincoln chatting away with a modern tourist in a cable-knit sweater, transcending not only place but time. Good, bad, and indifferent, these statues succeeded in engaging the public anew. Tourists flocked to the sculptures to admire or be photographed alongside these new images (usually shown life-size these days, and at ground level so eager tourists can pose with them).

Back in Washington, the U.S. Lincoln Bicentennial Commission spearheaded an effort to fund, under the leadership of my co-chairmen, Illinois Senator Dick Durbin and Peoria Congressman Ray LaHood, the restenciling of the faded words of the Gettysburg Address and Second Inaugural inside the Lincoln Memorial. Thomas Ball's once-ostracized Emancipation Group became the central gathering spot for the annual celebrations commemorating emancipation within the District of Columbia.

Moreover, these statues again proved capable of arousing not only admiration and curiosity, but also indignation. In April 2003, the onetime Confederate capital of Richmond unveiled a statue of Lincoln and his son Tad—shown yet again on an irresistibly inviting bench that left plenty of room to accommodate photo-happy visitors. It was installed behind the old Tredegar Iron Works (now a Civil War Museum and historic site) that had served during the Civil War as the major manufacturer of armaments designed to kill Lincoln's soldiers. For some local residents—Sons of Confederate Veterans and their friends—this was apparently too much, too soon. Though the project had been conceived as a gesture of reconciliation—it had, after all, been 128 years since Lincoln and Tad had walked through the conquered city in the final days before Lee's surrender at Appomattox— some people in the community objected. Loudly.

I was privileged to attend the dedication day ceremonies and to speak on behalf of the historical community. It had been ten years since my book on the Lincoln-Douglas debates had aroused the interest of C-SPAN, whose broadcast plans in turn inspired the re-created debates, which happily led to the Lincoln sculpture boom in Illinois. The event in Richmond would surely bring the resurgence to new levels.

It did—but somehow, not as I had imagined. As I took my place on the dais on a hot, sun-drenched spring day, I found myself seated between the descendant of a Richmond slave and former Virginia Governor L. Douglas Wilder, the state's first—and so far, only— African American chief executive. Could there be a more inspiring demonstration of how far Virginia society had come in a century and a quarter? But not everyone shared my enthusiasm for this symbolism.

As I rose to give my talk, a small one-propeller aircraft buzzed overhead, dragging behind its tail a long streamer marked with the

words John Wilkes Booth had shouted from the stage of Ford's Theatre after shooting Abraham Lincoln: "*Sic Semper Tyrannis*" (Thus
Ever to Tyrants). When the lady who could remember her grand-
mother speak of her enslavement followed to the platform, demon-
strators in the front rows of spectators shed their jackets and turned
their backs to reveal T-shirts emblazoned with the message, "Booth
was right." As the poor woman tried to share her memories of a person who had actually suffered in bondage, the sound of rebel yells
could be heard from protestors in the hills beyond. We had come a
long way. But apparently not far enough.

Still, there were two distinct ways of reflecting on the events that
day in Richmond. One was to rue the intolerance that still ruled so
many hearts. The other was—perhaps guiltily, for this student of iconography and American memory—to cheer the renaissance of public
Lincoln sculpture and celebrate its renewed ability to both inspire
and irritate. Paintings and photography could still trigger protests.
Television bloopers might trigger the ire of professional censors. But
there was still nothing like public sculpture to arouse admiration, indignation, and just plain attention. We had indeed come full cycle,
and once again public sculpture was at the forefront. What was old
was new again.

That is why this is an absolutely perfect moment for my friend Jim
Percoco to publish this riveting, uplifting account of his personal and
professional journey not only to view the venerable classics of Lincoln
sculpture, but also to engage young Americans—his students—by introducing them to these monuments as well.

We all remember our unforgettable encounters with great teachers. In my own case, I was lucky enough to have a fifth-grade teacher
named Henrietta Janke who encouraged my early interest in Lincoln—and offered praise enough to offset indifference by subsequent
"educators." Jim Percoco's students are luckier than most. They had
a committed, scholarly, adventurous educator who not only shared
his enthusiasm, but took it—and them—on the road for firsthand, up
close, and personal examinations of the sculptures themselves and
the cities and towns that had commissioned them. He not only offered them his interpretations and historical insights—all of which
adorn this volume—but also asked them provocative questions that
elicited memorable responses. Such exchanges revealed these sculptures, and their young viewers, in surprising new ways.

The result is a narrative of unusually compelling variety and substance. Part iconographical history and part travelogue, it allows modern readers again to understand—to feel—the power of these silent monuments to our greatest president, and to comprehend the reverence that inspired his countrymen to finance them, search for the best artists, and invite the greatest speakers to dedicate them. Moreover, it provides old hands like me, who tend to take these works of art for granted and assume their pride of place, to see them anew through the eyes of others.

If there is indeed an ongoing renaissance in the tradition of public statuary, then this book is destined to be one of its essential bibles. To see the heroic Lincoln as others saw and honored him, and to experience the confrontation of modern young viewers with these timeless results, is to appreciate Lincoln's reputation with fresh eyes, then and now, and measure his enduring impact on our culture.

At one point, this pied-piper teacher leads his flock toward a particular statue, ever curious, ever enthusiastic, and confides, "As we cross the street, Lincoln looks ready for us." As this book demonstrates so capably, Lincoln remains ever ready. It takes many villages, and one tireless and creative teacher, to remind us.

PREFACE

SINCE JUNE 2002, the last day of school has always played out the same way for me. The hallways are empty of students, and the debris they have scattered marks their frenetic exit. I tidy up my room for the last time, putting away in a cupboard a small replica of Daniel Chester French's seated statue of Abraham Lincoln. It was a gift from students. In ten weeks I will see this Lincoln up again on my desk as a talisman for the next school year.

Summer beckons with relaxation and renewal. But for the last four summers, while most folks dived into the neighborhood pool or hit the beach, I have taken a different kind of plunge and hit an unusual sort of trail: a Lincoln adventure.

It goes back, I suppose, in part, to being raised Catholic and taught in Catholic schools surrounded by statues of saints and other religious figures. When I was seven, my father took me to the New York World's Fair. I insisted that the first place we visit was the Vatican Pavilion. My quest at that tender age was to look at Michelangelo's *Pietà*, that classic sculpture from St. Peter's Cathedral. I looked—did I ever look. Time and again I stood in awe on the moving walkway that brought us into a dimly lit blue room, with sparkling lights on the ceiling, where Michelangelo's masterpiece was bathed in the most magnificent light. I remember not wanting to leave. The years of looking at a small replica in my school hallway and at color photographs on the bulletin board now came full circle in reality. I was overwhelmed. In 1972, when a crazed man attacked the *Pietà* in the Vatican and shattered part of Mary's face and hands with a sledgehammer, I grieved.

Three years after my trip to the World's Fair, I begged Dad to take me to Gettysburg. I was fascinated by a battlefield map from the 1930s that depicted all kinds of monuments dotting the tour route. I had to see them. On our visit I stared wide-eyed at one of the largest sculpture gardens in America. There was nothing static to me about a bronze or stone infantryman or general on a horse. They spoke to me.

My love of heroic sculpture had been dormant as I went to college, secured a teaching job at a suburban Northern Virginia public high school, got married, and began raising a family. It was not a case of no longer noticing statues—it was just that life had gotten predictable.

Then on a trip to northern New England, driving north along Interstate 91, I was intrigued by a sign to Saint-Gaudens National Historic Site in Cornish, New Hampshire. I remembered somewhere that Saint-Gaudens was a sculptor, and I also recalled seeing pictures of his enigmatic *Adams Memorial.* Learning that the memorial was in Washington, D.C., I decided to pay it a visit in 1988. Before I did, I decided to read the late Burke Wilkinson's biography *Uncommon Clay: The Life and Works of Augustus Saint-Gaudens.* It changed my life and my teaching in more ways than I could ever imagine. The timing was fortuitous. I was asked to team-teach a combined U.S. history and American literature class for high-school juniors part whose focus was to examine American history and literature in the context of fine arts. After reading Wilkinson, I started looking for ways to incorporate monumental public sculpture into my teaching. Two months later, I visited the Saint-Gaudens National Historic Site. There, John Dryfhout, then the site's superintendent, gave me Wilkinson's phone number in Washington, and within a year Wilkinson spoke to my classes, encouraged my independent study of public monuments, and became a friend.

Later a phone call to Chesterwood, French's home and studio, a historic site in Stockbridge, Massachusetts, led me to Michael Richman, an art historian and the editor of the Daniel Chester French Papers who lived in nearby Takoma Park, Maryland. What I wanted from Richman was what was inside his head. He insisted that I read several books, and when we finally met in the living room of his house he insisted that I complete another assignment: he gave me a list of monuments to go look at in Washington and instructed me to report to him after I had done so. A dutiful student, I submitted my homework. He then asked me, "Which ones did you like and why did you like them?"

Stumbling over my words, I tried to give the right answers. I must have done well, for Richman took me under his wing and encouraged my enthusiasm. He has been my mentor ever since, advising, cajoling, challenging, nudging, and training a two-decade-long encounter with American monumental sculpture.

In 1989, I received a National Endowment for the Humanities and Council for Basic Education Fellowship Award for Independent Study in the Humanities. That summer I focused on three prominent sculptors of the American Renaissance: French, Saint-Gaudens, and John Quincy Adams Ward. My study took me to Chesterwood, where I rummaged around the storage barn, looking at some of the more than five hundred plaster models that French's daughter Margaret had preserved. Returning to Cornish, Dryfhout led me on a tour of their storage facilities, sharing Saint-Gaudens's works not on display to the general public. At Dartmouth College's Baker Library I pored over Saint-Gaudens's papers, while Richman granted me access to French's business correspondence and personal letters and Sherry Birk, curator at the American Institute of Architects in Washington, permitted me to see some of the architectural renderings created by Richard Morris Hunt for several of Ward's monuments.

From the grant's shot of energy emerged a high school course based on my summer's experience. I wanted to teach a course that would immerse my students as I had been immersed in rigorous research with a practical application. With a green light from my principal, over a period of eighteen months I created a course called Applied History to help students learn the craft of being a professional historian in a nontraditional way, a glimpse of what a historian does, in part by working as interns at local historic sites, house museums, and history-related agencies. In a combination of public history, museum studies, and historiography, I tried to weave classroom teaching and learning with the hands-on "stuff" of history. My regular U.S. history classes also benefited from this monumental mania as I infused monuments and their particular histories and meanings into the curriculum, sending or taking students into Washington to look at sculpture for both historic as well as aesthetic merit. In the great laboratory of Washington, my students and I would look at the monuments of the city, and the students would then design memorials that would be reviewed by historians, curators, and other professionals.

I realized the dramatic connection between sculpting and teaching. Both are complicated and labor-intensive. Both generate a ton of paperwork. Where a sculptor shapes clay to create works of art, a teacher works with real people, shaping and molding them to become good citizens, stronger of character, developing their minds and hearts. I began to realize that I was becoming a different sculptor of sorts, teaching American history while at the same time trying to change the world, inspiring young people.

At home, life changed, too. Summer vacations or anytime we were on the road we almost always had to include a stop so that I could photograph some statue. Much to my wife's amusement and chagrin, I discovered that AAA travel guides include "Monuments / Memorials" in their indexes. After that, Gina and my daughters, Stephanie and Claire, endured all manner of detours on road trips not previously planned. In the car was my camera, loaded with film and ready to shoot images that I could take back to my students. At home my personal library was filling with biographies of sculptors, catalogues of their works, and long out of date, hard-to-find monument dedications. I filled folders with copies of old newspaper clippings about monuments.

In 1997, at a symposium marking the centennial of Saint-Gaudens's memorial to Robert Gould Shaw and the 54th Massachusetts Volunteer Infantry in Boston, I experienced another epiphany. My first professional conference on monumental sculpture, the symposium made me keenly aware of the field of public memory and how memorials and their meanings often shift over time. There was now something new and important to consider, along with the works of art themselves, that altered my approach to monuments and memorials. I discovered that this aspect of heroic sculpture could work as well in my classrooms as a hook, engaging students to really think about history, construct, meaning, and memory, taking names, dates, and people well beyond mere historical facts, providing them with a dynamic kind of engaging force. Along the way I became a journeyman art and public historian, and, I believe, a better teacher.

In 2002 my focus shifted dramatically to Abraham Lincoln as depicted in public sculpture. I wanted to see and discover for myself, in a more serious way, whether my training and foundation of study had real, academic merit. As a teacher who sets an example, there is nothing that I ask of my students that I don't require of myself—and that includes reading, writing, and rigorous research. I also wanted to demonstrate, in a very public way, that high school teachers are also scholars, slaying the myth that "people who can't, teach." I did not become a teacher by default, and I know very few teachers who did.

From 2002 to 2006 I spent summer vacations studying sculptures of Abraham Lincoln, trying to uncover how his memory is preserved in a handful of the close to two hundred statues of Lincoln that dot the American landscape. Of the more than six hundred statues and memorials to American presidents, according to the Smithsonian Institution Inventory of American Sculpture, almost one-third are dedicated to Abraham Lincoln. Only a few are true masterpieces or possess a history that is singular to the Lincoln story and cultural memory. All date from an era when great civic sculptures were created, the late nineteenth and early twentieth centuries. American painting, art, and architecture flourished during this time, which art historians have called the American Renaissance. These public sculptures to American heroes, including Lincoln, helped define an American identity and a particular vision of the nation in the years after the Civil War.

Other parameters defined my search as well. I wanted to examine only sculptures created by sculptors who were born in the same century as Lincoln and those monuments whose dedication services included Civil War veterans. Created by America's greatest sculptors, the seven statues I chose to include in this narrative also embody distinctive aspects of Lincoln's identity. These seven statues flesh out singular thematic aspects of Lincoln's identity: Great Emancipator, Youthful Visionary, Rough-Hewn Frontier Politician, Statesman, War-Weary Commander in Chief, Meditative Contemplative / Man of Sorrows, and Democratic Icon.

French, Saint-Gaudens, Gutzon Borglum, George Grey Barnard, Thomas Ball, Paul Manship, and James Earle Fraser each attempted to create the ideal Lincoln statue. Unlike the biographer or historian who gets hundreds of pages to tell a story, the sculptor gets one shot. Those sculptors had to capture for all time, in one creation, the embodiment of the figure whose memory they were trying to preserve.

Sculpture is an extremely labor-intensive process requiring multiple steps. The sculptor must work with the client or memorial commission that contracts him. Working out the initial design in small clay sketches called maquettes, the sculptor secures approval from the patron and then moves on to the enlarging process, creating working models of varying sizes in clay and plaster. At the heart of the sculptural process is the modeling of clay. Here is where the sculptor employs the synergy of imagination, intellect, and creativity. The design process takes months or even years. Once the full-scale working model is completed, the artist sends the work to the foundry to be cast, or to a stone carver, where it is pointed up by use of a device called a pointing machine that extracts measurements from the model that are transferred to the stone and then carved.

In the case of the seven Lincoln sculptures I visited, the complete paper trail, photographic inventory, and models exist for only French's and Bacon's. But the process was the same with the works by Saint-Gaudens, Barnard, Fraser, Borglum, and Manship. Some primary records of these artists still survive but remain incomplete. Ball, for instance, had been working out an idea for a monument to celebrate the Emancipation Proclamation long before he was contacted by the Western Sanitary Commission, the eventual patron. It was fortuitous that they were more than satisfied with what they saw with the smaller conception he had cast in bronze.

To understand Lincoln iconography, I read Merrill D. Peterson's *Lincoln in American Memory*, David Blight's *Race and Reunion: The Civil War in American Memory*, and Barry Schwartz's *Abraham Lincoln and the Forge of National Memory*. But I was looking for more. I wanted to touch these works in a personal way to see what these sculptures said to one middle-aged, balding teacher living in the early years of the twenty-first century. For four summers it was a pure joy to be able to climb into my car; poke around archives from the Manuscript Room of the Library of Congress to the Chicago Historical Society to the basement of Harvard's Houghton Library; ramble on to look at statues; and then write about my findings and experience.

However, there was a rub. I had to be careful to avoid hero worship. Lincoln was not a god, but a mortal. As president, he endured his share of criticism from the press, his own cabinet and party, and the military. But right after his assassination the veneration started. He was placed on a pedestal where people could honor his memory, propelled by martyrdom. Joseph Campbell observes, "People reinvent their myth or legend in order to fill a void in their present." Is the Lincoln we know more myth than man? As a flesh-and-blood human being, Lincoln was imperfect. He was susceptible to melancholy, insecure with himself, and sensitive about his background. As a politician, he waffled on slavery. He contended with a difficult relationship with his wife, lost two children to illness, and had an estranged relationship with his oldest son. He could be distant from people. David Herbert Donald argues that Lincoln never really had a good close friend after his roommate of four years, Joshua Speed, got married. Donald claims that what Lincoln needed during his adult life was a "chum." Lincoln, himself, may have been a bit prophetic when he said, "We will be remembered in spite of ourselves."

Americans are not the only people who are drawn to this complex man. David Lloyd George, speaking in London at the July 28, 1920, dedication of a replica of Augustus Saint-Gaudens's *Standing Lincoln* given by the United States in friendship to the British people, said, "In life he was a great American. He is no longer so. He is one of those giant figures, of whom there are very few in history, who lose their nationality in death. They are no longer Greek or Hebrew, British or American; they belong to mankind." Mario Cuomo added long afterward, "Lincoln's humble beginnings as the descendent of immigrants and pioneers made him the natural favorite of the generation of seekers and strugglers who have built this nation and continue to strengthen it. His high intelligence, powerful sense of practicality, elegant speeches and writings, and his general deportment—which created an impression of rock-solid honesty, integrity, and strength wrapped in a charming, soft persona—added to his attractiveness."

I, too, turned out to be one of these "seekers." Like any pilgrim about to venture on a long journey, I planned. I immersed myself in reading about Lincoln. Poring over the works of David Donald, Douglas Wilson, Gabor Boritt, Doris Kearns Goodwin, and others I came to understand how Lincoln is regarded by contemporary biographers and historians, what they like about him and what conclusions they were able to draw from wrestling with some of the more complex aspects of his life. I also read what his contemporaries said about him. I met with such Lincoln scholars as Harold Holzer, Matthew Pinsker, Ronald White, Dan Weinberg, and Frank Williams. In Springfield, Illinois, I visited the only home Lincoln owned and walked where he walked. In Freeport, Illinois, site of one of the Lincoln-Douglas Debates, I came to know George Buss, a Lincoln presenter, and the late Rich Sokup, who interpreted the life of Stephen A. Douglas. I will always relish the moment when, at the site of the debate, they immediately went into character as if I were not there. I attended any Lincoln seminar or lecture I could, particularly intrigued by the work of Allen C. Guelzo on Lincoln and emancipation.

Americans have had mixed feelings about Lincoln statues and what they mean. "You will find monuments to Lincoln all over the states,"

wrote an acquaintance to journalist Carlos Seitz. "The favorite subject is Uncle Abe striking the shackles off of Sambo. . . . All this Lincoln bunk has been built up, and kept alive by the Republican Party,
to perpetuate the party, and it has proven a life saver." What is so
interesting about this letter, probably written in the 1920s, is that the
author implies that Lincoln statues were sprouting up everywhere,
complete with an African American figure as part of the composition.
I uncovered only a handful of these statues in the United States. As
of 2007, too, only four of the former states of the Confederacy are
home to bronze Lincolns. The most recent one, dedicated in April
2003 in Richmond, Virginia, reignited "old wounds," as protestors at
the dedication, some dressed in period costumes, waved Confederate
battle flags and, the *Washington Post* reported, carried signs reading,
"Hitler / Paris 1940. Lincoln / Richmond 1865. Any Questions?"
while a wanted poster held aloft by a small boy bore Lincoln's face
reading, "Wanted: For War Crimes." Flying above the ceremony was
a single-engine plane trailing a banner that read *"Sic Semper Tyrannis* (Thus Always to Tyrants)," the state motto of Virginia and the
words shouted by Lincoln's assassin John Wilkes Booth as he leapt
onto the stage at Ford's Theatre after shooting Lincoln.

From 1867 to 1932 there were three distinct periods of Lincoln
sculptures, depicting Lincoln the emancipator or Lincoln the preserver of the Union and statesman, along with sculptures completed
for the centennial of his birth or shortly thereafter. The first generation of Lincoln statues, erected in the years immediately after his
death, celebrated him as the Great Emancipator. They include
Thomas Ball's (1876), featured in this book; Vinnie Ream Hoxie's
tribute inside the Rotunda of the U.S. Capitol (1871); Randolph Rog-
er's statue in Philadelphia (1870); and Larkin Mead's (1874) sculpture, which graces Lincoln's tomb in Springfield. In each of these,
Lincoln holds a copy of the Emancipation Proclamation and/or the
pen that signed that document. Only one of them, Ball's, includes an
African American figure.

In the second phase, marked by the dedication in Chicago of the
Standing Lincoln (1887) by Saint-Gaudens, there is a shift in Lincoln
monumental memory. Reconstruction had come to an end, African
Americans gradually were forced into second-class citizenship, and
Americans twenty years after Lincoln's assassination began to focus
on his role of savior of the Union. This Lincoln was more comfortable

in a changing social climate. With the emergence of a Jim Crow South, Lincoln as the patron of blacks was no longer needed nor wanted.

The second generation of Lincoln statues belongs to Saint-Gaudens, whose magisterial bronze graces Lincoln Park. French, Borglum, and Barnard's statues are the third generation of sculptures, springing up in the atmosphere generated by the 1909 centennial of Lincoln's birth. Manship's and Fraser's round out the last generation of the sixty-year span, dedicated in the 1930s.

The journey for me needed to be more than just me engaging with the monuments, for teaching and learning have never been solitary acts. I need to share what I have learned. Although I never intended to do it, I always ended up teaching at the foot of these monuments. When I could, I brought my students with me. If none were available I would find new ones, as I did with twelve-year-old Christopher Monte from Hillsborough, New Jersey, who met me with his parents at Fraser's *Lincoln the Mystic* in Jersey City. In Chicago, at the foot of Saint-Gaudens's *Standing Lincoln*, I met a visitor from China, also a teacher, and we not only talked shop but also talked Lincoln. I also tracked down one of my favorite students, who I had not seen in fifteen years, and we met at Borglum's statue of Lincoln in Newark, New Jersey. There was one addition to my summer road trips. During spring break one year I convinced fifteen seniors and their parent chaperones to give up their last holiday of high school and spend it with me on a bus—a Lincoln pilgrimage. On our way to Springfield, we detoured to Cincinnati, Ohio, to see George Grey Barnard's controversial *Lincoln*, where we also met up with fifty members of the Association of Lincoln Presenters, men who find their passion in portraying the sixteenth president in pageants for schools and civic celebrations. We ended that pilgrimage paying homage at Lincoln's Tomb in Oak Ridge Cemetery in Springfield.

Part of the deep joy I felt during this four-year odyssey was in reconnecting with young people. Growing older, and as I began to teach the children of students I taught when I was a novice, I was beginning to think I was losing my touch. A new generation of youngsters walked the halls of West Springfield High School, plugged into iPods, MP3 players, and cell phones. Many of them have heroes that I'm not comfortable with from the arena of popular culture. The worlds of MySpace, Facebook, and YouTube trouble me, as does the culture of full disclosure. My hope was to demonstrate looking at Lincoln as a man of substance, worthy of study, as opposed to individuals who lead seemingly shallow lives. Tapping into Lincoln in this quirky way proved a vehicle where I could reach students differently from the way I had hitherto done.

My students view me as a bit of an oddball or history geek, but they find that charming and genuine. I've been able to laugh with my students as I share my stories of assorted Lincoln adventures. At the same time I've been able to get my students to understand Lincoln better and appreciate the complexity of public memory and Lincoln's place in American and world history. Lincoln, who loved to tinker with new inventions and believed education to be the most important aspect of national life, would, I think, approve of my approach to reaching out to the latest generation.

The chronicle here fittingly begins and ends in summertime and Washington. As much as I discovered Lincoln, I also confirmed myself. Without anticipating it, I forged a unique relationship with Lincoln, the same kind of teacher-student relationship I pride myself in developing with my students.

On a broader level, I learned that people all over America have fashioned similar relations with Lincoln and his monuments. We remember Lincoln as we do because at some level many of us want to emulate the best of his qualities: compassion, resolve, wisdom, perseverance through hard times, and a commitment to a higher ideal, in doing so we can hope to make a difference in our small part of the world by living a Lincolnesque life.

Shortly after his historic 1860 speech at New York City's Cooper Union, where he delivered a crucial speech, Lincoln found himself on a speaking tour of New England. Shuttling by train through Connecticut, Rhode Island, Massachusetts, and New Hampshire, he confided in a traveling companion, John Gulliver, the secret to his success at self-education. He told Gulliver that as a young boy, he would take the object of his study and make sure that he "bounded it North, and bounded it South, and bounded it East and bounded it West" until he understood it. That was my goal on this journey; to bind it as he bounded his interests and understand these sculptures not just as works of civic art. I wanted to know why America venerated Lincoln with more monuments than any other American, what those statues say to us today, and who owns Lincoln's memory.

Saint-Gaudens once said, "Monuments are put up for all ages, while men and nations pass away." It must also be true that as time progresses, the meanings of these monuments must also change. No one is now able to look at the Lincoln Memorial without considering Marian Anderson and Martin Luther King Jr. and how their stories, in that setting, shaped two generations of Americans. While Borglum's *Seated Lincoln* can be interpreted as a relic of the Progressive era, it still draws people who come to sit and pose with a very human President Lincoln. In Fort Wayne, Indiana, *The Hoosier Youth* continues to fill a regional need.

These sculptures are not anachronisms that serve well as roosts for pigeons. They speak to us today, perhaps with different sensibilities from when they were dedicated, but they still speak.

Through my travels I was able to reconcile both aspects of Lincoln, the man and the myth, finding them of equal importance and in doing so confirming my roles as teacher and scholar. It was a very good journey. As with all pilgrims I followed my heart, letting it take me to places never before imagined. I have cherished my summers with Lincoln.

ACKNOWLEDGMENTS

THIS BOOK'S BIRTH has involved not just me but many players. At the outset I would like to thank Michael Richman, editor of the Daniel Chester French Papers, who has shepherded my study of public sculpture for almost two decades. Michael not only took me under his wing as an apprentice art historian, but also trained my eye in the critical understanding of the aesthetic merits of sculpture. He encouraged the project all along and read the manuscript, making valuable suggestions. His help has been indispensable, and I cherish his friendship.

During innumerable "editorial meetings" held at various Northern Virginia coffee shops, biographer James McGrath Morris constantly encouraged my writing, discussed my conclusions, and nudged me along in the way that only a good friend and fellow practitioner of the craft can.

Author Jerry Ellis, upon whose own writing I drew inspiration for this book's concept, always checked in on me, whether he was far afield or at home in Alabama. When I reached several low points in my work, he consistently supported my efforts and helped to fuel my persistence.

Matthew Pinsker, of Dickinson College, read the entire manuscript as well insuring that my material on Abraham Lincoln the man was accurate and that my historiography was appropriate to the subject matter. Youhuru Williams, of Fairfield University, also read the manuscript in its entirety, making cogent suggestions as to the conclusions I drew regarding Lincoln and race. Other scholars who read specific chapters germane to their expertise or made suggestions include Frederick C. Moffatt, professor emeritus of art history at the University of Tennessee; Barry Schwartz, professor emeritus of sociology at the University of Georgia; Kirk Savage, an art historian at the University of Pittsburgh; and Christopher Thomas, an art historian at the University of Victoria, British Columbia. Each of them offered solid criticisms and suggestions that enhance the book. I am also indebted to Scott Sandage of Carnegie Mellon University for providing me essential primary material relative to the story of Oscar Chapman and Marian Anderson's 1939 Easter Concert at the Lincoln Memorial. Of course, I assume responsibility for all conclusions drawn.

I thank Sarah Irvine Belson, dean of the School of Education at American University, who appointed me as History Educator-in-Residence and invited me to join her faculty as an adjunct professor. Robert Griffin, chair of the History Department at American University, granted me permission to teach a course on Lincoln's legacy, where I tried my teaching craft in a different venue and found remarkable success.

Darrel Bigham, professor of history at the University of Southern Indiana, and Rhode Island Supreme Court Chief Justice Frank J. Williams, both members of the Abraham Lincoln Bicentennial Commission, have supported this project from its inception, as has the commission's co-chair, Harold Holzer who so graciously provided the foreword. Jennifer Rosenfeld, deputy director of the commission, has been an enthusiastic supporter, as has Dan Weinberg, proprietor of the Abraham Lincoln Book Shop.

Of great help were librarians and archivists at a number of institutions who fielded my many phone calls, replied to numerous emails, diligently tracked down items they thought might be of interest to me, and provided me access to needed documents: Joan Miller, Wesleyan University Cinema Archive; Sarah Hartwell, Baker Library, Dartmouth College; Maureen O'Rourke, New Jersey Historical Society; Cindy VanHorn, Lincoln Museum; Bruce Brandt, New Jersey Room, Jersey City Public Library; Jennie Rathburn and Rachel Howrath, Houghton Library, Harvard University; Kate Chase, Westport (Connecticut) Historical Society; James Lewis, Charles E. Cummings New Jersey Information Center, Newark Public Library; Kay Peterson, Smithsonian Museum of American History; Wendy Hurlock Baker, Smithsonian Archives of American Art; Karen Spilman and Jonathan Nelson, Dickinson Research Center, National Cowboy and Western Heritage Museum; and Sarah Hutcheon, Schlesinger Library, Radcliffe College. Kim Bauer, former curator of the Henry Horner Lincoln Collection at the Abraham Lincoln Presidential Library in Springfield, Illinois, was always gracious with my requests and provided tremendous help, particularly with the primary material of Robert Lincoln. Robin Borglum Carter, granddaughter of sculptor Gutzon Borglum, graciously let me use photographic images from the Borglum Archives. Andrea Paredes-Herrera of American University always handled my repetitive questions about securing needed primary material via electronic server with great patience and made certain that requested material was always delivered to me in a timely fashion. Her indefatigable assistance was always professional and generous.

The mother-and-daughter team of Sylvia Walsh and Kathleen Smith, congregants of All Souls Bethlehem Church, formerly All Souls Universalist Church in Brooklyn, granted me access to needed primary material to the church, its former pastor Cornelius Greenway, and his relationship with sculptor George Grey Barnard. My conversation with them in their kitchen was warm and engaging.

In the arena of public history I would like to thank B. J. Dunn, Gregory Schwarz, Henry Duffy, and former site superintendent John Dryfhout at Saint-Gaudens National Historic Site, Cornish, New Hampshire, for their interest and support as well as that of Lisa Niven, Executive Director of the Saint-Gardens Memorial. The same holds for Timothy Townsend at Lincoln Home National Historic Site, Springfield, Illinois. At the Smithsonian Institution's National Museum of American Art, Susan Nichols and Christine Hennessey provided important support and interest. Former director Paul Ivory and archivist Wanda Styka, who helped clarify some primary source issues, always encouraged my work at Chesterwood. Filmmaker Paul Sanderson also provided encouragement.

At West Springfield High School, where I have hung my hat since 1980, two principals, Glynn Bates and David Smith, played crucial roles in permitting me and supporting my independent scholarly pursuits of American sculpture and writing; for that I am most grateful. Also in communion with me were my colleagues in the Social Studies Department who remain one of the most professional and intellectual groups of high-school educators I know. Within the mix of my West Springfield family were student teachers Erin Murphy and Bradley Swain, who completed some fact-checking for me and accepted my immersion of them in Lincoln studies. Applied History students Robyn Adams and Cristina Peterson each did a stellar job compiling relative information about Lincoln sculptures from the Smithsonian Institution's Inventory of American Sculpture database.

Priya Chhaya, also a former Applied History student, designed my webpage with terrific care and energy. I am indebted to the numerous students who appear in this book, joining their quirky teacher on a fair share of Lincoln pilgrimages. Tom Parrett, my Applied History parent emeritus, deserves kudos for his steady friendship and support of the way I approach the teaching of history and for continuing to journey with me and my students long after his daughter, Jessie, graduated from West Springfield High School.

Editor Gregory McNamee respected my manuscript with a clear and kind eye. Gratitude is also due to Robert Oppedisano, director of Fordham University Press, who immediately understood the vision I had for this book and permitted me the latitude to see it through. Working with the entire staff at Fordham has been a great pleasure.

Last, but certainly not least, are the three most important women in my life: my wife Gina and my daughters Stephanie and Claire. It was their fortune—or misfortune, depending on the day—to have Abraham Lincoln move into the house with them. They did not ask for his presence; rather, he appeared in all manner of forms from paintings and photographs that line the wall of my den, dozens of Lincoln titles that crowd my bookshelves, and several statues of Lincoln that peer out at them. They understand that Lincoln is here to stay.

LIST OF PHOTOGRAPHS

Summers with Lincoln

Emancipation/Freedmen's Monument (Smithsonian American Art Museum)

1

Charlotte's Seed

Thomas Ball's *Emancipation Group* / *Freedman's Monument* (1876), Washington, D.C.

SUMMER IN WASHINGTON always means the triple H's: heat, haze, and humidity. The surest way to tell summer has arrived in the nation's capital is by the proliferation of ubiquitous corrugated metal fireworks concession stands that populate just about every strip mall parking lot in Northern Virginia, where I live and teach. Graduation was last Tuesday. It is now Sunday, and I am with five of my former Applied History students, all recent graduates, in search of Abraham Lincoln, a mile east of the domed U.S. Capitol. Here in Lincoln Park stands an early monument to Lincoln's memory, Thomas Ball's *Emancipation Group*, also called the *Freedman's Monument*.

My eclectic band of students reflects the growing ethnic diversity of the region and the nation and how multiculturalism is increasingly playing a role in our schools and public life. Enzo's parents are from El Salvador, Dhrupad's parents hail from India, Bryan's dad is the pastor of Kirkwood Presbyterian Church in Springfield, and Leslie's folks are retired military, as are Michelle's. The different backgrounds of my students are not lost on me as we make our way from Northern Virginia across the Potomac River into the District of Columbia. Riding in Clio Car, my self-appointed chariot of time (this, the third incarnation, a cherry red Hyundai Elantra), paying homage to the Muse of History, complete with vanity license plate announcing its presence, I anticipate an engaging experience. It would have been easy for these teenagers, now full-fledged high school graduates, to tell me, their quirky history teacher, to take my Lincoln obsession and go packing. But they don't. Somehow I sense that they have come to appreciate that I am teaching about building bonds that last far beyond the halcyon days of high school. In history we have found a common passion which has led them to eagerly follow the Pied Piper in my soul, which manages to manifest itself on serious road trips. Four months earlier I had led these students and twenty of their peers on a civil-rights pilgrimage to the Deep South. Singing freedom songs such as "Ain't No Body Going to Turn Me Around" and "We Shall Overcome," we walked, in commemoration, from Brown Memorial Chapel across the Edmund Pettus Bridge in Selma, Alabama, retracing the footsteps of those courageous souls who made a difference with their voices and feet in 1965. Those marchers continued the work Lincoln had begun a century earlier. It seemed fitting that our last collective visit should be to a statue that honors Lincoln and arguably his greatest act, emancipation. My students' sensitivity to racial issues today would boggle some of the minds of those involved in the erection of this statue.

I ease Clio Car into a perfect parking space on the edge of the park. It is just after 6:00 p.m., and the heat begins to dissipate. With the drop in temperature, there's now the possibility of us dodging a pesky pop-up thundershower, always a potentiality during a Washington heat wave. Judy Collins's jaunty version of "Hey Nellie, Nellie," a vintage civil rights anthem invoking Lincoln's memory, fills my car with an appropriate theme.

The students are not surprised to see me sporting a Lincoln T-shirt that I picked up at Tinsley's Dry Goods Store on one of my forays to Lincoln's hometown of Springfield, Illinois. In fact, last year I had a running joke with Enzo about historical T-shirts. I picked one up for him, too, and presented it to him one day at the beginning of class. The silkscreen artist, Thomas Trimborn, using pen and ink, depicted a provocative image of the sixteenth president—a composite, based on the last known series of photographs taken of him, in Alexander Gardner's Washington studio in early 1865. Lincoln's cockeyed face in a thoughtful pose, complete with his lazy left eye drifting upward, imparts a warm attitude of the subject. My students responded as I presented it to Enzo with a chorus of, "Now *that's* a cool Lincoln T-shirt."

In some ways, the teens with me are kind of history geeks, like their teacher, and they don't mind talking about things that matter: what makes good history, the civil rights movement, policies of race and slavery, and the tricky ground of public memory. That is why I asked them to give up part of their weekend and join me. I know their comfort levels. The conversation would be inspired and passionate, and my fleeting moments with these young, diverse Americans would conjure up a kind of collective visit to a sacred site.

Historian Nicolaus Mills contends, "We do not visit a memorial to engage in a critique of it. Instead we bring a sense of history with us when we come to a memorial and we expect that as public art, the monument will lead us beyond its own materiality and back in time to the person or event it commemorates."[1] I agree with Mills but take him one step further, for I view visiting public art as an act of deliberate engagement. Public monuments work best when those visiting them leave their experience somehow richer and better informed about the historical moment or person they celebrate. At the same time their experience should also challenge them to consider the meaning imparted by the work of art. I want my students to understand this, and I want to take them back to a time and place where small-scale public sculptures were meant to be visited in a thoughtful manner. The German word for monument, *Denkmal*, literally means "thought object." For the past two decades I have been using "thought objects" to teach American history. They have had a profound impact on my instruction and on my students, making them aware of not only the emotional power of such monuments, but also how that power is constructed, physically as well as metaphorically.

Ball's sculpture was erected in the horse-and-buggy day, when people passed leisurely and not in a whirlwind. Today, most folks zip by Lincoln Park on their way to work at the Capitol, the Supreme Court, and the nearby Congressional Office buildings without even giving a glance to Lincoln and the Freedman. Unlike the monuments on the Mall, like the new National World War II Memorial or the Korean and Vietnam War memorials, which by virtue of their location and design requires active public participation, Ball's sculpture is a throwback to a different era.

Reaching the pedestal that supports the heroic-size Lincoln and Freedman, I open my copy of Thomas Ball's autobiography, *My Threescore Years and Ten*, to the photograph of the sculptor and pass it around to the students. He looks like Rasputin. They laugh at the image of Ball, agreeing with my assessment of his looks. Ball, like many American artists of the mid-nineteenth century, was an expatriate American, born in Massachusetts, worked at his craft, shuttling back and forth between the United States and Italy, establishing an

opulent and luxurious residence and studio, Villa Ball, on the crest of
a hill overlooking Florence. He sought inspiration from the works of
the great Italian sculptors, particularly Michelangelo and Donatello.[2]
"Ball is a man of great talent and versatility—a fine musician, an excellent painter and an admirable modeler," reported *Ballou's Pictorial Drawing Room Companion.*[3] By the time Ball received the
commission for the Freedman's Monument, he was best known for
his heroic equestrian statue of George Washington, dedicated in the
Boston Public Gardens in 1869.

The sculptor learned about Lincoln's assassination while en route
to Munich, and shortly thereafter he began to dabble with some
ideas, "a study, half life size, of the 'Emancipation Group' which had
been impatiently bubbling in my brain ever since receiving those hor-
rible tidings."[4]

Thinking like historians, the students eagerly take up my directive
to spend some serious time looking at Ball's composition and then
weigh in with their assessment. As they take a deeper look at the
sculpture, I hear them talking and making comments about the pose
of the figures, particularly the Freedman, which Ball posed for by
using two mirrors and kneeling down in front of one to capture the
posture he was seeking.[5] They also make observations about the assorted symbols Ball used in his design.

Finished, the students gather around me, wanting to know more
about the sculpture, anticipating a good story. Sometimes the stories
of their creation are as compelling as the monument. These students
have taken to heart one of the tenets I teach, about the construction
of history and historical memory.

We sit in the shade of the trees and I tell the story of Thomas Ball
and his creation to my fellow sojourners. In many ways this story is
so typical of the history of white-black relations in America, a history
with which my students are familiar. Freedmen wanting to honor the
man whom many referred to as "Massa Linkin" or "Father Abraham"
were upstaged by white "do-gooders," the "friends of the freedmen,"
willing to accept the cash donated principally by former members of
the United States Colored Troops, but paternalistically unwilling to
let them participate in the process of who would "determine the
character of the monument." Given the tenor of the times, African
Americans accepted the image, cheering at the dedication as they did

Emancipation/Freedman's Monument (Michael Richman); inset: Thomas
Ball (Archives of American Art)

when the Thirteenth Amendment, abolishing slavery, was approved by Congress on January 31, 1865.[6]

April 14, 1876, eleven years to the day since Lincoln was assassinated, found a large throng gathering at the intersection of East Capitol and Eleventh Streets, waiting for the dedication to commence. Among them were representatives of Washington's diplomatic corps, assuring that Abraham Lincoln belonged to not only America, but also the world at large. The *Baltimore Sun* reported it "the event of the day."

The sun struggled to appear for the 2:00 p.m. dedication as the sky threatened showers. Large numbers of African Americans, "resplendent in all manner of regalia, the Pioneer Corps of Alexandria uniformed in black pants and blue shirts, the Knights of St. Augustine sporting black hats with yellow plumes and blue, sword-ensheathed baldrics," representing twenty different Negro charitable and civic organizations from Washington and Baltimore, assembled in the vicinity of Seventh and K Streets.[7] At noon they headed out on a circuitous route heading down K Street to Seventeenth Street, crossing over to Pennsylvania Avenue through the White House grounds, past the grand and stately Willard Hotel along Pennsylvania Avenue toward the Capitol, where, after a few quick turns, they found themselves on East Capitol Street and headed to Lincoln Park on a direct access to the Capitol. Marching bands were mixed in among the groups. Banners were proudly unfurled. Keynote speaker, orator, and writer Frederick Douglass, the most strident voice for abolition and the rights of African Americans during the nineteenth century, rode in a carriage in the parade not far from his home at 318 A Street. I once drove, as best I could, the procession route in the ever more security-conscious capital, navigating the approximate route. It took more than a half hour to make the drive, which was somewhat less than five miles long, even well after rush hour. Marchers in 1876 completed the loop in two hours.

When the procession arrived, Douglass joined on the dais President Ulysses S. Grant, members of his cabinet, members of Congress, and the Supreme Court. Despite the distinguished company on the rostrum, the day belonged to Douglass and Lincoln.

That November, the contested election between Rutherford B. Hayes and Samuel J. Tilden would effectively end Reconstruction, dashing any hopes that Douglass and the African American community had for future progress. Within a generation Jim Crow would become the ruler in the South, while Douglass fumed at what he saw as a sellout to African Americans in the name of Blue-Gray Reunions. Twenty years later the case of *Plessy vs. Ferguson* would legally codify the doctrine of "separate but equal."

In 1903, the same year Douglass's heir to civil rights concerns, W. E. B. DuBois, published his landmark *Souls of Black Folk*, arguing that the problem of the twentieth century was the color line, fellow sculptor and art critic Lorado Taft called "Ball's conception of Lincoln a lofty one, which he has conveyed in a language intelligible to all. . . . The Lincoln monument is one of the inspired works of American sculpture: a great theme expressed with emotion by an artist of intelligence and sympathy, who felt what he was doing."[8] At best Taft's assessment is a qualifying statement skirting any real criticism of a statue that aesthetically falls short of the mark. Nevertheless, Ball's sculpture is important to consider in the realm of Lincoln public sculpture because of the tale of its creation, Frederick Douglass's complex and intriguing remarks regarding Lincoln's memory at the dedication, and the way the sculptural image suffused and reinforced for several generations the "Great Emancipator" sobriquet. In an episode of art imitating art, the same year, Thomas Edison would glean from Ball's Lincoln statue to conclude his five-minute short *Uncle Tom's Cabin*. In doing so, Edison was the first to integrate Lincoln's image in motion picture, using a facsimile inspired by Ball's monument.[9]

By today's conventions and sensibilities, no sculptor would attempt a composition portraying Lincoln and the Freedman as Ball did. His composition is anachronistic. Art historian Kirk Savage accuses the sculpture of being a "hybrid of allegory and realism" and a "failure to imagine emancipation at its most fundamental level, in the language of the human body and its interaction with other bodies."[10]

The project's stewards—the energetic President James E. Yeatman and fellow commissioner, Unitarian minister, and college president William G. Elliot of the Western Sanitary Commission, headquartered in St. Louis—insured that the undertaking would not fail. During the Civil War, the Sanitary Commission served as a wartime volunteer relief agency responsible for philanthropic endeavors dedicated to alleviating the suffering of troops and thousands of displaced refugees in the Mississippi Valley and the Western theater of the war. By the end of the Civil War, the Sanitary Commission began to focus its energies on caring for black orphans. As a final tribute to the people they had served, the commission undertook sponsorship to see a fitting tribute raised to Lincoln and the Freedman.[11] The plaque affixed to the front of the pedestal of the monument relates the moving story of Charlotte Scott's role in the history of the monument and the seed money she contributed that jump-started the project.

Scott's deep sense of loss and respect for the slain president provided an impetus for the monument's seed money as the first financial contribution. The apocryphal story, most likely comfortable to paternalistic whites and retold on the bronze plaque, tells how Scott, a former slave, employed in 1865 as a washerwoman in Marietta, Ohio, scraped up her first few meager savings—five dollars—upon hearing about the assassination "to build a monument to good Massa Lincoln." However, a deeper look indicates otherwise. Scott really said, "The colored people have lost their best friend on earth. Mr. Lincoln was our best friend and I will give five dollars of my wages toward erecting a monument in his memory."[12] Her owner, William P. Rucker, a pro-Union man who had fled from Virginia to Ohio, freed Charlotte in 1862, but she continued to live with the family. At the Ruckers' urging Scott entrusted the money to Marietta minister C. D. Battelle, who collected other offerings from the black community. "I received her offering," he said, "and gave notice through the press that I would receive other donations and cheerfully do what I could to promote so noble an act."[13] Shortly, news of the grassroots monument movement caught the attention of Brigadier General T. C. H. Smith, commander of the St. Louis garrison. Smith convinced the Western Sanitary Commission president, James E. Yeatman, that this was a worthy project and that the commission should see it through, arguing, "Such a monument would have a history more grand and more touching than any of which we have account."[14] A letter sent from Rucker to Yeatman urged that "every dollar should come from former slaves."[15] Yeatman sent out a call through local newspapers and letters to the white officers of black regiments, soliciting donations. By December 1865, more than $16,200.00 poured in to the St. Louis office.

Not much of this story is conveyed on the plaque. Like all history, the truth can only be found by digging.

My students are impatient with the story. Holding a thoughtful pose, Bryan starts the conversation rolling. "Face it. Scott's gift far exceeds its monetary value," he says emphatically. "Its importance lies in the fact that it represents Scott's own reverence to Lincoln's emancipation of her race. The Western Sanitary Commission's stereotype of Scott into the atypical, uneducated former slave devalues not only her act, but also her humanity." We are on a roll, but I have to remind the students to avoid the temptation to impose our values on those living in the past. While the actions of the Western Sanitary Commission seem paternalistic to us, the sense of their benevolence was genuine.

"Color," Bryan continues, "is not the measuring block of a person's value, a lesson that even today we struggle with in post Civil War, Reconstruction, and Civil Rights Movement America. It is the future that matters." Bryan is onto something nuanced but important. Hope for the future lies within the very spirit that motivated past generations toward change despite fear, violence, and hatred. It is in the past that we find heroes in the faceless thousands who inspire us to continue their work simply by their determination and example. The history of the United States has always looked for the proverbial "better tomorrow" because we yearn for human equality.

Without trying to be an iconoclast, Leslie poses the following. "Okay, Mr. Percoco, blacks weren't allowed to pick the design of the statue they paid for: that just goes to show that the black people could work so hard, but not succeed to the fullest, and not for lack of trying either. It's completely unfair that those without vested interest in the sculpture would be the ones to pick it. What's that fable or whatever . . . about the animals that did not help the mother hen harvest the wheat to make her bread, but they heartlessly ate all of the finished product, while she sat by and watched all of her hard work disappear. Sad. I think its bittersweet irony that in an attempt to make Charlotte's words sound foolish as they thought black dialect should be the white people who distorted her comments appeared the bigger fools." Her peers nod their heads in agreement.

Leslie's sentiments are filled with a sense of prescience as well as a particular kind of intellectual hindsight, the tyranny of present-mindedness, often hard even for adults to overcome when trying to be objective in studying history. I sometimes wonder if objectivity should be left aside when examining our past racial history. That, however, would only spiral down into the blame game. At some point we need to have a true national discussion on race and its long-term place in American history. Perhaps the generation I am speaking with will have the courage to move the conversation forward.

Enzo's eyes, shaded by the brim of his Minnesota Timberwolves cap, the doo-rag beneath it capturing the sweat on his brow, brings a spin to the story. "I see the story of Charlotte Scott differently," he says with a sense of purpose. "The first thing I thought of was one word: 'typical,' because the population and the mindset of folks back then would have thought that since this was a statue of Lincoln freeing the slaves, 'Yes, let's give them *some* sense of importance and a feeling like they actually are making a contribution.' But behind closed doors however they would be the ones running everything. Bottom line, they were still in control no matter what the circumstance and they were the ones calling the shots and pulling the strings. But from the public's vantage point it might have seemed like the African American community was doing a lot of the work for this project. This mentality fits."

Then, pausing and holding his thought in his mind, spinning it around before he speaks, Enzo continues. "The other thing that strikes me is perhaps they never wanted the African Americans to plan the monument and do nothing more than pay for it so they [the Western Sanitary Commission] wouldn't have to."

"That might sound a bit harsh," he says, "but in times when anything was possible and blacks had no rights and were treated as second class citizens, as horrific as it sounds, it just might be true. I think it was methodically planned out and understood by all the key players that the African American community and any former slaves would not take part in anything else except for payment." Ironically, the *Newark Daily Advertiser* reported, "The colored people of the District of Columbia will today unveil the new Lincoln statue in Lincoln Park."

Standing before the statue, we see Ball's attempt to bring the Emancipation Proclamation to life through the metaphor of sculpture, providing a different kind of resonance than the document or the act itself. At the unveiling, the African Americans who participated in the dedication cheered. It was, after all, a celebratory occasion. They had ample reason to cheer, since the African American community shelled out the funds to make the statue a reality. The cheering, a matter of civic pride, was touched perhaps with a sense of some measure of recognition. Frederick Douglass, though, chided the design because "it showed the negro on his knee when a more manly attitude would have been indicative of freedom."[16]

Erecting public monuments in post–Civil War America was just as complex and complicated as it is today. Process always precedes product. Winning or receiving a Lincoln monument commission was a boon to one's career. Other sculptors soon entered the Lincoln monument fray. Within three years of his assassination, sculptor Clark Mills proposed a massive sculpture of epic proportions to Lincoln. A local sculptor, whose studio and foundry stood on nearby Bladensburg Road in Maryland, Mills was best known for the 1853 equestrian statue to Andrew Jackson that guarded the White House from its perch across the street in Lafayette Park and his 1860 mounted sculpture of George Washington riding his steed in Washington Circle. In one of American history's greatest ironies, sculptor Thomas Crawford sent to Mills's foundry from his studio in Italy his plaster version of *Freedom*, designed to crown the dome of the Capitol, where Mills's slave labor cast it in five large separate sections. Mills's proposed Lincoln Monument consisted of a pyramidal structure arrayed with more than two dozen various figures of important statesmen, civic leaders, and Union generals. At the apex of the pyramid sat a figure of Lincoln in the process of signing the Emancipation Proclamation, with allegorical figures of liberty, time, and justice resting against the plinth on which Lincoln sits.[17] Beneath the figures of the period statesmen and civic leaders is a triptych with an allegorical depiction of the story of emancipation. Once again, the black figures are overshadowed by their white deliverers. A stereo photograph sent to potential subscribers included the following inscription, "The first . . . presents the slave in the most abject state, as when brought to this country. Here we behold him nude, deprived of all which tends to elate the heart with any spirit of pride or independence. The second represents a less abject stage. Here he is partly clad, more enlightened, and hence, realizing his bondage, startles with a love of Freedom. The third . . . is the ransomed slave, redeemed from bondage by the blood of Liberty, who, having struck off his shackles, holds them triumphantly aloft. The slave is pictured gratefully bowing at her feet."[18] In our time this reads like patronizing pap, but those who wrote it in 1868 were generous, sincere, and heartfelt. There were, however, objections to Mill's proposed composition, but not because of how it portrayed the freed race. William G. Elliot, writing to Yeatman while vacationing in Florence in November 1869, complained, "I almost wish that the Washington monstrosity would fall through. . . . It will be a stupendous pot-pourri, in honor of everybody and therefore nobody. . . . Pour cold water on it if you can." His concern was more focused on the aesthetics as opposed to the design. "Moreover, Mills had acquired an infamous reputation in the art establishment as a philistine who won popular commissions by pandering to popular taste," opined the *Evening Star*. In the end, Mills's "Washington Folly" failed to materialize.

For Elliot, the failure of the Mills proposal would set in motion the process for the sculpture that stands today in Lincoln Park. In the same letter to Yeatman, an enthused Elliot admits visiting Villa Ball. "Mr. Ball," he wrote, "has a small group, half life size, of Lincoln and a slave, which I like very much. I shall send you a photograph of it. It is in marble and very well executed." In this version the Freedman wears a Phrygian cap lettered with the word "Liberty." Lincoln's right arm and hand, holding a wreath, rest on a kind of national shield bearing the stars and stripes. Eliot continues, "The Negro's chain is broken and the African type is well maintained without overdoing. The likeness of Lincoln is softened, but perfectly correct. Price $2,000.00."[19] Ball, moved by news of Lincoln's death, was inspired to create a fitting tribute to the martyred president.

On a scouting mission to Harvard University once, I was granted permission to see Ball's 1865 model. Past row upon row of old and rare books and manuscripts, stacked like sarcophaguses, I was led to the Lincoln Room, so designated by only by a small typed piece of paper taped awkwardly to the door. A special key was needed for entry. As the heavy metal door pushed aside, my palms sweaty and my adrenaline racing, I prepared to see the Holy Grail. I crossed the portal but was sadly disappointed. Crowded in among all types of Lincoln and Civil War ephemera and rare books and raised off the floor by only a small wooden pallet, stood a bronze and not marble reduction. To study it effectively I had, like the enslaved figure, to get down on my hands and knees. Lincoln's words from the last clause of the Emancipation Proclamation are indeed on the base of the reduction, but part of the clause is missing. Conveniently omitted was the phrase "sincerely believed to be an act of justice, warranted by the Constitution, upon military necessity." Revisionist history is obviously not a new phenomenon.

Two years later, Elliot wrote Ball in Florence, after the commission had agreed to move forward using the sculptor's image. "I received a letter," gushed the sculptor in his autobiography, "from Rev. Mr. Elliot. . . . He had visited my studio and had always pleasantly remembered a small group of Abraham Lincoln and a liberated slave, and that he was one of the committee of the 'Freedmen's Memorial Society,' empowered to select a design for the memorial; requesting me to submit to the committee photographs of the above group, and my terms for furnishing the same in bronze, nine or ten feet high. This I did with alacrity, and a favorable answer came by return mail. They were delighted by the group, and hoped that I would be pleased to accept the amount at their disposal ($17,000). . . . Of course I accepted their offer, for you must remember that every sent of this money was contributed by the freed men and women." By now the story of Charlotte Scott was rock solid, as Ball concluded, "The first five dollars of this fund were brought to the colonel of a negro regiment by a poor negro woman, 'to buy a monument for Mas'r Lincoln.'" After enlarging the model to ten feet, Ball sent the finished product off to Munich, where it was cast in bronze and then shipped to the United States.[20] For such an important commission, Ball set aside only a few pages in his autobiography to discuss this project, leaving his personal record of working on the monument rather thin.

Congress appropriated a site in a neighborhood that was becoming increasingly residential and approved three thousand dollars for the pedestal. Ironically, no one involved in this project mentioned or discussed the connection between the year of the statue's dedication and the nation's centennial celebration. As well intentioned as everyone was, they all missed a great opportunity to draw some deep and reflective parallels.

Interestingly, too, the Commission bypassed what could have been a golden opportunity for race and memory in American history. Initially they selected the diminutive but high-spirited expatriate Harriet Hosmer as their sculptor of first choice, believing that her model of the proposed monument was "the greatest achievement of modern art." Hosmer's composition, reminiscent of Mills's design, consisted of a multitiered memorial. Unlike the memorial Mills proposed Hosmer placed allegorical African Americans figures as a central component to the memorial. Angelic figures representing "mourning Victories," holding reversed trumpets symbolically representing Lincoln's martyrdom, kneel on four pentagonal columns offset from the main structure. Set back from the Victories and elevated on four circular columns are four freestanding figures of African Americans, one figure a seminude slave manacled at the wrist, described by Hosmer as "exposed for sale." Juxtaposed with the slave on the opposite axis is an African American Union soldier at parade rest. The other two figures on the pedestal represent a field hand and a "contraband" slave. This figurative cycle represents the story of African American liberation by their own hands. Beneath them is a bas-relief tribute to the life and death of Lincoln. Above the four freestanding African Americans is a drum that supports the central column on which rests a sarcophagus with a recumbent figure of Lincoln. On the drum is a frieze of thirty-six allegorical female figures representing the states in the Union at the time of the Civil War. The drum also supports four columns, creating a circular temple-like space for the Lincoln sarcophagus, which is capped by a dome. While honoring Lincoln, this memorial also asserts the role of African Americans in securing their own liberation.

It is an interesting approach, given that the Western Sanitary Commission did not permit the financial contributors a say in the design. Savage argues that Hosmer's design envisioned "not only a new African American man, but a new American society in which he can find acceptance. . . . Her decision to install this imagery at the heart of her memorial structure—the black figures occupy the center of the imaginary pyramid of space—was a radical proposal for it insisted on the centrality of the African American subject, when only a short time before that subject was, sculpturally speaking invisible."[21] The *Independent* reported, "It has spoken at last—to a negro woman whom Lincoln emancipated—by Harriet Hosmer the New England artist." Critics were well aware of the implications of the African American centrality to the monument arguing that the four freestanding black figures were the seminal part of the design. It was easy to doom such a project under the guise of projected anticipated costs.

The combined efforts of the African American community and the Western Sanitary Commission were not the first attempt to raise a monument to Lincoln's memory in Washington. By 1876 the Capitol rotunda housed the only sculpture Lincoln posed for from life, by young Vinnie Ream Hoxie, while Lot Flannery's tribute, dedicated on April 15, 1868, the third anniversary of Lincoln's death, graced the steps of city hall. Others, including members of the African American community led by Henry Highland Garnet, wanted to create a kind of living memorial to the martyred president. Garnet's organization, the Colored People's Educational Monument Association, proposed the erecting a national school for freedmen in Lincoln's name.[22] But a typical heroic bronze or stone monument was more in line with the expressions of Frederick Douglass, who argued that African Americans should have a place in the venue of civic monuments particularly if they were funding the project.[23] In the end, Douglass would be the victor arguing in the *Anglo-African* that a monument raised to Lincoln and paid for by blacks "would express one of the holiest sentiments of the human heart." Two months later, in the same journal, he equally supported the idea of a combined monument subscription program of "a people's monument to Abraham Lincoln without distinction of color." For Douglass the issue was far more than color: "the fact of my being a negro," he argued, "is far less important in determining my duty than the fact that I am a 'man,' and linked to all mankind as a man and a brother."

My students listen with heightened interest. I next share with them the story of the African American Freedman figure that sculpturally complements Lincoln. Ball relied on photographs of Archer Alexander, the last slave returned to slavery under the Fugitive Slave Act, for the modeling of the Freedman's Face. This story, like others with the Freedman's Monuments, is replete with contradictions. Ironically, Alexander was a servant of William G. Elliot, and so, according to the *Anglo-African*, "the inevitability of subservient relationship of the former slave to the monument's sponsor was, in a sense reencoded in the design of the monument." In another twist, Alexander was a runaway slave from Missouri, a state not bound to the legalities of the Emancipation Proclamation.

In a small volume published in 1885, *The Story of Archer Alexander*, Elliot not only outlines the convoluted circumstances connected with Alexander's escape and subsequent liberty, but also whitewashes the truth. "His freedom came directly from the hand of President Lincoln," the author contends, "and his own hands had helped to break the chains that bound him."[24] The Proclamation in fact, as meted out in Missouri, would have retained Alexander in slavery. So much for the report offered by Philadelphia's *Daily Evening Bulletin* that the statue "represents poor President Lincoln breaking the chains of the African slave."

Elliot's conclusion rocks my students' sensibilities. Showing Alexander a photograph of the Freedom Memorial after the dedication ceremonies, Elliot reports, "I explained to him its meaning, and that he would thus be remembered in connection with Abraham Lincoln, the emancipator of his race, he laughed all over. He presently sobered down and exclaimed, 'Now I'se a white man! Now I'se free! I thank the good Lord that he has 'livered me from all my troubles, and I'se lived to see this.'" Sixteen years after the dedication, the *Boston Evening Transcript* noted that the pose was suggestive of the Freedman "blackening Lincoln's boots." Over time, African Americans grew indignant with the artistic rendering that echoed the *Evening Telegraph*'s sentiment, mockingly asking, "Shine, sir?"

If truth be known, the historical record is fairly clear that when Lincoln entered Richmond, Virginia, the capital of the defeated Confederacy on April 4, 1865, former slaves flocked to his side, one genuflecting as he passed. "Don't kneel to me," said the president. "That is not right. You must kneel to God only, and thank Him for the liberty you will enjoy hereafter."

"Funny," says Dhrupad, the most serious of my pilgrims, finally weighing in. "The monument may have been supported initially by black freedmen, but it was the whites who seem to have shaped its meaning, figure, and destiny. It was Ball who shaped the monument, using the likeness of Archer Alexander, to suit his own needs. One could say the blacks were ripped off, as it was their idea and their money, but the final result was something to satisfy whites instead. Unfortunately, it was whites who designed and shaped the meaning and glory of the monument."

Dhrupad's assessment supports the following reported by the *Washington Evening Star*, "There would be a beautiful fitness, a degree of rare poetic justice in such a monument being raised by the voluntary contributions of the freedmen and women, who, having lived contemporaneously with their benefactors, have learned to know and revere them."

"Ha!" Leslie emphatically says. "This memorial would have Alexander appear as if he owed his freedom and life to Lincoln, when in fact he was completely unaffected by Lincoln's act. Ball modeled a story that never really was, and those in charge preferred it that way. Alexander's story reflects how the whole black race's ability to affect its own destiny got swept under the rug in order to make room for Lincoln as savior in the history books."

As the sun begins to dip over the Capitol, the sky takes on a lovely pinkish orange tone. I am anxious to generate a conversation about the pose. Ball's composition places Lincoln standing erect above and to the right of the Freedman. Lincoln's right arm extends downward holding in his hand a scrolled Emancipation Proclamation, the wrinkles along the coat sleeve adding a sense of realism, though the rest of his buttoned frock coat and trousers "are simplified to the point of monotony."[25] The hand rests on the top of a podium adorned with a bas-relief medallion of George Washington. Lincoln's left arm is extended out over the kneeling Freedman with his palm facing down, providing a sense of drama, as if to personify the actual freeing of a slave. The crouching or kneeling Freedman holds a broken shackle in his right hand and looks not at the Great Emancipator but directly ahead. He is draped in a stereotypical loincloth and is naked from the waist up. Other sculptural symbols complement the piece. Behind Lincoln and the Freedman is a whipping post with blooming roses creeping up and entwining the physical pillar of the institution of slavery. A broken lash and fetter that cannot be viewed easily from the ground symbolize the end of slavery. To see them, I have to hoist myself up on the pedestal, wondering, as I strain, what was the point of sculpting them if no one can see them to understand their symbolism. Collectively the sculpture represents Lincoln's actions in manumitting the slaves. It is quite simplistic and didactic. In raised twelve-inch block lettering, the word "Emancipation" adorns the bronze plinth between the top of the ten-foot pedestal and base of the sculpture. Other than the plaque affixed to the pedestal, there are no other inscriptions.

The posed figures do not relate to one another in the story of emancipation. Clearly, this ensemble demonstrates a belief of the sculptor as well as the Western Sanitary Commission that African American emancipation was solely the by-product of white beneficence. There is no evidence here that illustrates the roles African

Americans had in securing their own freedom. This idea of white beneficence would carry on well until the 1960s, until the height of the
modern civil rights movement. It is true that President Lyndon Johnson signed into law the Civil Rights Act of 1964 and the Voting Rights
Act of 1965, but the people who made those pieces of legislation a
reality were not government officials, rather African Americans and
their white allies who marched, boycotted, and demonstrated to demand what should have been given to them long ago. Those laws
were won on the backs of living witnesses to Eugene "Bull" Connor's
fire hoses and dogs in Birmingham and on the wrong end of Alabama
state troopers' billyclubs in Selma, not because of LBJ's signature.

"One of the issues is that no one is certain of Ball's intent of the
pose of Freedman," I point out. "Is he rising, or is he kneeling in
homage to Lincoln, who appears like Father Abraham delivering the
gift of freedom? One might argue that this sculpture smacks of the
sentiment of white beneficence." Vintage newspaper reports on the
Washington statue and the unveiling of its duplicate, in Boston in
1879, offer differing opinions as to the Freedman's posture. My students look at me for an answer that is not forthcoming. "Ball," I contend, "makes no mention in his autobiography as to the meaning of
the pose. So what do *you* think?"

A lively discussion ensues. Some of the students say that Lincoln is
bidding him to rise to accept his freedom, while others are not so
sure. Bryan, arguing deliberately like a cool and calm debater, employing logic rather emotion, tries to persuade the others. "From afar
it looks as if Lincoln is repressing him. But on closer inspection it's
more of a freedom thing with the shackle broken." Leslie disagrees.
"He doesn't look like he's in the act of rising," she complains. Michelle offers an answer that lets everyone, including the sculptor, off
the hook. "Maybe," she says, "he left it open for interpretation."

I find all of this a bit amusing. Lincoln scholar Gabor Borrit believes that one of the most important ideas Americans should take
from studying Lincoln's life is Lincoln's fervent belief in what he
called "the right to rise."[26] For Lincoln it was America's gift to the
world to allow the common man reach for uncommon heights.
Against Ball's sculpture, Borrit's assertion takes on a whole new
meaning.

One critic of the sculpture wrote that the monument "converted into the literal truth of history.[27] "Raising the stakes, I ask the students to respond. Dhrupad takes the cue. "The monument shows the truth of how black men had been regarded in society before, that the whites were supreme over the blacks. Here we see a figure of a white man towering over a kneeling black man. The black man was meant to show gratitude to Lincoln, but then blacks always had to show their gratitude to whites."

"Mr. Percoco," Leslie interjects, "history is written by the winners. In the case of this monument 'the winners' translates to history being portrayed by those in power. During the memorial-making process, the 'winners' were the white people at the head of the Sanitary Commission, in the sense that they had control over what the statue would look like. Because they had control, they were able to portray something a bit less than accurate. That's how the white people in charge wanted it. That's how history was streamlined to make it easier and, ergo, history is written by the winners."

For me the figure is rising, perhaps being bidden by Lincoln to do so, which is problematic. But it *is* called the Freedman's Monument, not the Lincoln Monument, so it is fair to say that Ball must have intended the crouching figure to be depicted in the process of rising. Granted it is not self-emancipation nor does the monument allude to the role that African Americans played in many cases in being self-emancipated persons. Frederick Douglass, like many others trapped in bondage, made the deliberate choice of his own volition to flee. There is not even a hint of the Underground Railroad here. Memorials to the Underground Railroad and the African Americans who led the movement would not become fashionable until after the modern civil rights movement.

What if the donors had had a say in the design? We will never know the answer, of course. But returning to Hosmer's conception, it might be fair to assume that a design African Americans had accepted would prove less problematic.

The conversation shifts to a focus of the portraits of Lincoln and the Freedman. There is again vigorous debate among the students. With the sinking sun behind the sculpture, Lincoln's brow is strengthened, shadowed, and deepened by the play of light. First we look at the eyes, and I point out that Lincoln's pupils are more developed than those of the Freedman. His eyes are modeled using a technique commonly found in classical or neoclassical works called "the blank stare," depicting no pupils. Bryan sees a relationship between the expressions on the faces of both figures. "The message," he says, "exchanged by their looks does not necessarily have to be one of celebration." Everyone agrees that Bryan has raised an interesting point.

Enzo again offers a different slant. "The Freedman," he says, "is looking at the sky, almost as if he's saying 'Now the sky's the limit.'" For Leslie, "the eyes of the Freedman, without their pupils, make him look like he has no direction or focus." Michelle thinks that the lack of pupils is something symbolic. "They represent the masses of freed slaves," she asserts.

Our thoughts drift toward the Emancipation Proclamation, which, like Lincoln, is shrouded in a kind of mythical aura. Most Americans think that Lincoln freed all the slaves, which is far too simplistic. And herein lies part of the problem with Americans and their collective sense of our history. Dhrupad reminds us that Lincoln was first a man dedicated to preservation of the Union before he became the Great Emancipator. The proclamation he signed on January 1, 1863, freed the slaves only in areas of the Confederacy under rebellion. It did not apply to the four slave states that remained in the Union: Delaware, Maryland, Kentucky, and Missouri. Many historians have been critical of the limits of the proclamation, as were African American activists of the time, particularly Frederick Douglass, who argued, "Had there been one expression of sound moral feeling against Slavery, one word of regret and shame that this accursed system had remained so long the disgrace and scandal of the Republic, one word of satisfaction in the hope of burying slavery and the rebellion in one common grave, a thrill of joy would have run round the world, but no such word was said, and no such joy was kindled."[28]

Times have changed little. Varying groups have sought an official apology for slavery. More recently, Lerone Bennett Jr., in his *Forced Into Glory: Abraham Lincoln's White Dream*, provokes the reader to reject Lincoln as the Great Emancipator, claiming, "Racism was the center and circumference of his being."[29] For Bennett and other Lincoln debunkers, Lincoln issued the Emancipation Proclamation solely for political reasons.

It might be prudent to argue that Lincoln's early opposition to slavery was based on the potential economic restraints of free labor that the institution of slavery posed as opposed to sympathy for enslaved blacks, but Lincoln the Illinois prairie state assemblyman was not Abraham Lincoln the president of the United States, who told his friend, Illinois congressman Isaac Arnold, in the aftermath of signing the Proclamation, "Now we have got the harpoon fairly into the monster slavery."[30] He understood what he was doing. The record, though, is clear that Lincoln was consistently personally opposed to slavery. Morally he was opposed to slavery. A look at the evidence makes that obvious. As a twenty-eight-year-old delegate to the Illinois legislature, Lincoln voted against a resolution condemning abolitionism, arguing, "The institution of slavery is founded on both injustice and bad policy."[31] In his 1854 speech in Peoria, Illinois, he repeatedly voiced his personal opposition to slavery. When Lincoln wrote his friend Albert Hodges in April 1864, the president remarked, "I am naturally anti-slavery. If slavery is not wrong, nothing is wrong. I cannot remember when I did not so think, and feel."[32]

A very human Lincoln emerges from Arnold's postwar reminiscences. "I could not for a moment control my arm," he told Arnold. "I paused and a superstitious feeling came over me which made me hesitate." Lincoln had been greeting New Year's well-wishers to the White House. "I have been receiving calls and shaking hands till my arm is stiff and numb. I never in my life felt more certain that I was doing right than I do in signing this paper. They will say," he continued, "he had some compunctions. Anyway, it is going to be done." With a firm resolution Lincoln spelled out his full name rather than with his customary "A. Lincoln." "That will do," he simply said.[33]

His resolve to change the focus from a war of preservation of the Union to a war of liberation had taken time to germinate, and Lincoln had grown in the two years since he assumed the presidency. One of the reasons I have made Lincoln the totem of my classroom teaching is because of the growth of the man. I want my students to understand that an individual's life is dynamic and not static and that one can mature in outlook and vision well into adulthood.

Was Lincoln a bigot? By our standards, yes, but let me qualify that. True, he told "darkie" stories in caricature dialect, and when challenged on the race question was always quick to respond, "I do not understand that because I do not want a negro woman for a slave I must necessarily want her for a wife,"[34] and in the infamous Matson Case he defended the rights of a slave owner to keep his "property." But in spite of these contradictions, there is no proof that Lincoln ever saw African Americans as less than human beings entitled to the ideals outlined in the scripture of the Declaration of Independence. Historian James Oakes admits to this dichotomy but argues, "If it is difficult to square the public with the private Lincoln on the question of race, it is even more difficult to reconcile his endorsement of racial inequality with his vehement antiracism of which there is a good deal. He once pondered the absurdity of race as a justification for slavery in a way that made the very concept of race absurd. He made the humanity of blacks central to his antislavery argument. He insisted that the Declaration of Independence, with its promise of fundamental human equality, applied to blacks and whites alike."[35] With regard to race Lincoln grew and his outlook changed during the course of the Civil War. That is really what matters.

Alan Guelzo claims that there are eight myths or "lies" about Lincoln and the Emancipation Proclamation. He believes that Americans should consider them as a whole if they really want to understand Lincoln, his Proclamation, and the Civil War era. First, Lincoln was a racist. Second, the Proclamation did not free any slaves. Third, the Proclamation was purely a political gesture. Fourth, Lincoln dragged his feet on the path to Emancipation. Fifth, the Proclamation had no eloquence in its language because Lincoln was indifferent to emancipation. Sixth, the Proclamation was an attempt to rally support in the North. Seventh, the goal of emancipation was to prevent foreign intervention in the war. And eighth, slaves performed their own acts of emancipation and did not rely on Lincoln's Proclamation.[36]

The students are well aware of my interest in historical myths and how we construct our history, particularly in a public space. In bringing such issues to bear in history instruction, teachers challenge students to grow as thinkers and constructive critics and develop a deeper appreciation for living in the present within the context of history. In the best of circumstances this can lead to a burgeoning sense of empathy for today's issues as well as for historical personalities. At a long-forgotten and somewhat obscure sculpture to an American who is layered in mythology, these arguments take on much more powerful and greater meaning.

For historian James O. Horton of George Washington University, "It was Abraham Lincoln's capacity for personal growth that moved him from a mild opponent of slavery to the man that radical abolitionist William Lloyd Garrison finally came to call 'the Presidential chainbreaker of millions' and Frederick Douglass came to call liberator and friend."

Horton is well aware of the problems of presentism, too, when it comes to Lincoln, reminding me in an interview:

> In this age, when some charge any revision of political position as a "flip-flop" and consider thoughtless consistency a praiseworthy political attribute, we would do well to remember one of the most important political figures in American history, President Abraham Lincoln, a man who learned from personal experience and changed his mind. Although Lincoln had opposed slavery from a very young age and even vowed to move against it if and when he had the chance, before the Civil War he believed it was protected by the Constitution and was willing to tolerate its existence in the South. He was not a racial egalitarian and said so publicly. The events of the Civil War, including the military service of two hundred thousand black soldiers whom he credited with playing a major role in saving the country and his personal relationships with Frederick Douglass and other African Americans, changed his mind. Ironically, Lincoln's public change of stance on the question of slavery and racial progress provoked his assassination. After his Emancipation Proclamation, Lincoln became an advocate of the 13th Constitutional Amendment that finally brought the federal protection of slavery to an end. In his last speech, in 1865, Lincoln advocated voting rights for many blacks.

The fact that Lincoln stood by his 1864 reelection platform, knowing full well that to not do so might cost him the election, and did not drop the Thirteenth Amendment and emancipation from the Republican Party plank, gives credence to his powerful moral center. Lincoln could have backed off on emancipation, for political reasons, but he would rather have been right rather than to sell out those to whom he had become entrusted.

Edna Greene Medford, associate professor and director of graduate studies in the Department of History at Howard University, has a bit of a different slant on Lincoln as the Great Emancipator. She once told me, "It is problematic to ascribe to a single individual responsibility for the freedom of nearly four million enslaved people. Undeniably, Lincoln's actions during the war facilitated freedom for African

Americans. However, there were many men and women who pressed him to move forward, including enslaved people themselves, who very early on saw the war as an opportunity to overturn slavery."

Lincoln knew what he was doing when he signed the document. The fact that two years later he symbolically signed thirteen copies of the Thirteenth Amendment, which by law he was not required to do so, resonates with the kind of nuance Lincoln was famous for and girds the argument that he was acting by this point in time as a humanitarian.

Within the context of today's political milieu, Lincoln's memory is further challenged, particularly from his own party. Eric Foner, writing in *The Nation*, claims,

> Most striking, the party of emancipation and Reconstruction has become deeply hostile to civil rights enforcement, affirmative action— indeed, any measures that seek to redress the enduring consequences of slavery and segregation. Republicans, George W. Bush acknowledged in his recent speech before the NAACP, have 'not always carried the mantle of Lincoln.'[37]

My mind drifts back to something that occurred at school several years before. The memory seems quite appropriate, given the setting. Students from the History Honor Society wanted to paint a mural in the social studies wing of our school. They asked me about their design, which was to spell out the word "History," using characters and images from the past. For the letter "H," students wanted to paint a picture of Abraham Lincoln shaking the hand of a slave. They requested drawings or illustrations of slaves from which they could model their painting. These particular students were very industrious and highly motivated. As we hashed out some ideas, it suddenly dawned on me that Lincoln should not be shaking the hand of just any slave, but rather that of a dignified Frederick Douglass, leveling the playing field. The History Honor Society leadership seized upon the idea, and every time I walk past the mural I think about how a high-school history teacher and some students got it right for Lincoln, Douglass, and our school community. A hidden hope of mine is that years from now teachers and students at West Springfield High School will view that mural not only for its initial worth, but also for how ideas and viewpoints of history are reinterpreted and shaped over time. The juxtaposition with Ball's Emancipation Group could not have rung any clearer.

Medford, concurring, told me, "Given the contributions of African Americans as fighting men and in myriad ways as civilians, a fitting image for the Freedmen's Monument would have been the depiction of the newly emancipated as partners with Lincoln in the cause of Union and freedom." Her solution is much more rooted in the true antebellum abolitionist world than the staid old-fashioned device offered by Ball.

Snapping me out of my reverie, the students want to weigh in on other sculptural devices, particularly the roses and their entwining the whipping post. Enzo thinks that the whipping post was deliberately placed in the rear of the group because Ball was trying to cover up the past. "The whipping post is covered with roses," Michelle says, "but people forget about the thorns until they are bleeding." I like her use of imagery and the sense on irony she brings to bear on her analysis. Bryan agrees, "The flowers may be pretty but one can still get stung by the thorns." Ever dispassionate, Michelle reminds us once again not to be present-minded, imploring us to look at the entire sculpture "through the views of the time when it was dedicated." I remind them that all the components of the sculpture are part of a narrative, an attempt to tell a story in bronze.

Michelle provides the perfect segue to read some excerpts from Douglass's dedicatory address. I show them the copied original text that I secured from the Library of Congress. A certain kind of energy seizes all of us as we study the elegantly handwritten words. Standing in the park where he delivered this same speech, looking at his handwriting, brings to the moment a special kind of historical immediacy.

I ask the students to step back in time, place themselves among the crowd, and imagine what it must have been like on that cloudy April day, watching events unfold. The Marine Band strikes up "Hail Columbia," opening the ceremony. Prayer is offered. A reading of the Emancipation Proclamation is received by all with "as much enthusiasm as if it had just been issued." The band plays the "Marseillaise." Yeatman, representing the Western Sanitary Commission, makes brief remarks. Presiding officer John M. Langston, dean of Howard University's law school, represents the African American community at large and graciously thanks the commission for its work. "In behalf of the entire nation," he says, "in behalf especially of the donors of the fund with whose investment you and your associates have been charges, I tender to you, sir . . . our sincere thanks for

the prompt and wise performance of trust and duty committed to
your care. The finished and appropriate work of art presented by you
we accept and dedicate through the ages in memory and honor of
him who is to be forever known in the records of the world's history
as the emancipator of the enslaved of our country." Finished, he
turns and asks the ever-reticent President Grant to pull the silk cords.
Silence ensues. The draped American flags part. Lincoln and the
Freedman are revealed to the world; spontaneous applause and
cheering breaks out. Cannons boom. The band strikes up "Hail to
the Chief."[38]

Douglass, remarks in hand, stands erect, his head of hair grown out
into a great mane. He begins speaking. His melodious baritone voice
booms over the crowd and carries across the fields of this residential
part of the District of Columbia. It was fitting in more than one way
that Douglass delivered these remarks. Both he and Lincoln were
self-made men, for the most part self-educated and fond of the classics. Both were keenly aware of their respective roles in history.

By the end of the Civil War, Douglass had grown himself in his
admiration and estimation of Lincoln. During the war he had met
with Lincoln at the White House on three occasions. Lincoln took
Douglass seriously and consulted him. The relationship between
both men was pivotal to each of them and to the success of the Union
cause. At some level their relationship remained a reflection of America's racial ambiguity. Even though he chided Lincoln in his dedicatory address, Douglass was clearly pleased that this particular day had
arrived. "Friends and Fellow-Citizens," he opened, "I warmly congratulate you upon the highly interesting object which has caused you
to assemble in such numbers and spirit as you have to-day. . . . Wise
and thoughtful men of our race, who shall come after us, and study
the lesson of our history in the United States: who shall survey the
long and dreary spaces over which we have traveled: who shall count
the links in the great chain of events by which we have reached our
present position, will make note of the occasion: they will think of it
and speak of it with a sense of manly pride and complacency."

Invoking the sentiments springing from Lincoln's Second Inaugural Address, a speech that he told Lincoln was "a sacred effort,"
Douglass looks to the future for all Americans, saying, "I refer to the
past not in malice, for this is no day for malice: but simply to place
more distinctly in front the gratifying and glorious change which has

come both to our white fellow-citizens and ourselves and to congratulate all upon the contrast between now and then: the new dispensation of freedom with its thousand blessings to both races and the old dispensation of slavery with its ten thousand evils to both races—white and black."

Douglass extols the virtues that have brought the monument to its creation and the memory of the man who stands before the dignified crowd in bronze. But he is careful in his remarks about the connections between Lincoln and those whom he liberated and he clearly speaks from the soul and with the voice of a nineteenth-century African American. "We claim for ourselves," he argues "no superior devotion to the character, history, and memory of the illustrious name whose monument we have here dedicated to-day. We fully comprehend the relation of Abraham Lincoln both to ourselves and the white people of the United States. Truth is proper and beautiful at all times and in all places, and is never more proper and beautiful when speaking of a great public man whose example is likely to be commended for honor and imitation long after his departure to the solemn shades, the silent continents of eternity." Moving forward, the great orator admits his view of the truth of Lincoln. "It must be admitted, truth compels me to admit, even here in the presence of the monument we have erected to his memory. Abraham Lincoln was not, in the fullest sense of the word, either our man or our model. In his interests, in his associations, in his habits of thought, and in his prejudices, he was a white man." I wonder what was going through the minds of those white men sitting on the platform listening to Douglass. Did they cringe? Did they flinch? And more important, did they, in my student's parlance, "get it?" No, not given the dim record of the federal government in the aftermath of Reconstruction.

"He was pre-eminently the white man's President," Douglass intones, "entirely devoted to the welfare of white men. . . . The races to which we belong were not the special objects of his consideration. . . . First, midst and last, you and yours was the object of his deepest affection and is most earnest solicitude. You are," he reminds whites in the crowd, "the children of Abraham Lincoln. We are at best only his step children: children by adoption, children by force of circumstances and necessity." Interestingly in 1865 Douglass called Lincoln the "black man's President." Eleven years after Lincoln's death Douglass changed his viewpoint. It may be that as Douglass moved away in time from the living Lincoln he adjusted his views through a different lens, owing to the social and political changes between 1865 and 1876. An even more provocative possibility is that Douglass's comments about Lincoln are more about himself and his times than they are about Lincoln.

But Douglass is willing to give Lincoln credit where credit is due. "Viewed from the genuine abolition ground, Mr. Lincoln seemed tardy, cold, dull and indifferent: but measuring him by the sentiment of his country, a sentiment he was bound as a statesman to consult, he was swift, zealous, radical, and determined."[39] This was, after all, the president and man who had invited Douglass to the White House, shaken his hand, and called him "my friend, Douglass."[40] Strange that no ardent abolitionist like William Lloyd Garrison, an ally of Douglass, ever made such a claim. But then again, Garrison called for the Union to let the South go after shots were fired on Fort Sumter rather than fight to keep it in the Union. For Douglass this was anathema, a sellout to the four million souls fettered in chains.

When Douglass has finished, the band strikes up the "Sicilian Vespers" overture by Rossini, and Dr. J. P. Newman offers the benediction concluding the program. "The occasion," editorialized the *Washington Chronicle*, "could not fail to impress everyone with feelings of the most profound respect for a people in whom the sentiment of gratitude is so strongly ingrained as it is in those whose voluntary contributions paid for the magnificent memorial which commemorates the crowning act of Lincoln's life."[41]

The students' attention has been rapt. I can see that in their minds they have time-traveled. Finishing, I ask the big question, the one I always spring on my students: "So, what do you think?"

Leslie is the first to respond. "I can see Douglass's perspective," she says. "Lincoln was not a great moral crusader. Douglass says, where do we go from here?"

"Black people," Enzo offers, "need a black person to step up and take them forward."

"So when did that happen?" I ask.

"It would take another hundred years," says Enzo, "when King becomes the African American community's 'man and model.' But Lincoln took the first step. Now others need to pick up the cross, so to speak. People then" he continues, "realized that slavery was wrong but in actuality its still there with the oppression blacks still felt. It's still going on today with all kinds of people and groups." With regard to the statue, he concludes quietly, "Why celebrate? This was just the beginning."

"Okay, but what about King's replacement of Lincoln as the 'man and model' for African Americans? How does this change things?" I venture. "What does this say about King's leadership?" I ask.

Leslie doesn't miss a step. "If people think that it was Martin Luther King's movement, then today they—young people—are more likely to say, 'Gosh, I wish we had a Martin Luther King here today to lead us.' If people knew how the movement started, then the question they would ask themselves is, 'What can I do?'"

I nod in silent agreement, as do the four other students. Maybe the whites on the platform with Douglass and the Western Sanitary Commission never "got it," but Leslie, Enzo, Bryan, Dhrupad, and Michelle have. They are not at all surprised when I inform them of a recent check I conducted on the Inventory of American Sculpture. Of the close to two hundred statues to Lincoln in the United States, only a handful includes an African American figure or other sculptural devices to suggest slavery.

It is fitting that as we leave Lincoln Park, the sky quite dusky, I am reminded of the line from William Cullen Bryant's poem "Abraham Lincoln":

> Thy task is done; the bond are free:
> We bear thee to an honored grave
> Whose proudest monument shall be
> The broken fetters of the slave.[42]

One man had made a difference in the world simply by the stroke of a pen. Although he might fairly have been criticized by contemporaries and Monday-morning quarterbacks, at least he did something. How much different would the world be if all of us simply did something? For my young historians, that is what Lincoln's legacy means.

Lincoln the Hoosier Youth (author)

2

The Hero of Hoosierdom

Paul Manship's *Lincoln the Hoosier Youth* (1932), Fort Wayne, Indiana

FIVE HUNDRED AND TWENTY-EIGHT MILES and ten and a half hours by car away from home, I find myself in downtown Fort Wayne, Indiana. Saddle-sore from the marathon ride, I am alone. I miss my students. There's no band of teenage historians here for me to lead frolicking to some hidden Lincoln monumental gem I have discovered. "Too bad," I think, "the kids could easily have connected with Paul Manship's *Lincoln the Hoosier Youth*." As the sculptor envisioned him, this Lincoln is the same age as the high-school students I teach.

Named after the Revolutionary War hero "Mad" Anthony Wayne, Fort Wayne has a downtown right out of Sinclair Lewis's *Main Street*. The beautiful dome of the Allen County Court House graces the cityscape, the art deco Lincoln Tower pierces the small skyline, and Victorian homes line the streets. The 2000 census reports that more than 200,000 people live here, but the empty avenues suggest that the city has seen better days.

A beautiful mid-July day, not unlike the day of the dedication of Manship's masterpiece, greets me. I glide my car alongside the curb on Harrison Street and park directly across the street from the headquarters of the Lincoln National Life Insurance Company. My tight neck needs to be cracked. I exhale, stretch, and rotate my head as my spine releases pressure to a popping sound. It feels good. For a brief moment I look across the street at the Doric-style Indiana limestone building. I adjust my vision to the heroic monument centered at the top of the steps that lead into the building, a space that was deliberately designed with a statue in mind. The bronze figure offset against the light stone walls stands out. The base, made of Crotch Island granite from Maine, protrudes out over the steps, and its pinkish gray color sparkles with pigmentation. It sits flush with the elevated entrance plaza also formed with the same stone. The statue is the right size in this space, symmetrically sited within the enfolding wings of the building. The 14.5-ton pedestal, seated squarely in the center of the base, measures six and a half feet high and is five feet square. It has an olive-gray tone with black flecks sprinkled throughout. Quarried in Conway, New Hampshire, the granite can endure all kinds of weather and reflects a particular kind of solidity and strength.

Upon the pedestal rests Lincoln. Two workers are cleaning and buffing the statue. The sculpture has a fresh glow. Employees of the Lincoln National Life Insurance Company hustle their way up the stairs and then disappear into the four-story building, a pace that strikes me as being rather quick for the Midwest.

Before I get out of my car, I listen to the final portion of the tape in my player. The narrator of Sandburg's *Lincoln: The Prairie Years* closes out one section on the audio book I have brought along. Despite the long drive, I've made only a small dent in volume 1. The tone of the story and the narration is right and puts me in a good frame of mind to pursue my interest.

> The years pass and Abe Lincoln grows up, at 17 standing six feet, nearly four inches, long armed with rare strength in his muscles. At 18 he could take an ax at the end of the handle and hold it out from his shoulders in a straight horizontal line, easy and steady. He could make his ax flash and bite into a sugar maple or a sycamore, one neighbor saying, "He can sink an ax deeper into wood than any man I ever saw."[1]

I drop a few coins in the meter, hoping that I've paid enough to cover me for a couple of hours. When on the trail of Lincoln sculpture, I never know how long my wanderings will take.

As I cross the street, the two workers eye me. Maybe my pace has caught their attention. My camera, slung over my shoulder, bounces off my hip as I approach the curb. One of the two workers looks older, probably close to my age; the other fellow appears to be in his early twenties. A smile flashes across the face of my contemporary, a sign I take for a welcome. For about ten minutes we chat about their work, the Lincoln Life, and the waning economic state of Fort Wayne. As we talk, Glenn continues to buff the bas-relief panel of "Fortitude." He leans back and looks at his work with a critical eye and smiles. "Just like waxing a car," he says proudly.

I start photographing the statue. Within a few minutes someone from the insurance company comes out the main entrance and stops me. I explain my mission. He's a pleasant enough chap but still asks me to come in the building and check in with security. I oblige, wondering if the security guard is going to make me take off my shoes. He doesn't, but he places a call upstairs anyway just to cover himself. After a brief explanation he smiles with a nod, giving me the go-ahead to resume my work. Back outside, I try my best to make a conversation with Doug, Glenn's assistant.

My efforts are futile. "It's just a job, man," he says to my inquiry of what it's like to be cleaning a great piece of public sculpture. "Well then," I ask, "what's it like to be cleaning Abraham Lincoln?" He gives me a quizzical look that I read as, "Dude! Don't you get it? I don't care. What are you a weirdo? Get a life!" I take the hint that Doug could not care less about Lincoln and sculpture.

The youthful and nearly handsome face on the monument strikes me. This gentle Lincoln is not the oft-depicted gawky, gangly youth who moved to New Salem, Illinois, in 1831. A sturdy young man powerful in demeanor and form stands before me. The torso and muscular limbs suggest a kind of hearty frontier stockiness, the rugged constitution the result of hours of manual labor on the Lincoln Homestead, splitting rails and plowing fields for his father, Thomas. No doubt his foray down the Mississippi River to New Orleans, working on a flatboat in 1828, helped develop his singular arm strength.

I follow the maxim I always give my students when visiting a monument or historic site: "Take yourself back in time to the past and see what only your mind can envision." For a moment I pause and let my mind's eye wander. My imagination carries me back. I find myself on Friday, September 16, 1932, a glorious sunny day in downtown Fort Wayne, Indiana. The country is enduring one of the worst years of the Great Depression, the farm belt in particular bearing a heavy burden. Despite the hard times, residents and visitors pour into Fort Wayne to witness the dedication of the nation's newest statue of Abraham Lincoln, Manship's *Lincoln: The Hoosier Youth*.

Four thousand men in their fedoras and straw hats and women in their calf-length dresses fill Harrison Street and the plaza in front of the Lincoln National Life Insurance Company. Newsreel cameras capture the event, and a national radio audience is tuned in via the National Broadcasting Company through its local affiliate, WOWO.

Amplifiers are set up for the remaining six thousand people who cannot get close enough to see the dais or hear the speakers and their remarks. Among those seated in the crowd are aging Union Civil War veterans, members of the Grand Army of the Republic, who live in and near Fort Wayne. They, too, are being honored this day. These men, accorded special reserved seats in the grandstand, are here to remember the service they had rendered to their commander-in-chief. Four of the oldest living residents of Indiana, Illinois, Michigan, and Ohio, who have actually seen Abraham Lincoln, have also been invited to the ceremonies by the Lincoln National Life Insurance Company. Thomas Gilmore, aged 101, from Macomb, Illinois, is the senior member of this contingent. Boy Scouts serve as ushers and pass out programs. Even their aging leader, the still vigorous eighty-two-year-old Daniel C. Beard, National Scout Commissioner, is on hand for the day's events. His afternoon address, "Lincoln the Youth," delivered at a special tribute program designed specifically for Fort Wayne's young schoolchildren, will promote Lincoln's legacy among Indiana's youngsters. Like all students, they are happy to have been released early from their classes.

Eighty-four-year-old Mrs. M. O. Smith, the former Louisa Vandersloot, from Hanover, Pennsylvania, also has made the journey to Fort Wayne. As a fifteen-year-old schoolgirl from Gettysburg's neighboring town, she sang in the chorus at the November 19, 1863, dedication of the Gettysburg National Cemetery, where Lincoln delivered the Gettysburg Address. Seventy years later she still recalled the moment. Extending his long arm over two of the older girls selected to sing, Lincoln reached out to Vandersloot and in "his great warm, all-enveloping hand took hold of my little one and almost crushed it." Again that night at a reception the president singled her out and again firmly grasped her hand. She reported that she "tingled all over" as Lincoln held her, feeling his "kindliness and greatness of soul."[2]

These elderly Americans have more than just personal reasons to be in Fort Wayne. They represent to the majority of younger folks in the crowd not only the vestiges of a bygone era, but also a living connection to the man everyone is honoring.

Other dignitaries, from across the United States, are in town to witness the unveiling, and speak at any one of the numerous programs scheduled to honor Lincoln and his place in Indiana lore. In another nod to young people, Lincoln biographer Ida Tarbell speaks at the Second Annual Lincoln Students' Luncheon. U.S. Senator James E. Watson of Indiana brings a special message from President Herbert Hoover to read. U.S. Secretary of Agriculture Arthur M. Hyde presents the keynote address. With him on the rostrum are Otto L. Schmidt, president of the Illinois Historical Society, and Louis A. Warren, the director of the Lincoln Historical Research Foundation, which played a singular role in getting the sculpture erected. The invocation, delivered by Joseph R. Sizzo, pastor of the New York Avenue Presbyterian Church in Washington, D.C., which President Lincoln occasionally visited, adds a spiritual touch to the celebration. In addition, Sizzo reads a personal message from Mary H. Lincoln, the widow of Robert Lincoln, the only Lincoln son to live to full adulthood. In 1905 he granted the Lincoln National Life Insurance Company permission to use the Lincoln image. The junior Lincoln had carefully managed and cultivated his father's image and public memory. He often commented on the attempts of different sculptors to capture his father's persona and essence in public sculpture. On most occasions he chided the artists and their efforts, thinking very little of portrait sculpture. "It seems to me impossible that a bronze heroic statue can ever be a faithful likeness of the subject,"[3] he wrote a friend in 1881. Now he was dead, and Manship could breathe a sigh of relief, knowing that the most critical of all Lincoln sculptor critics was unavailable to critique his work.

Arthur J. Siebold, manager of the credit rating bureau of the Retail Merchants' Association, has asked all Fort Wayne businesses to display their flags. Hunter's Clothing Store more than obliged by taking out a three-column ad in the *News-Sentinel*, celebrating the event and claiming with a nod to Lincoln, "Clothes may not make a man, but they help a lot."

At 12:30 the official dedication ceremonies commence. Arthur F. Hall, president of Lincoln Life, introduces the sculptor, forty-seven-year-old Paul Manship, who speaks briefly. The important task of pulling the drapes from the sculpture falls upon Hall's five-year-old grandson. The appearance of the young Hall, who was the great-grandson of the chairman of the board and great-great-grandson of Lincoln's secretary of the treasury, Hugh McCulloch, makes for a family affair. It takes him two tugs on the cord to unveil the youthful

Lincoln. When the drapery finally parts, the crowd responds with enthusiastic applause and cheering. The band strikes up "America," which is followed by the presidential salute of twenty-one guns employed by the National Rifle Corps of the American Legion, Post 47.

For the next hour the crowd listens intently to a series of speeches that present the rags-to-riches story of Abraham Lincoln. Given the time, they are words that the audience longs for and wants to hear.

At the conclusion of the speeches, Beard, as representative of the Boy Scouts of America, places a wreath at the foot of the statue as a tribute from that organization. Within two years the Boy Scouts will begin an annual long-term program in Fort Wayne that spreads to other parts of the country, known as Lincoln Day Pilgrimages.

Over the next several days, nearly one hundred telegrams from all across the nation pour into the Lincoln Historical Research Foundation. The radio coverage has secured a national interest as governors, Lincoln buffs, teachers, and all manner of government officials send their congratulations to Fort Wayne.

The Detroit News sums it up best: "A new and different statue of Abraham Lincoln was unveiled here today. . . . It is a likeness of Lincoln at 21; a stalwart Indiana frontiersman, unburdened by his country's problems."

I snap out of my time-travel reverie and once again focus on the present moment. My thoughts focus on the idea of meaning. Civic monument dedications on this scale remain as important today as they did in 1932. Collectively, these ceremonies remind us of what we share in common with each other and with the past. They help us focus on ideals we cherish and collective memories we value, and they give us hope for the future. At a more academic level, such practices are vital in creating a construct of history acceptable to the masses. With regard to public memory, the United States is no different from the ancient cultures of Greece and Rome nor other nations and empires past or present.

Lincoln the Hoosier Youth echoes a theme similar in sentiment to other tributes to the young Lincoln. A book in his hand and the traditional ax affirm a decision to exchange manual labor for intellectual pursuits. It is a robust figure, mirroring what he wrote in an 1860 autobiographical piece for John L. Scripps. "A. though very young, was large of his age, and had an axe put into his hands at once; and from that till within his twenty-third year, he was almost constantly handling that most useful instrument."[4] Lincoln's hands, always an important component in any figurative sculpture, are well balanced; one rests on the ax handle, while the other is gently placed on the head of a hound. The ideal sleek art deco quality of the statue reflects all that Lincoln dreamed of becoming as he fixes his gaze forward, toward the future. The four medallions, all of which include idealized figures, adorn the pedestal, suggesting in their idealization the qualities that would shape Lincoln's character and the eventual destiny of a nation. Above each medallion, etched in stone, are words that define each image. Justice, on the south side of the pedestal, represented by the typical figure of a blindfolded female, carries in her right hand the evenly balanced scales of justice, while her left hand holds a sheathed sword. On the northern side of the pedestal is Fortitude, whose strength is demonstrated threefold by a lion upon which he sits, a Doric column that he grasps in his right hand and arm, and a shield cradled under his left arm. Charity faces the building on the eastern facade of the pedestal, represented by a mother watching over three small children. A heroic, muscular American eagle representing patriotism rounds out the medallion series on the western side of the pedestal, the same side on which Lincoln gazes out at the world. The rich bronze tones of the figure play off the limestone of the Lincoln National Life Insurance Company in a way that brings the eye of the visitor to the statue, almost as if it were saying, "Look at me if you want to know what this company stands for." Its quasi-neoclassical style captures if not the true young Abraham Lincoln, then certainly the sentiment of many of his countrymen living at the time of its dedication, honesty, integrity, and rugged individualism. His portraiture reflects an interest in formal sculptural values as opposed to the subject's personality. But with it the sculptor did give us an insight of the early visionary persona of the Hoosier youth.[5]

The sculptor, with a $75,000 commission in his pocket, took his Lincoln work seriously, touring Kentucky and Indiana, Lincoln's homes as a youth. Louis A. Warren accompanied the sculptor and helped him to fashion an appropriate image of a young Lincoln. They toured related historical sites and talked of Lincoln. Manship read biography after biography and interviewed Lincoln scholars Carl Sandburg and Ida Tarbell, better known as a muckraking journalist who took on Standard Oil, but an equally enthused Lincoln buff. Their input helped the sculptor settle on his particular vision of the youthful Lincoln. Tarbell's remarks at the Second Annual Lincoln Students' Luncheon, the afternoon of the unveiling, reported in the *News-Sentinel*, are laced with mythical phraseology as "son of the Republic," and "his words are simple, natural, like the man." Of the new bronze image of a youthful Lincoln, she said, "Until now that youth has been the victim of over-much pitiless and unimaginative realism. Mr. Manship has stripped away the sordid and ugly details under which the real boy was all but buried, and by his simple, noble, truthful art has given us a Hoosier youth in whom we can see the man we know," asserting a truth that would have been hard for the sculptor to uncover."

There is no photographic evidence of Lincoln before 1846, when he was thirty-seven. This proved to be Manship's biggest frustration. So Manship pored over Lincoln family genealogy and studied dozens of photographs to get a better grasp of his subject. On one occasion the sculptor visited the grave of Lincoln's beloved mother, Nancy Hanks, in the southeastern corner of the state to draw inspiration. From that moment on he understood his charge. "The desire to represent the young Lincoln as a dreamer and a poet rather than as the rail-splitter was uppermost in my mind."

"Everyone has heard or read the stories of Lincoln's youthful physical prowess," Manship said, "and so we have depicted Lincoln as the brawny youth that he was. The axe tells the story of his rail-splitting days. The book symbolizes his intellectual faculties; and the dog reminds us of his exceptional love for animals as well as the greater feeling of human sympathy and protectiveness." As to the hound dog, Manship relied on the story as related by William Herndon, Lincoln's younger law partner in Springfield, Illinois. The tale concerned Lincoln's rescue of a dog in the Wabash River when the Lincoln family moved in 1830 from Indiana to Illinois. "I could not," recalled Lincoln, "endure the idea of abandoning even a dog. Rolling off socks and shoes, I waded across the stream and triumphantly returned with the shivering animal under my arm. His frantic leap of joy and other evidence of a dog's gratitude amply repaid me for all the exposure I had undergone."[6] History aside, this episode may really be a fable. Manship obviously liked the story because he found a dog "from across the Ohio River from the place of Lincoln's youth, and . . . just the type" to use as a model for his statue. He brought the dog with him to his Paris studio and began working on the sculpture in 1929.

Lincoln the Hoosier Youth (author)

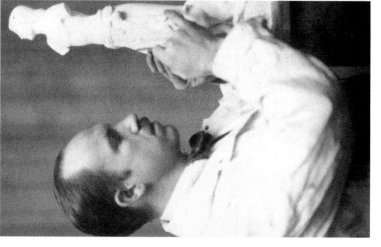

Paul Manship (Smithsonian American Art Museum). Right: Dedication of *Lincoln the Hoosier Youth*, September 16, 1932 (The Lincoln Museum, Fort Wayne, Indiana)

Three years later, after it had been cast at the Compagnie de Bronzes in Brussels, Belgium, it was unveiled. The public could now see for the first time Manship's "Lincoln, clad in linsey-woolsey shirt and butternut trousers," resting "at ease against an oak stump, axe at his side, his right hand holding a book into which the index finger is thrust to mark his page, while the left hand rests upon the head of the dog. In it we have the earnestness and seriousness of a thoughtful youth, and we also see the melancholy aspect which was characteristic of the subject throughout his lifetime, and which has been depicted by the artist with rare subtlety," as scholar F. Lauriston Bullard wrote.[7]

Manship's Lincoln is twelve feet six inches tall. From the pavement to the top of the pedestal there is an additional ten feet making the total height twenty-two feet; within the confines of the expansive courtyard, the scale of the figure is almost perfect. Sculpture and architecture harmonize quite nicely.

The company decided on a more youthful, virile interpretation of Lincoln than the standard presidential portrait would have it, one with which Hoosiers could identify. Lincoln spent his adolescence living and working in Indiana, for one thing, and it makes sense that an insurance company would select a vigorous and healthy rendition of Lincoln, filled with vitality, to help promote its product. For a moment I consider what Lincoln might have thought. More than likely, his shrewd side would give it a nod, complete with some related joke or anecdote.

I cannot help but be drawn to Lincoln's right hand, which holds a book. His ambition to learn and better his lot in life through reading is the stuff of legend. I recall a quote of his that I like to share with my students: "I will study and be ready; then maybe the chance will come"[8]—still solid academic advice for the twenty-first century. I recall Sandburg's narrative from my drive:

> Education came to the youth Abe by many ways outside of schools and books. As he said later, he "picked up" education. He was the letter writer for the family and for neighbors. As he wrote he read the words out loud. He asked questions, "What do you want to say in the letter? How do you want to say it? Are you sure that's the best way to say it? Or do you think we can fix it up a better way to say it?"[9]

I imagine that the book in his hand might be one of his favorite reads. Perhaps it's Bunyan's *Pilgrim's Progress* or Parson Weems's *Life of*

Washington. These were stories that fortified the young Lincoln. Weems's particularly helped shape his outlook on America. Then again, it might be a book of poetry. Lincoln loved poetry, even dabbling in verse himself. He read Shakespeare and Thomas Gray. In particular he found an affinity for Gray's "Elegy Written in a Country Church-Yard," reflecting perhaps his propensity to depression, what he termed "the Hypo." One verse resonates with me:

> Here rests his head upon the lap of Earth
> A youth to fortune and fame unknown
> Fair science frowned not on his humble birth,
> And melancholy marked him for her own.[10]

When you really look at Manship's Lincoln, you have to consider Lincoln's rejection of his roots. One can sense it looking at the face. Lincoln's eyes, locked in a forward blank stare, reflect a kind of dreamy longing for something better. He wanted so much more than what a hardscrabble life had to offer. He preferred intellectual to manual labor. Books and learning became his ticket from the backwoods to prominence. Lincoln even rejected his father and his lifestyle. When time came to pull up stakes a year after the family relocated from Indiana to Illinois, Abraham Lincoln never looked back. He didn't even attend his father's funeral.

"Every man is said to have his peculiar ambition," Lincoln wrote on a circular in 1832 to the people of Sangamon County as a first-time candidate for a seat in the Illinois legislature. "Whether it be true or not I can say for one that I have no other so great as being truly esteemed by my fellow men, by rendering myself worthy of their esteem. How far I shall succeed in gratifying this ambition, is yet to be developed."[11] Here in Fort Wayne, it appears that Lincoln got pretty far.

There is much more to this bronze Lincoln than just the statue and the artistic patronage of the Lincoln National Life Insurance Company. Like Lincoln it is a great American story involving the patriotism of the Boy Scouts of America and the development of one of the nation's premier Lincoln museums.

In 1931, Dr. Louis Warren opened the Lincoln Library and Museum to allow public access to the collections of the Lincoln Historical Research, now the Lincoln Museum of Fort Wayne, Indiana. It purports to be the caretaker of the largest private collection of Lincoln memorabilia in the world. The insurance company and the museum work together to promote the legacy of Abraham Lincoln, the sculpture being just one of many public collaborations. As a result of Daniel C. Beard's dedication addresses at the unveiling of *The Hoosier Youth*, Warren wrote an article in *Lincoln Lore*, the museum's newsletter, published by the insurance company. He followed it with a letter to Boy Scout councils encouraging pilgrimages on February 12 to Lincoln statues located within their perimeters. These pilgrimages started here in Fort Wayne in 1934. Since then, depending on the weather, upwards of three thousand Scouts from northeastern Indiana participate in this annual ritual in Fort Wayne, which has spread to other parts of the country.

That first assembly of three thousand uniformed Boy Scouts must have been quite a sight. I can relate to the name, too—Lincoln Day Pilgrimage, for am I not in my own way engaged in the same sort of venture? Even if we are a secular country that professes no state or official religion, all of this hints at some sort of civic prayer.

I knew I would want to speak with someone here about what the statue means today, so before heading out I called the information office of the insurance company and was put in contact with Lowell Tillman, a retired employee who keeps an eye on the condition of the statue, the Boy Scouts, and the museum. We arrange to meet at the statue. As I am standing there, admiring Manship's work, Tillman playfully sidles up to me and, before introducing himself, says, "He looks better from up top." After a hearty handshake we talk. "That statue," he proudly states, "means something to me and the community. I just enjoyed the heck out of looking at it for all those years I worked here." His eyes brighten and twinkle as he talks with great animation, the gold embroidered Lincoln Museum golf shirt accenting the conversation. Lincoln is his hero. Several times he uses the phrase "charged up," in recounting his delight.

"Two decades ago Lincoln was turning green," he says. "A St. Louis firm was brought in to remove the oxidation and restore the patina. After the cleaning, I was able to look down at the statue from the second floor." Pausing and recollecting, a small smile crosses his face. "It looked like pure gold," he says, beaming. His pride in his company's conservation and care for the statue are evident.

Tillman's favorite anecdote about the statue centers on the ax handle of the Manship sculpture, initially miscast backwards. Had Lincoln used that ax, the Railsplitter would have chopped off his foot with the first swing. You can see the original ax and Manship's model in the Lincoln Museum gallery. Manship, a great artist, took the time to correct his mistake.

"The face is rather handsome for a Lincoln, don't you think?" I inquire, striking a nerve.

"Well sure," he says, "but you have to remember that this is a young Lincoln. This is not the Lincoln who was yet roughed up. President Lincoln's face was shaped by his years of hard work on the prairie. Guys got busted up doing that kind of work."

Tillman's comments reminds me that years later, poet Walt Whitman often watched President Lincoln's carriage ride in the summer as he commuted between the White House and his summer cottage on the grounds of the Old Soldier's Home. In a letter, Whitman called Lincoln "a perfect Hoosier Michelangelo,"[12] no doubt a reference to the size of their respective noses.

Tillman adds, "He probably got a busted nose, too."

Any discussion of present-day insurance company employees and their reverence for their sacred namesake and corporate logo saddens the retiree. He tells me, "I think people know it's Lincoln, but they don't know the history and impact of this place." With a heavy countenance, he reckons that half of the current employees of the company have never been to the museum to share in its rich treasures. He's distressed by what he sees as a lack of interest or care in Lincoln and his memory. Tillman believes that Lincoln was a model of self-improvement, a person that we should all emulate. In part that is why the Manship statue resonates with him. "An awful lot of people in this country," he emphasizes, "have done that just as Lincoln did. In some other countries you don't have that option. Some people here don't think you have that option," he adds quietly.

For Tillman, Lincoln remains an iconic figure, the embodiment of someone who pulled himself up by his bootstraps and made something of his life, someone who knew that in his legacy there must be a kind of purpose. I hope that my presence and journey here assures him that part of my quest as a teacher and lover of public sculpture is to bring life to the overlooked and forgotten.

Manship's statue connects with this community. This Lincoln, a regional hero of the Midwest, makes sense to local folk. People react differently because his roots are here. Part of the appeal of the *Hoosier Youth* is that it connects him with the region. Time spent in Indiana was crucial to Lincoln's development. These were hard years that shaped Lincoln physically and emotionally and that may have been the toughest of his life. Lincoln's great physical strength developed as the result of manual labor stemming from chopping wood, splitting rails, working a frontier farm, and laboring on a Mississippi flatboat. He lost his mother at age nine and helped his father fashion her coffin. Then his sister, Sarah, to whom he was very close, died ten years later. It was also here that he learned to make acquaintances, play jokes, and tell stories that drew people to hear him. All of this part of the Lincoln story played itself out against the backdrop of the Lincoln family struggling to eke out an ordinary life in Indiana. It is not surprising, then, that New Hampshire abolitionist Jesse Hutchinson inserted a lyric in the 1860 Lincoln campaign song "Lincoln and Liberty": "We'll go for the son of Kentucky, the hero of Hoosierdom, too."[13]

Lincoln recalled years later, "In the fall of 1844, I went into the neighborhood in that state in which I was raised, where my mother and only sister are buried, and from which I had been absent about fifteen years. That part of the country is, within itself, as unpoetical as any spot of the earth; but still seeing it and its objects and inhabitants aroused feelings in me which were certainly poetry; though whether my expression of those feelings is poetry is quite another question."[14] In reaction to his visit, Lincoln penned "My Childhood's Home," a twelve-verse anthem to his Indiana experience, which opens,

> My childhood's home I see again,
> And sadden with the view;
> And still, as memory crowds my brain,
> There's pleasure in it too.[15]

Lincoln understood the place of Indiana in his development. His voice, not the mythical baritone suggested by actors Gregory Peck or Raymond Massey that have fused into popular culture, was a high-pitched, nasal Hoosier twang. Whenever I try to imitate Lincoln's voice in my classes my students are shocked. They are convinced that the robotic Lincoln of Disneyworld or Disneyland has it right, when nothing could be farther from the truth.

But something else is afoot in Fort Wayne with Lincoln. Here we find the foundation for utilizing the Lincoln image as a marketable enterprise. As a progressive Whig, Lincoln would most likely have approved. Since 1905, more products have been sold using the Lincoln name than any other personality in American history. As my market-savvy students have often pointed out, it makes sense. Lincoln represents honesty and integrity. Even the Lincoln Museum honors Lincoln the salesman, with an extensive exhibit that includes a potpourri of products he has been used to hawk. The twentieth century alone gave us Lincoln Logs, the Lincoln Continental, Lincoln oranges, Lincoln appliances, and Lincoln tobacco and liquor. In the museum one can find a sign for "Abe's Bail Bonds" and a Budweiser T-shirt in which Lincoln's trademark stovepipe hat is replaced with a can of beer. Beneath Lincoln's face the shirt reads, "All beers are not created equal." (Lincoln would not have been amused. He neither smoked nor chewed tobacco and was a well-known teetotaler.) Corporations have cashed in on the Lincoln image and continue to do so. Today Lincoln and a talking beaver hawk a prescription sleeping pill, and the Lincoln Financial Group runs television ads showing a retiree golfer being followed by Abraham Lincoln on the golf course. In another version, Lincoln rides in a gondola on a Venetian canal with a retired couple. Here Lincoln ensures viewers that in retirement it's good to have Lincoln behind you. This particular insurance company has been at it for over one hundred years. Since 1905 it has been using the Lincoln profile to protect folks against all manner of maladies or threats.

But one has to really wonder then if this practice of wrapping corporations in Lincoln, like the American flag, has trivialized the man to the point that we have really become blind to his true virtues. Does this behavior with Lincoln's memory also turn folks off from trying to understand the reality of the man? Have we have done Lincoln a disservice by placing him on the shallow mantle of cult celebrity status? In the end, does it not really honor Lincoln but cheapen him in the American marketplace? Are Americans willing to make the effort to look beyond the billboards and car advertisements that appear to be typical in mainstream America? Can we as a culture look past the President's Day flyers adorned with images of Abraham Lincoln and George Washington peddling sheets, dishwasher detergent, and other creature comforts? In some ways all of this runs counter to the other very American tradition of civic pride, pageantry, and ceremony so central not only to a monument's dedication, but also to the enshrinement of our heroes and leaders.

Manship's sculpture reflects the era in which it was dedicated and how people viewed life. It marks Lincoln's time in this state and has some universality of the story of the self-taught man having few advantages. Making something of his life is one of the many stories of the Lincoln image that is very germane to his Indiana years; it is the story of an ordinary person who grows up to live an extraordinary life. If I were teaching this young Lincoln in my classroom today, he would be defined as a gifted child. On the steps of the Lincoln National Life Insurance Building we commemorate a Lincoln of sublime simplicity and humility, absent of naïveté. What one does not get in Manship's work are Lincoln's complexity and seeming contradictions.

While those contradictions don't manifest themselves in *Lincoln the Hoosier Youth*, they are present in American life. On the same day that the Manship was dedicated, United Press International reported that Frank Tucker, twenty-four, a "Negro," was lynched by a mob of five hundred people for stealing ten silver dollars from the town bank and slashing a deputy with a razor in Crossett, Arkansas. *The News-Sentinel*, the afternoon paper from Fort Wayne, never made the connection between the lynching and the legacy of the life that was honored in a grand All-American ceremony.

Paul Manship provides for us, in bronze, a glimpse into the early life of Abraham Lincoln. Through the power of his art we can tap into the early ambition of the sixteenth president. Lincoln's rejection of manual labor for intellectual pursuits is most evident as is Lincoln the visionary and dreamer. As a young man, Lincoln began the long road to achieve his peculiar ambition, a road that finds, in part, its origin in the Indiana soil. From here he would move on to greatness. But first he had to find success as a politician and prairie lawyer.

Other sculptors would take up the charge to define those images as well. Those sculptures are waiting for me. I eagerly hop back into my car, ready to continue the quest.

Barnard's *Lincoln* (author)

3

A Different Kind of Civil War

George Grey Barnard's *Lincoln* (1917), Cincinnati, Ohio

I'm PLAYING PIED PIPER AGAIN and glad to be doing so. This time I deliberately set out to see if I could bring a Lincoln statue to life in a way that I had never done before. My proving ground would be George Grey Barnard's *Lincoln* in Cincinnati's Lytle Park.

Thirteen seniors and seven of their parents agreed to give up half of their final spring break to go on a Lincoln Pilgrimage Road Trip. Just after daybreak in Virginia, they board a white charter bus along with my student teacher, Brad, and me. Nine hours later, we arrive at our destination, the Quality Inn and Suites in Norwood, Ohio, a suburb of Cincinnati. Road-weary but still enthusiastic, my travel companions squeal with delight when they see a large hotel sign heralding our arrival: "Welcome Association of Lincoln Presenters (ALP)." Boasting more than 160 members, the ALP is an organization dedicated to preserving the life and legacy of the sixteenth president through dramatic presentations. Its members dress up and role play Lincoln for civic groups, schools, nursing homes, and churches, bringing him to life. It's a privilege for them to live out their motto, "In Lincoln's Image." Not even our founding fathers have such a group of boosters.

Two years before our excursion, I traveled to Vandalia, Illinois, to attend the ALP annual conference, oddly convening each year on the closest weekend date to that of Lincoln's actual assassination. Held in the old state capitol, it was a delightful experience, augmented by its members' willingness to embrace the history teacher in their midst. I promised myself at the time that somehow I would get my students to connect with this interesting group of fellows. Cincinnati and Barnard afforded me that opportunity. The moment had arrived.

As the bus wheels hummed along the interstate, the little reading lights above each seat glowed as students and parents scanned the material I prepared for them for our trip. A month prior to our departure I constructed a short historical treatment on Barnard's Lincoln, traveling to New York in Barnard's footsteps, closely pursuing and sleuthing the tale of his creation in preparation for our pilgrimage. The story unfolded, for me, as I stood on the corner of Ocean and Ditmas Avenues in Brooklyn across from the brick and stucco All Souls Universalist Church. Standing there, I mentally took myself back in time. Although the Cincinnati Lincoln sculpture was dedicated in March 1917, it was February 14, 1932, that would prove in many ways monumental. On that Sunday's Valentine's Day, with temperatures hovering around freezing and a stiff breeze cutting across New York harbor and the East River, the mercurial sixty-eight-year-old sculptor, George Grey Barnard, with his shock of white hair and weather-worn face not unlike Lincoln's cockeyed visage, entered the sanctuary to deliver a "Lincoln Speech." It was appropriate timing. Two days before, in the age before the combined President's Day honoring Lincoln and George Washington, had been a legal holiday, Lincoln's Birthday. In the sanctuary, beneath a copper-sheeted octagonal dome-shaped cupola, more at home in New England than Brooklyn, sat some three hundred congregants. The dark wood-grained interior provided a warm, spiritual atmosphere.

Barnard had been invited to speak by the charismatic pastor, Dr. Cornelius Greenway. Known to his congregation as Connie, the popular minister had a passion for the pulpit that only slightly edged his great interest in history, particularly with regard to the lives of heroes. An avid collector of signatures of the famous, Greenway had written *Hunting Big Game with a Fountain Pen*, the story of his pursuit for historical autographs. In his heart, Greenway had a special place for Lincoln. And to Greenway, Barnard was a "preacher who carved sermons in stone," an allusion to his skill as a monumental sculptor.[1]

Barnard and Greenway were longtime friends. The sculptor, almost always in chronic debt, turned to Greenway for counsel in 1930. On the verge of being evicted from his thirty-year-old monastery-like home and studio at 700 Washington Avenue, perched on the cliffs of upper Manhattan overlooking the Hudson River, Barnard needed Greenway's help. Much of Barnard's debt was the result of his insatiable appetite for collecting medieval art. His quest and subsequent collection became the foundation for the Metropolitan Museum of Art's Cloister Museum. "His life," Greenway said "was like a river that had broken its levees. He swept us all along with him. No one was given time to get a second breath—his art was at stake and he enlisted us in the cause."[2]

In many ways it made sense to have Barnard deliver a Lincoln sermon in a holy place. For Barnard, "God fills our sails if only we hold them to the mast."[3] He believed he was gifted and divinely inspired and keenly felt it was his responsibility to pay homage to his Creator through his work. All Souls, through its pastor, had been fortuitous to have engendered and cultivated a special relationship with the Bohemian artist. In gratitude for the church's support of his struggle to save his home and workshop, during what Greenway called, "the lost cause," he had given to the church two samples of his famous works of sculpture; the original model for "Brotherly Love," a Michelangelo-esque type work of two people reaching out to embrace one another though constrained by the stone that separates them and "Descent from the Cross," a bas-relief panel. On this Sunday, Barnard watched as six men struggled to place in the church chancel a massive marble head of Lincoln, created after he finished the Cincinnati commission, that he was loaning to All Souls.

As Barnard climbed the four steps to the pulpit, he must have had much on his mind.[4] Life was crowding in on him. His beloved home and studio in Manhattan was again under threat of foreclosure. And aging had not been easy. Arthritis increasingly interrupted his work, afflicting his hand and finger joints. But any fleeting thought of difficulty may have disappeared as Barnard stepped up to address one of his particular obsessions. Fifteen years earlier his heroic but controversial statue of Lincoln for Cincinnati had consumed him and much of the art world. Like all sculptors, Barnard was happy to have been awarded a Lincoln commission. But Barnard was a bit of a rebel as well as a rascal. As a neophyte sculptor at the École des Beaux Arts in Paris, an institution committed to the academic training of artists, Barnard was straddling an age between sculptural work that depended on a delicate balance between the real and ideal in human form. Some, however, were moving toward modernism and more impressionistic work.

The public and vitriolic struggle he endured in 1917–18 over his interpretation of Lincoln became an international cause célèbre.

Even his friend Isadora Duncan, the dancer whom he had watched perform many times, grew frustrated with Barnard when Lincoln got in the way of a mutual pet project. It had been Duncan's hope that together she and Barnard would collaborate on a sculpted tableau vivant centered on Walt Whitman's "I Hear America Singing," which would be called "I See America Dancing."

"Ah, George Grey Barnard," Duncan said, "we will grow old, we will die, but not those magic moments we spent together, I the Dancer, you the Magician who could have seized his dance through its fluid reflection—you the Master Power to send the lightning stroke of the moment down to Eternity. Ah, where is my master-piece—my chef d'oeuvre—'American Dancing'? I look and encounter the gaze of Human Pity—of his colossal statue of Abraham Lincoln dedicated to America—the great brow, the furrowed cheeks, furrowed by tears of Human Pity and Great Martyrdom—and I the slight, futile figure dancing before this ideal of superhuman faith and virtue."[5] In spite of the past, it was clear that this Sunday did, however, belong to him and Abraham Lincoln.

Barnard's small stature may have come as a surprise, given his reputation, to those gathered in the pews to listen. The daughter of his playwright friend Percy MacKaye, Avia MacKaye Ege, had once been impressed with his looks. "He is marvelous," she wrote, "very beautiful, almost like a Greek statue, with a radiant piercing sweetness, eyes which are like mirrored sparks and give the effect of light. As you are blinded by their radiance, you cannot see the thing which produces it behind. He has an extraordinary grace; an elusive cast in the eye, for one eye seems to wander. His big voice is of like quality, large—very large, with such resonance that, in a small room it fills it to discomfort, but vibrant, sweet penetrating, a marvelous musical instrument."[6] Coincidentally, Barnard's left eye wandered, as did Lincoln's. In some ways Barnard looked like a Bowery pugilist, short and stocky like the actor James Cagney. And in spite of his sizable ego he was likable.

Like Lincoln the president, who held the helm over a divided nation, so too would Barnard's Lincoln preside over a split that would pit those in favor of a more traditional interpretation of "President Lincoln" rather than a homespun prepresidential Lincoln. As with the charges levied against Barnard's Lincoln, reflecting "hobo-democracy," a kind of uncouth, rough-hewn version of the American dream, we still debate the meaning of art, particularly commemorative works. Art, like history, is not uncontested ground.

Played out in the national press, this particular struggle, spilled over from a charged debate between two period journals, *Art World: A Monthly for the Public Devoted to Higher Ideals* and *Touchstone.* Led by editor and sculptor Frederick Wellington Ruckstull, *Art World* between June 1917 and March 1918 ran seven issues containing extensive brutally scathing editorials against Barnard's Lincoln. As a strident defender of the artistic values of the American Renaissance, Ruckstull raised his voice against what he feared to be an onslaught of works contrary to academic merit and values.

To Ruckstull nothing less than the moral compass of the role of art in a democracy was at stake with Barnard's Lincoln. Proponents of modernism and radical art must not be permitted to gain the upper hand. It was a classic case of reaction to the fin de siècle of the age. To this end, *Art World* published altered photographs and paintings of Lincoln, as well as published photographs of Barnard's work, in unfavorable light. The use of these images made this a classic case of bending the truth to achieve a particular objective.

In the other corner was *Touchstone*, edited by New York socialite and art critic Mary Fanton Roberts. It employed two heavyweights, Lincoln biographer and muckraking journalist Ida Tarbell and unofficial poet laureate Edwin Markham. Before the dust finally settled, many national newspapers and weeklies, former presidents Theodore Roosevelt and William Howard Taft, scores of artists, noted British satirist George Bernard Shaw, aged friends and acquaintances of Abraham Lincoln, and his only surviving son, Robert, weighed in on the row.[7] Even the venerated Volk life mask and how to interpret it was cast into the debate. In a way, the raucous and vigorous debate foreshadowed future brouhahas concerning American civic sculpture and public memory. Various newspapers including the *New York Times* and the *Philadelphia Evening Telegraph* ran public opinion polls about Lincoln statues, adding fuel to the controversy. Not only was art at stake, but also at issue was the still running debate of how Abraham Lincoln should be remembered. This story added another layer to the mythology that so often surrounds the sixteenth president.

Like most stories about civic monumental sculpture, it started innocently enough. Charles P. Taft, the younger half-brother of President William Howard Taft, and his wife, Anna Phelps Taft, were wealthy Cincinnati patricians and part of the city's established elite. For them the time was right to give a gift to their beloved city. Their enthusiasm for a tribute to Lincoln intended to put that city on the map.

Lincoln visited Cincinnati twice as an attorney. In 1855 he was humiliated by his future secretary of war, Edwin Stanton, at the celebrated McCormick Reaper Trial, and he watched the proceedings of the trial relegated to the courthouse gallery. To friends Lincoln later remarked, "I have nothing against the city, but things have so happened here as to make it undesirable to ever return here."[8] He returned to Cincinnati once more as a politician in pursuit of the White House and then later as president-elect on his inaugural train ride to Washington.

A Republican, much in the mold of his conservative older half-brother, Taft was educated at Yale and Columbia. In 1895, after dabbling in Ohio politics, he was elected to the U.S. House of Representatives. His fortune rested on his father-in-law's shoulders as the manager of his vast entrepreneurial enterprises, including "transportation, utilities, amusements, and newspapers." Cincinnati's premier paper, the *Cincinnati Times-Star*, was part of the Stinton holdings. When David Stinton died in 1900, his fortune, properties, and home reverted fully to Charles and Anna.[9]

In the years after the Civil War Cincinnatians vigorously pursued the same status enjoyed by Boston, New York, Philadelphia, and other American cultural centers. In 1871 the Tyler Davidson Fountain was unveiled in the city's downtown, marking the beginning of a period of active civic art patronage. In the late nineteenth and the early twentieth centuries, Cincinnati continued to enrich its increasingly urban landscape with works of public sculpture and institutions devoted to the arts. For the Tafts this included the acquisition of personal art works to reflect their place among Cincinnati's social elite. Between 1902 and 1920 the Tafts amassed a huge collection of European masters, including works of Van Dyke, Turner, and Gainsborough. As proud art patrons, the Tafts enjoyed sharing their possessions. They often loaned works of art to various exhibits and graciously opened their home to connoisseurs and the press.[10]

As the centennial of Lincoln's birth loomed, Cincinnati, like other major cities, sought to erect a suitable monument to his memory. In 1907 Charles Taft found himself as one of thirty-five prominent citizens named to the Committee on a Permanent Memorial of the Lincoln Centennial Memorial Association. In 1909 the Committee found itself with a $100,000 windfall, the contribution of a wealthy widow, Mrs. Frederick H. Alms, whose husband, a Civil War veteran, held Lincoln in high regard. For Eleanora Alms this was a worthy project that would honor not only her husband but also the "man he and his soldier comrades worshipped."[11] Her only stipulation for the donation was that the city maintain, repair, and clean in perpetuity the Lincoln statue.

The Alms Committee and the Tafts would have to contend with the eccentricities and egos of two sculptors, Barnard and the fiery and pompous Gutzon Borglum, both of whom believed he was the most qualified to create a fitting and heroic Lincoln statue. Each artist believed that he had reached such artistic heights and stature that to place his name in competition would be undignified. From October 1909 until December 1910 a kind of frenetic correspondence ensued between Borglum and the Alms Committee and to a lesser extent between the committee and Barnard. Feelings were hurt, egos bruised, promises broken, characters assassinated, contracts written and declared null and void, and rules changed to an increasing cacophony of charges and countercharges. Initially the Tafts backed Barnard, asserting as a defense premise that Barnard's "total disregard of time and labor proved him to be a passionate creative being who, in obvious contrast to Borglum, gave no thought to commercial interests. From Borglum's perspective, the contest was one in which a man of "prolific, poetic character" faced the "bluster and brag" of a bankrupt and failed artist.

In the end, the commission went to Barnard, but not before a frustrated and exasperated Charles Taft admitted in a letter to William, "I have been so mad today that I have not been able to do anything . . . if ever a confidence game has been practiced we are certainly in it."[12] At one point it was even intimated that Barnard held a kind of Svengali power over the Alms Memorial Committee. Poor political maneuvering and costly miscues cost Borglum his chances. In early

December 1910 four members of the Alms Committee awarded Barnard a contract. Alms, reported the *Cincinnati Times-Star,* was assured that Barnard's Lincoln "will redound not only to the glory of Cincinnati, but would be a lasting and worthy memorial to your beneficence." But on December 15, Barnard signed a second Lincoln contract with the Tafts, who offered him $100,000. An incensed Borglum returned to Cincinnati and publicly accused the Tafts of treachery. The *New York Times* ran a headline, "Borglum Attacks the Tafts."[13]

On December 16, Barnard returned to New York. For the moment he was financially sound. But only for the moment. He decided to move forward with the Taft Lincoln. The sculpture would be sited in Lytle Park, directly across the street from the Tafts' home.

One can understand Borglum's bitterness. By now he had successfully sculpted two critically successful portrait statues of Lincoln, one for the Rotunda of the U.S. Capitol in 1908 and one for Newark, New Jersey, in 1911. Barnard was not known for portraiture or commemorative works. Principally a sculptor of allegorical subject matter, he first gained recognition with the piece *The Struggles of the Two Natures of Man* (1894), acquired by the Metropolitan Museum of Art in New York City as a gift. Best known for the massive marble ideal pieces he sculpted to grace the entrance to the Pennsylvania State House in Harrisburg, Barnard, excelled at sculpting allegorical figures. He often fell behind in his work, made enemies, had contractual problems, and let his expenses accumulate. Simultaneously, his quest as an art dealer and collector of assorted works from the Middle Ages proved a distraction. The project was colossal and involved two separate treatments for either side of the main entrance to the statehouse. The work, called *Love and Labor: The Unbroken Law,* was to be placed on the north side of the staircase, while the south side was graced with the *Burden of Life: The Broken Law,* each a cornucopia of allegorical and ideal figures. While this work was on exhibition in Paris, Charles Taft first encountered Barnard's work and guaranteed Barnard that he would be awarded the Alms Lincoln contract.[14]

The Lincoln commission was something of a departure for the forty-seven-year-old Barnard, but he poured his whole heart and soul into the project. He carefully studied the life mask of Lincoln made by Chicago sculptor Leonard Volk in March 1860. Lincoln agreed to endure the grueling process and in his own way thus played a hands-on role in his legacy. Securing for successive generations the exact dimensions of Lincoln's face, Volk's handiwork would prove to be a terrific tool for sculptors. The mask was dynamic, vigorous, and strong, with supple muscle tone. In his typically self-deprecating manner, Lincoln exclaimed, "There's the animal himself!" Captured for all posterity was the odd curvature of Lincoln's face with which sculptors would have to contend. There was the natural curve from the crown down to the chin, but there was also a curve across the face most articulated by the off-center alignment of Lincoln's nose. This created two distinct hemispheres of Lincoln's face. His right side was more relaxed and fleshy, reflecting perhaps his innate compassion and flexibility, while his left side offered a tighter musculature, suggesting Lincoln's resolve to preserve the Union.[15]

"An imaginary Lincoln," Barnard said, "is an insult to the American people, a thwarting of democracy." Hearkening to his own self-proclaimed providential calling, Barnard continued, "No imitation tool of any artist's conception but the tool of God and Lincoln made—Lincoln's self—so that all form had been obliterated. . . . To most, the life mask is a dead thing; to the artist life's architecture." To Barnard, the essence of Lincoln was in the mask and it was his sacred trust to interpret it. "We and future ages," he said, "have this life mask to fathom, to interpret, to translate. Art is the science that bridges 'tween nature and man. Sculpture being a science to interpret living forms, hidden secrets of nature is revealed by it."

A democratic vision, Barnard observed, was rooted in Lincoln and reflected in his facial structure. "Lincoln's life mask," he said, "is the most wonderful face left to us, a face utterly opposed to those of the emperors of Rome or an assertive over others; Lincoln's commanding self for the sake of others, a spiritual will based on reason. His powerful chin is flanked on either side by powerful construction, reaching like steps of a pyramid from chin to ear, eye to brain, as if his forces took birth in thought within, conceived in architecture without building to the furthermost limits of his face."

"For one hundred days," Barnard pondered while carefully scrutinizing Lincoln's features, "I sought the secret of this face in the marvelous constructive work of God. Here is no line, no form, to interpret lightly, to evade or cover. Every atom of its surface belongs to some individual form melting into a larger form and again into the form of the whole. The mystery of this whole form nature alone knows—man will never fathom it, but at least he should not bring to this problem forms of his own making." Barnard never recognized the irony of his own words.

"Art's virtue," Barnard believed, "is to reveal not obscure. It is a power to make plain hidden things. Art is not nature, the mask of Lincoln not sculpture. The mask controls its secrets. Lincoln's life revealed them, as the sculptor must reveal the power and purpose of this wondrous mask."[16]

Barnard worked exclusively on Lincoln's facial portrait in 1911 and 1912, cultivating a mystical bond with the subject. Each morning he would eagerly enter his studio to take up his day's work. "I cannot wait," he wrote, "to wash face, hands and especially shave in the mornings, I am so impatient to get to the studio. Each day it is the same passionate tempest of concentration from 9 a.m. to 6 p.m., only eight or ten minutes for eating my sandwiches." Later he said that his work on Lincoln's head had "more great art in it than anything I have done."[17] By 1912, Barnard, too, decided that his statue would be a Lincoln before he assumed the presidency, what he called a "Lincoln of the People." The sculptor's hope was to have the completed bronze figure cast by October 1913.

Commensurate with a project of this scale and scope, Barnard labored in his New York studio making numerous clay sketches and maquettes of varying sizes, moving from smaller versions to larger impressions. From clay he moved to plaster and by 1913 settled on a heroic size of a fourteen-foot standing Lincoln.

That same year he opened a national search for a suitable model that read "Wanted—A man of the Abraham Lincoln type, facial resemblance not desired, giant in stature, six feet three inches or more, big-boned, sinewy, age 40 to 50 years, to pose for Lincoln statue at $10 per day. Several months work." Thinking he might have luck finding someone Lincolnesque from Lincoln's home state the same add was placed in the *Louisville Courier-Journal* and Barnard eventually traveled to Kentucky to conduct interviews. Answering the ad was forty-four-year-old Charles Thomas, whose home was not far from Lincoln's birthplace. With Thomas, Barnard claimed to have found the perfect figure in that of the unskilled railroad worker, who, coincidentally, was employed by the same railroad company Lincoln had worked for as an attorney, the Illinois Central Railroad. To the

sculptor, Thomas was another lean, lanky, and self-professed railsplitter who reminded him of Lincoln and tangentially of Christ. Barnard
said that Lincoln's "unshapely feet trod the winepress of God's judgment on a land; whose ungainly hands plucked thistles and planted
flowers in their stead; whose unsightly back bore the bruises of a nation's chastisement; whose uncomely face bore the prints of vigil and
scars of grief; a face more scarred than any man's save One, and save
that One a face more beautiful."[18] Thomas had an odd curvature of
the upper back, a forward tilt in his neck, was of the right height, and
was clean-shaven. Of Thomas, Barnard said, "I have seen the models
of Europe—men of Greece and Italy—symmetrical and beautiful in
a classical way but nothing ever appealed to me like the form of this
Kentuckian."[19]

In its execution, the tall gaunt figure, with his arms crossed in front
of the body's midline reflected, perhaps unconsciously, the gothic
figures found on the medieval tombs of nobility many of which Barnard encountered on his art collection forays through Europe. Aesthetically problematic, particularly when viewed from the side,
Barnard's hunchback Lincoln suffers from the same issue that de-
tracts from Daniel Chester French's 1912 statue of Lincoln on the
statehouse grounds in Lincoln, Nebraska. In both instances, Lincoln's physiognomy looks awkward and freakish.

Perched on top of the torso was a faithful treatment of Lincoln's
face, complete with oversized ears, creases, moles, lips, and bone
structure. Barnard struggled with Lincoln's neck anatomy, and he
would be singularly criticized for Lincoln's neck and the sharp protu-
berance of his Adam's apple and accompanying thyroid cartilage.

A combination of health factors, including an acute bout of arthritis
in Barnard's hands and a serious fall in his workshop that hospitalized
him, led to missed deadlines and haggling between the client and patron over payment installments. In 1913 he went on an extended
shopping spree for medieval antiquities in Europe and was focused
on finishing the building of the Cloisters, the museum that would
house his ever-growing art collection. Running a large workshop like
other sculptors, he assumed other projects, including that of a fifteen-
foot plaster portrait bust of Lincoln that he called *Lincoln in
Thought*.

These diversions consumed him until the middle of 1915, when he
once again committed his energy on the Taft Lincoln. In November

1915 he launched the first of several public relations campaigns for his statue. The full-scale plaster model was exhibited to special guests, including Theodore Roosevelt. Denver attorney L. Ward Bannister thought that Barnard's Lincoln struck a chord reminiscent of the Illinois Republican Senate candidate who challenged Stephan A. Douglas for that seat in 1858. In a letter to a friend, Bannister wrote that Barnard depicted Lincoln "stooped as to shoulders, wearing clothes more or less ill fitting and shoes of the coarse heavy type then worn in country districts. The hands, large and rough, are crossed in front, and the expression of the face especially the eyes is that of sadness and isolation. The very homeliness of the garb and posture accentuates this expression and makes Lincoln to be all the more in Art what he was in nature—the embodiment of a great but as yet in many ways uncultivated democracy. If the American people fail to appreciate this statue it will be because they do not know themselves."[20] Other visitors expressed their delight to the sculptor as well calling the figure "original and individual." Some said it was "the greatest Lincoln that had ever been produced in this country."

Another visitor to the Fort Washington studio, Frank M. Chapman, a good friend of Theodore Roosevelt, wrote the Tafts shortly after a visit, "I congratulate Mr. Taft in having been privileged to give his country so impressive a statue of its first citizen that its resting place would always be a mecca for every lover of liberty and freedom."[21] The encouraging responses pleased the patrons.

Acrimony, however, again entered the picture over payment schedules even as the plaster components were ready for casting at the Roman Bronze Works, with the clients hoping for an October 1916 unveiling. And in August, Barnard's wife, Edna took ill forcing Barnard to attend to his wife's recuperation. In late October the foundry completed the casting process. By early November, Barnard was badgering his client for a release of additional funds to help with a temporary exhibition of the assembled work in New York. The conniving Barnard arranged for a private visit to the Roman Bronze Works of Philadelphia *North American* editor Leigh M. Hodges, who penned an enthusiastic review, "A New Tradition in American Art," for his November 25 edition. Most telling was Hodge's assessment of Lincoln as an icon of democracy, writing that the sculptor was "stirred by a passion for democracy and a profound reverence for Lincoln as its prophet." Hodge concluded that Lincoln's feet were like roots "spreading into the common soil." This Lincoln, the editor contended, was the work of a genius who understood America at its fundamental core and it embodied the soul of America as kind of a "sacred legacy through one soul to millions of souls."[22] The ploy worked. Publication of the article convinced Taft to release the necessary funds so that the sculptor could temporarily exhibit his work in New York City before it was shipped to Cincinnati.

Two other allies whom Barnard discovered during this phase of the work included an actual Lincoln appointee to the United States Custom Service, Harrison W. Gourley, and a former president, Theodore Roosevelt. Gourley, fifty-one years after Lincoln's assassination, was still with the Custom Service. He claimed that Barnard had reincarnated his former boss and gave thumbs-up to the depiction. Roosevelt, who loved public commemorative sculpture and was always intrigued by works representing Lincoln, told Barnard, "I have always wished I might have seen him—and now I do. . . . At last we have the Lincoln of the Lincoln-Douglas debates. How long we have been waiting for this Lincoln! I feared that with the passing of the years it would never come; but here it is—the living Lincoln. Lincoln was never done with a beard, it hid his character. But now after long waiting here he is, the true Lincoln. This statue is unique; I know of no other so full of life. The greatest sculptor of our age has revealed the greatest soul of our age. One is worthy of the other. (I commend Barnard with all my heart.) He has given us Lincoln, the Lincoln we all know and love."[23] Roosevelt almost always gushed over any statue of Lincoln. In 1911 as the dedication speaker for Borglum's Lincoln in Newark, New Jersey, he similarly praised that artist's interpretation.

Thirteen days after Hodge's piece appeared, workers from the Roman Bronze Works hoisted the sculpture into place in the courtyard of Union Theological Seminary. Barnard was ebullient. He had his temporary exhibition. The exhibition opened to the public on December 12, and by the time the statue was crated and packed away by the end of February nine thousand people—ordinary citizens, interested journalists, wealthy business tycoons, artists, the literati, politicos, and pundits—had viewed Barnard's work.[24]

However, much as the Civil War consumed Lincoln, Barnard's Lincoln continued to be at the forefront of a set of competing interests, both aesthetically and ideologically. At issue was not only an artistic interpretation, but also the question of who owned Lincoln's memory. Barnard's vision of a rumpled hick rankled those who believed that Lincoln should be afforded greater dignity in a public sculpture. To them, Barnard usurped Lincoln's image, denying him the dignity befitting a great man and president. The ruckus that would soon break out would explode not only in the United States, but would also have international complications at a critical juncture—namely, America's entry into World War I.

An initial flurry of positive and favorable commentary helped bolster Barnard's position. New York's *Outlook* reported, "The creative power of the American sculptor has revealed the vision of the real Liberator."[25] One admiring woman wrote that "tears sprang to my eyes—whilst my heart leaped in gratitude to know that there was one in our midst who could portray to posterity the soul of our martyred Lincoln." Another claimed he was "struck by [Barnard's] noble mastery, your spiritual insight, and your poetic powers. Fellow artist Abbott Thayer gushed this Lincoln to be, "an exquisite art miracle like a Beethoven andante . . . the very note it strikes in Being rather than Seeming." Illustrator Charles Dana Gibson weighed in, saying, "It seems foreordained by history that at this supreme moment you should bring forth your great statue of Lincoln the Democrat."[26]

But Barnard made a critical error in judgment in his attempt to secure the needed Taft funding for the exhibition. A Philadelphia newspaper scooped the New York journals with access to the foundry exhibit secured by Barnard.[27] To this end, *New York Times* publisher Adolph Ochs, a defender of progressive and controversial public sculpture, remained mostly silent on the exhibition. Barnard's naïveté in public relations matters cost him. Sculptors such as Borglum and French understood that the key to securing a sculptor's reputation and work was predicated not so much on the quality of the work but rather with how the press managed public relations efforts. Not unlike the man all three captured in marble and bronze, Borglum and French were sagacious with regard to public opinion: "He [Barnard] knew it to be especially foolhardy to permit one newspaper to receive privileged access to information."[28]

Complicating matters was a photograph attributed to the sculptor that found its way into the New York press. The picture, a distorted full-length portrait of the statue taken at an unusual angle, was not flattering. The *Literary Digest* reproduced the image for a national audience. In faraway Wisconsin, the editor of the *Milwaukee Sentinel* fired an opening salvo at Barnard's Lincoln in what would become a barrage in the art war that dominated the art press through the second half of 1917 and the early part of 1918. "The question arises," the *Sentinel* queried, "is it realism at all? Is it a faithful presentment in bronze of the real Lincoln? . . . There are entirely credible and competent witnesses now living who knew Lincoln in the flesh and remember perfectly well how he looked—no difficult thing for 'Old Abe' was a striking figure that, once seen was never forgotten."

In an informal survey, the *Sentinel* polled some of these Lincoln witnesses as to the reality of Lincoln as compared with Barnard's bronze. "The consensus of usually indignant testimony is that it is fearfully and wonderfully unlike Lincoln as they knew him," the paper opined, adding, "The finished artistic result of these processes is one that so far as our own inquiries go, is calculated to stir wrath and resentment those who knew Mr. Lincoln in life and must be admitted to be competent witnesses as to his personal appearance." Adding insult to injury in its stinging conclusion, the *Sentinel* claimed the figure more akin to Ichabod Crane, the hapless schoolteacher in Washington Irving's *Legend of Sleepy Hollow*.[29] Nobody seemed to notice or care that everyone remembers differently.

Again Barnard did nothing to further his cause when he granted an interview the day after the opening exhibition to J. M. Allison, editorialist for Taft's newspaper. Barnard exulted in his work of sculpture's being of providential means. The design, he observed, was not really his but evidenced the hand of God at work on his Lincoln. "It was created," he confided in Allison, "utterly without vanity itself." The finished product "was beyond mere sculpture," and it was not Barnard's place "to say my works are good or bad. . . . There are things made by the human hands which speak of mysteries unrevealed. . . . Those are the things in which the hand has been guided by an inspiration which may not be defined."[30] Too late, Barnard realized his mistake, knowing that his remarks would be hard to swallow by the general public at large. When other newspapers carried the *Times-Star* article, Barnard argued in writing in his defense that he had been misquoted and then begged that his denial not be circulated, particularly in Cincinnati. Barnard had undermined himself.

Financial issues once again hounded the sculptor as Barnard's mortgage holder threatened to foreclose on his home and studio in early January 1917. Once more Barnard went begging for Taft to help bail him out of his straits, even suggesting that Taft pick up the mortgage. Taft released another five thousand dollars to defray the cost of the owed property taxes.

Frederick Wellington Ruckstull, the high-minded editor of *Art World*, exerted some influence in the National Sculpture Society, of which Barnard was a member. Ruckstull, their public sculpture project coordinator, wrote a piece in his journal, "A Standard of Art Measurement." "What the human soul really thirsts for," he wrote, "is not so much originality as—Beauty. If to Beauty is added Originality so much the better. But above all we must have Beauty. And the artist or epoch in art which forgets this fundamental law is in full decadence."[31] In June, Ruckstull would come out vociferously against Barnard and his Lincoln.

On the world stage, the United States edged closer to war with Germany as the late winter gave to spring. With the sculpture being prepared for its final destination, suggestions were raised in various progressive circles that duplicate casts of the Lincoln should be cast for foreign capitals. What better way for the United States to demonstrate its belief in democracy as a political institution in an age of dying monarchies than by presenting to the people of Europe a suitable image of America's "democratic icon"?

On March 27, four days before the statue's unveiling in Cincinnati, the city government of Paris officially accepted the gift, writing, "The committee believes that France is today fighting for the democracy of the world, she is fighting our battle. In appreciation of the gallant spirit of the French people, America presents this statue of Abraham Lincoln who was more than any man the truest representative of Western democracy." An additional cast was ordered for Russia, but when the United States declared war on Germany in April, these plans were laid aside. The idea of a third cast proposed for London as a gift from the American to the British people marking one hundred years of friendship remained a possibility for the duration of the war. After the Cincinnati statue was unveiled, members of the American Centenary of Peace Committee secured financial support from Taft. "Supposing that this offer came from the entire American committee instead of a fraction of its membership, the British committee accepted the offer and obtained an official designation of the Westminster site."[32]

Wrapped in cloth and perched on a three-foot-high crop of a Vermont pink granite boulder, the sculpture conspicuously graced Lytle Park on the morning of its dedication, Saturday, March 31, 1917. The location directly across from the front porch of the Tafts' home made it easy for the couple to admire their contribution to Cincinnati's public landscape. Barnard had originally opted for a more natural pedestal lower to the ground, arguing that this was more fitting for Lincoln: "he is too great a Human to stand on a polished base."[33] A raised platform festooned in flags and patriotic bunting stood just behind the sculpture. Cincinnati's newspapers had been eagerly following the story for months. Twenty thousand people showed up for the dedication ceremony scheduled to begin at 2:30 p.m. in the cool early spring afternoon. Of the throng of humanity were ten thousand schoolchildren who marched to the site. Military and civic organizations participated in the pageantry as well. Even Taft's rival newspaper provided extensive and front page coverage of the event. The *Cincinnati Enquirer* reported, "Red, white, and blue wave from every building and many downtown business houses put on gala attire in honor of the occasion." The newspaper invoked Lincoln's memory as America prepared for war: "On the eve of a national crisis which seems destined to become second only to that which Lincoln faced, former President Taft, making the principal address yesterday at the unveiling of George Grey Barnard's statue of Abraham Lincoln turned to the memory of the Emancipator as 'an anchor of hope and an earnest of victory' to the country in its impending struggle."

The hometown newspapers did not dwell so much on the litany of Lincoln's life and achievement as outlined in most of Taft's address, but rather focused on the present state of the American nation and people as war clouds loomed. "In a time such as this," said Taft, "when we are facing war for the vindication of our rights Lincoln is the figure that comes before our eyes." Skillfully, Taft used the Lincoln image and invoked his spirit and memory. "He is the ideal to whom we look and to whom we point our children. He shows the sacrifice," he said, "our country has the right to ask of us. His memory removes all dross from the fine gold of love of country. The thrill which Old Glory gives us as she floats in the blast of national danger and storm brings Lincoln to our eyes and thoughts." "The Stars and

Stripes, in their inspiring beauty," the newspaper continued, "shadow forth the lineaments of Lincoln' face to every true American."[34]

Far from retreating from the controversy raised by the sculptor's interpretation, Taft praised Barnard for his design: "The sculptor in this presentment of Lincoln which we here dedicate, portrays the unusual height, the sturdy frame, the lack of care in dress, the homely but strong face, the sad but sweet features, the intelligence and vision of our greatest American." Tapping once more into Lincoln's spiritual dimensions and legacy, he boldly declared, "He has with success caught in this countenance and this form the contrast between the pure soul and commanding intellect who belongs to the ages, and the habit, and garb of his origin and his life among the plain people—a profound lesson in democracy and its highest possibility."[35]

If they wanted, people could later secure a copy of the trim tan dedication book, embossed with gold lettering, bearing on the frontispiece an image of the sculpted portrait. Here they could read all of Taft's remarks, Barnard's view of Lincoln, the short acceptance speech by Cincinnati's mayor, and a poem, "Barnard's Statue of Lincoln," by Lyman Whiney Allen. Opening the front cover, readers found an indirect rebuttal to the piece written in the *Milwaukee Sentinel*. Robert C. Clowry, former president of the Western Union Telegraph Company, provided the following testimony: "The Barnard statue is a beautiful piece of workmanship and a perfect likeness of Mr. Lincoln. I was well acquainted with Mr. Lincoln during my residence at Springfield, Illinois before the war."[36]

On April 6, 1917, the United States declared war on Germany and entered the "war to end all wars." At the same time, Frederick Wellington Ruckstull, in June, followed by Robert Lincoln, declared war on any attempt to provide England with a duplicate of Barnard's cast.

Ruckstull's condemning article, "A Mistake in Bronze," was an eight-page screed against the Barnard, published in the June 1917 issue of *Art World*. Ruckstull wrote, "It is an axiom that when a man sets up a public work of art in a public space it becomes a candidate for public approval or condemnation. We are sorry we cannot approve this statue of Lincoln by Mr. Barnard." Ruckstull was particularly incensed with the pose and clothing arguing that Barnard's interpretation only reinforced the idea that "represented [Lincoln] as a 'slouch' as a 'hobo-democrat' and a despiser of elegant social forms, that it has found general credence among the unthinking—to the detriment of our country. . . . This 'slouchiness' of Lincoln is an absurd myth and a calumny." Ruckstull addressed the photographic record of Lincoln, employing five images taken after 1854. In one caption beneath an 1861 photograph, he wrote, "Lincoln was plain, not ugly; simple but not common and that he was careful in his dress whenever he appeared in public." The editor then asked readers to compare and contrast the Lincoln photos with photographs of the Barnard statue, saying, "Now notice the slouchiness of the dress on Mr. Barnard's statue. But note especially the deliberate pushing of the coat collar, making the latter stick out like an owl's ear, and calling attention to an occasional disarrangement of his collar, which was almost inevitable considering the peculiar collar then in fashion. Was this deliberately so composed by Mr. Barnard in order to accentuate the reputation of Lincoln for 'slouchiness' and devotion to a 'shirt-sleeve' and 'hobo' democracy? If so, it is a libel on Lincoln."

Arguing that there was a certain beauty of Lincoln's words, such as the Gettysburg Address, "the nation's Sermon on the Mount, which will inspire our people for all time to move on towards higher levels of thought and feeling," Ruckstull thought Barnard way off the mark and offered this challenge. "The question now is, should Lincoln be thus shown as a slouch? This is one of the most urgent and important questions for the American people to answer. For there lurks danger to our democracy in setting up a statue of Lincoln as a symbol of a *slouch*-democracy."

Ruckstull next attacked Barnard's modeling of the Lincoln's face. "In reality," he said, "he had one of the grandest faces ever modeled by a benign providence. . . . The face on the statue represents Lincoln as if he had been a melancholy, distrust-inspiring weakling which is utterly untrue" Fuelling Ruckstull further was Lincoln's neck. "Notice the enormously long, and scrawny neck giving the effect of the head of an anaconda struggling out of a hole in the ground. This is accentuated by the expression of sourness and a cadaverous accentuation of Lincoln's lack of flesh in the face."

The assault continued with heavy criticism on Barnard's treatment of the hands, legs, and shoes. "We see that nothing about this statue is true—neither the face nor the neck, shoulders, hands, feet, drapery or character—neither body nor soul."

Concluding with a slam at Barnard, Ruckstull said, "One has only to study the fine style, the beautiful artistry in Lincoln's speeches, public papers and even his letter to see that he had the fine soul of a great artist. And all great artists, by instinct, love order, elegance and beauty in all its forms." To Ruckstull, Barnard had presented a Lincoln reflecting, "radicalism in rags" and a "woeful, wallowing Willie," placing Lincoln on the altar of those who aspire not to beauty but to "the hobo-minded," forcing all people "to choose between a democracy smacking of the ugliness of the barnyard and an autocracy offering something more ideal and beautiful." Ruckstull had more faith in the people than he had in Barnard and in a final cudgel said, "men have always come back to the supreme pursuit of nature—the creation of the beautiful. That is the main reason why Mr. Barnard's statue is a mistake in bronze."[37]

Illustrating and bolstering his argument, Ruckstull published retouched photographs of Lincoln statuary, such as Augustus Saint-Gaudens's 1887 *Standing Lincoln* in Chicago, in which the statue is "enveloped in medium-soft illumination and burnished with affine granular patina" to heighten its effect. Later he would employ cartoons from *Life Magazine* and the British press lampooning the statue once he discovered that Taft had plans to present the sculpture as a gift to England and see it placed in London's Chancery Square next to Parliament.[38]

In the June 1917 and January 1918 issues of *Art World*, Barnard's sculpture was subjected to what amounted to a police lineup using seven images from different views Barnard had photographed while it was on exhibition at Union Theological Seminary. His lack of using proper photographic techniques and lighting did not do justice to the statue. Readers of *Art World* had to pass judgments based on what they saw in print. In November 1917, Ruckstull editorialized in a caption of one of Barnard's photographs by writing, "Looks Like Something the Cat Brought in on a Wet Night." In the same issue he raised the stakes. The statue was now "a calamity and an atrocity that ought to be finished—with dynamite."[39] In the December 1917 issue, Ruckstull excoriated Barnard personally. "We could name a sculptor of this city," he wrote, "who at one time, was a sober citizen, but gradually became a mere animal. He was one of the cleverest decorative sculptors, but he ventured into the field of portrait statuary and made a statue of a national character that everyone recognized as a dire failure. He was utterly unfit intellectually and spiritually to undertake that work but, because he was a clever decorator, he and his friends imagined he could make a fine portrait statue. We could mention a score of similar cases in this country and abroad. These facts account for the creation of so many mediocre monuments and mural decorations in this country and other countries which are often mere crimes in bronze and paint." At the end of the piece Ruckstull printed a series of letters to the editor supporting *Art World's* position, including several from one of the nation's foremost Lincoln collectors, Judd Stewart. Another editorial was provided by the librarian of the Iowa State Library who kept and submitted to *Art World* the names of fifteen other people who knew Lincoln in life and who condemned the Barnard statue as a "gross caricature." Additionally, he published a resolution from the National Academy of Design opposing sending the statue to England. The Academy, which comprised leading American artists, had considerable public influence.[40]

Art World continued to mount its campaign in severity, with Ruckstull writing, "The statue suggests that even in its greatest hero democracy breeds nothing but a stooped-shouldered, consumptive-chested, chimpanzee-headed, lumpy-footed, giraffe-necked, grimy-fingered clod-hopper, wearing his clothes in a way to disgust a ragman."[41]

Not everyone was condemnatory. Rallying to Barnard's defense was Mary Fanton Roberts, editor of *Touchstone*. Seizing the moment, she canvassed the arts community and secured support for the Cincinnati Lincoln from sculptor Frederick MacMonnies, Lincoln biographer Ida Tarbell, and poet Edwin Markham.

In the October 1917 issue Fanton, bringing her journalistic fervor to bear, defended Barnard, his work, and his interpretation against Ruckstull's and the *Art World's* hostility and arrogance. MacMonnies, a onetime student of and former assistant to Saint-Gaudens, argued, "The essence of art after all is the artist's vision of the greatness of his subject. George Grey Barnard's Lincoln in my estimation, is not only original, as every monument and work of art must be, it is also a personal vision, which all great art must be to be truthful. To me this statue is full of fine feeling of, nobility. He makes me understand his vision of Lincoln's greatness. I feel that through this monument, Lincoln has been immortalized for America and for all time. . . . After all what can any art do beyond creating a mood? And Barnard's statue of Lincoln does this. It puts one in a mood to understand Lincoln's achievement and character which produced this kind of achievement. . . . As for myself I am more than willing that Lincoln should be represented in England by George Gray Barnard."[42]

Two months later, *Touchstone* ran an editorial by Tarbell, "Those Who Love Lincoln: A Word For Barnard's Statue." Tarbell opened with a direct shot at *Art World* and levied immediate support for Barnard. "Those who interpret the leaders of men in art," she said, "have often played strange tricks through their desire to have them *look* something more than men. Sometimes the interpreter himself cannot face the fact. Again, he knows that if he does so, those for whom he is interpreting, will not accept the work." Clearly weighing in on the side of a homespun Lincoln, Tarbell continued, "To those of us who love Lincoln above all as a tremendous human being who has shown what a man can make of himself in spite of the hardest of fates, any attempt to shirk the facts of his life seems like a sacrilege."

Recalling Lincoln's frontier life, Tarbell resurrected an image of Lincoln appropriate to his humble background. "We want to know," she wrote, "all about him from birth to death. No detail of the simple rough pioneer life of his youth is either unimportant or ignoble to us. We treasure every story of the sorrow, hardship and defeat that followed him through manhood to his very grave. They are part of his making. We feel at home with one so familiar with the lot of the common man. He has known our handicaps and has overcome. He is a victor and one of us."

Barnard's Lincoln was no "slouch" or "hobo-democrat" to the class-conscious champion of the common man. It is amazing," Tarbell wrote, "to see this old dislike to leanness and poverty and rough clothes—this doubt that greatness can, or at least that it should come from where they exist—expressing itself in an organized campaign against an interpretation of Abraham Lincoln which not only admits the poverty and meagerness of his early life but glories in it; makes it a masterful feature of his interpretation. . . . There is not a touch of exaggeration or caricature in his statue."

Tarbell was unrelenting in her defense of the statue. "While the figure shirks nothing of the struggle of the man's life," she argued, "it has an inexpressibly touching dignity, patience and nobility. Is it," to the critics she challenged, "that they are wroth at the courage that insists upon telling the story of hardship and in showing boldly the part these hardships had in the making of the man?"

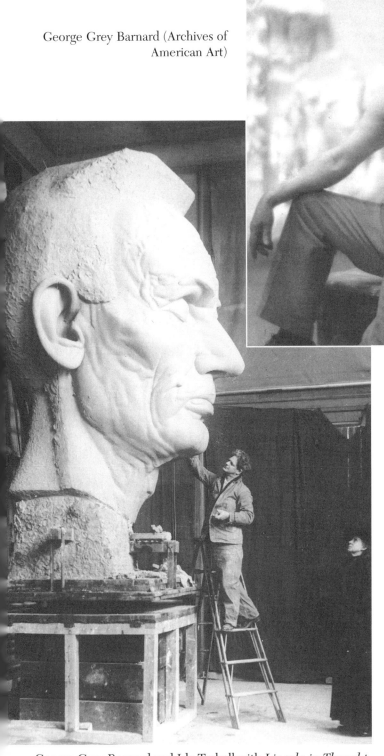

George Grey Barnard (Archives of American Art)

George Grey Barnard and Ida Tarbell with *Lincoln in Thought* (Archives of American Art)

Dedication of Barnard's *Lincoln,* March 30, 1917 (Cincinnati Historical Society)

Tarbell then upped the ante. "Trousers too wrinkled? I wonder did the critics ever read the scores of descriptions of wrinkled clothes and wilted collars, and ruffled hair that those who saw Lincoln in life, when traveling and lecturing, have left behind." She urged readers to glory in Lincoln's wrinkled and unshaven face, his lack of care for dress. For Tarbell the critics of the statue smacked of the critics of Lincoln who chided him during the Civil War. She recalled Lincoln's humiliation at the hands of Stanton during the 1855 McCormick Reaper Trial and indirectly cast Ruckstull and his allies into the camp of those who admonished Lincoln early in the war. "They could not believe it—these men of the east—that one who *looked* so could be a great man." And in a jab to Ruckstull's posture on democracy, she chided, "Of course, they called themselves Democrats; but to many of us, Democracy exists in no class below our own; or if by chance we have come up from the lower class, we are inclined to attribute it to some superior power in ourselves, something in us not in other men." Just as the statue drew recriminations, so too did Lincoln in his White House years as "he was made conscious of this difference; saw the half-contempt his appearance aroused." And like the statue, "This appearance brought him insults—and he knew them as insults—while he endured them for the sake of the Cause to which he had committed himself."

"This figure, full of nobility and resolution," Roberts reasoned, "has the pathos of one who has known what the leanness and struggle of life mean—of one who, in fact, was never able to escape intimate contact with human suffering and need."

Countering Ruckstull's assessment of Lincoln's head, Roberts argued, "How any mortal man can look into this face that the sculptor has wrought by years of loving and reverential toil and not be fully stirred to the depths, I confess I cannot understand."

Tarbell concluded, "those who do not see the great soul of Barnard's statue would never have seen it in the living man himself."[43]

Beneath Tarbell's defense ran a shorter piece by Edwin Markham. His credentials, he claimed, rested on his twenty-year "special study, of Lincoln, his life and his work, his words and his character. I have seen well-nigh all the notable statues of Lincoln," he said, "and I consider the Barnard statue at Cincinnati the greatest of them all." He openly allied himself with Tarbell regarding Lincoln's life on the frontier as one of having been shaped by a "dignity of labor." Equally

critical of Ruckstull's assessment, Markham countered that this particular "dignity of labor," was eloquently expressed by Barnard, "and
if that idea is a mistake, then our national principle is a mistake. If
the dignity of labor is merely a hollow phrase, then the democratic
ideal is a hollow bubble."[44]

As the artistic press war raged, into the volatile mix emerged Lincoln's sole surviving son, Robert. With this, the national press began
to pay attention. By 1905 Robert Lincoln had assumed the mantel as
guardian of his father's legacy. Never himself fond of public sculpture, he viewed sculpture as more or less for the decorative arts for
the home. However he was a bit more open minded when it came to
his father. While reticent about his father's legacy, as more and more
monuments peppered parks and public landscapes around the country, it was not possible for him to ignore them or for memorial associations to ignore him. Of all the Lincoln statues erected in his lifetime,
Barnard's disturbed him the most. He vigorously and openly opposed
the plans of the American Centenary of Peace Committee to provide
Barnard's statue as a gift of friendship from the people of the United
States to the people of England. To Robert Lincoln it was not so
much the idea of not giving a respectable statue to the people of the
United Kingdom, but rather that this particular image of his father
would be erected in the Westminster Enclosure near British statesmen of stature such as Benjamin Disraeli and Lord Palmerston.

In September, Lincoln sent Ruckstull a letter of thanks for *Art
World's* assault, writing, "I am still engaged in making a number of
efforts to prevent the consummation of Mr. Barnard of having this
dreadful statue set up in London. . . . I am making no secret of my
efforts."[45] Several days later, in a letter to New Yorker, Isaac Markens,
author of *Abraham Lincoln and the Jews*, Robert Lincoln lashed out,
"It is as grotesque a likeness of my father at any time." The artist,
Lincoln surmised, "might be suspected of having a 'screw loose." A
week later in another dispatch to Markens, Lincoln wrote, "You ask
whether I have seen the statue. I am glad to tell you that I have never
seen the beastly thing and I hope that I may never do so. I am quite
satisfied that the photographs I have seen do not lie in depicting its
various atrocities."[46] A month later, as the debate intensified and as
national newspapers, including the *New York Times*, which had come
out against the statue calling it "a long-suffering peasant," began to
poll the American public, Lincoln wrote to Charles T. White, "I think

I can say to you that my mail indicates that the public feeling of sending this statue to London is growing rapidly in very influential quarters."[47] The younger Lincoln's influence was strong enough to get the
U.S. House of Representative to pass a resolution requesting that
President Woodrow Wilson prevent the shipment of the duplicate
cast to London.[48]

There may be a reasonable explanation as to why the younger Lincoln had such difficulty with Barnard's work. The sculpture may have
reminded him of how his father appeared when he visited him in
1860 while enrolled in boarding school at Philips Exeter Academy in
New Hampshire. One of Robert Lincoln's schoolmates, Marshall S.
Snow, recalled,

> His hair was rumpled, his neckwear was all awry, he sat somewhat bent
> in the chair, and altogether presented a very remarkable, and, to us,
> disappointing appearance. . . . We sat and stared at Mr. Lincoln. We
> whispered to each other: "Isn't it too bad Bob's father is so homely?
> Don't you feel sorry for him?" Not ten minutes had passed before his
> uncouth appearance was absolutely forgotten by us boys and, I believe,
> by all of that large audience. For an hour and a half he held the closest
> attention of every person present. I cannot recall the details of his
> speech. We were carried away with the arguments, with the style, and
> with the rapid change, now and then, from earnest, serious argument
> to something with a humorous fashion that would illustrate the point
> he was endeavoring to make. His face lighted up and the man was
> changed. There was no more pity for our friend Bob; we were proud
> of his father.[49]

Barnard's statue may have invoked the memory of the embarrass-
ment Robert felt when his classmates first saw his father. The live
man could change a negative first impression to admiration, but the
statue locked that first impression forever in bronze. Lincoln scholar
and collector Frank J. Williams, chief justice of Rhode Island, in
whose chambers, on a pillar, stands a three-foot reduction of the Barnard, believes it "a wonderful realistic and earthy Abraham Lincoln
which probably was disliked by because of its true resemblance to his
father."

In the largest survey conducted by the *Philadelphia Evening Telegraph,* in late 1917 a total of 167,079 individuals responded to the
questionnaire about which Lincoln statue in America should be

presented to England. Of them, 96,112 voted in favor of the Saint-Gaudens statue in Chicago being duplicated, while only 2,016 respondents cast favorable votes for the Barnard. Polls taken by other publications were consistent with the result of the *Philadelphia Evening Telegraph*; Barnard's Lincoln was dead last in all of them. Writing to Shaw, Stewart was quick to point out the results of the Philadelphia paper, arguing, "This will give you a fair idea of how the American people view this matter. I think this newspaper vote is reliable because it represents the public—the people who view the statue; it is not as if it is a technical journal of sculpture had taken a vote which would have resulted in professional opinions only."

Barnard was incensed by the attacks on his creation. He accused Ruckstull and his allies of being akin to the Copperheads, the anti-Lincoln Peace Democrats during the Civil War. But there was little he could do to halt the efforts to undermine the duplicate cast for London. He wrote all manner of invectives laid out against Ruckstull that he, in a very Lincoln-like fashion, never sent. Keeping with the tenor of the times as American doughboys fought the Kaiser's troops in the war to "make the world safe for democracy," Barnard did take note that the *Art World* editor carried a Germanic surname. Though Ruckstull considered himself of Alsatian descent, he did change the spelling of his name from Ruckstuhl to the less Teutonic Ruckstull after the December issue. Twelve pages of disorganized comments, invectives, incomplete sentences, and numerous jumbled thoughts are laid out in a screed found among Barnard's papers that reflects his hurt and furor.[50]

A year later, the feelings still festered as Ruckstull rekindled rumors of Barnard's mental instability. In a letter he disingenuously claimed sympathy for the "half-witted of the race who will persist in going off a tangent and flying into a state of neurosis and demi-insanity and will swear that a totem-pole is finer than an Apollo Belvedere."[51]

Barnard believed that his fellow sculptors were lined up against him. In a letter that, too, was never sent, Barnard chided Daniel Chester French, who by this time was deep into his project for the seated Lincoln for the Lincoln Memorial. "Little did I dream," he wrote, "that while I was planning on giving my life to my country you and Rucksthul and others. . . . A plan was being made among sculptors to cast ignominy on my life's work, and bring disgrace before the world upon my name and my family. . . . I regret with all my blood and soul I am not at the battlefront, but grateful that I am here now to protect my life's work and my family's honor from the knife thrusts at my back."[52]

Mostly it came down to interpretation. In the end it was high idealism against realism. In a well-balanced interview provided to the *New York Times*, the painter Kenyon Cox offered a more gentle and reasonable take on the controversy. The interview was juxtaposed with four photographs, one of an 1861 Mathew Brady portrait of President Lincoln, one of Barnard's piece, one of the Borglum Newark statue, and one of the Saint-Gaudens. "It is easy to see what Barnard was trying to do and why," said Cox. "He was carrying out in his sculpture his ideal of Lincoln. Of course no artist can make a portrait of the 'real Lincoln.' Lincoln is dead; and in any case all that the artist can do is carry out his ideal. Barnard's was, as he himself has said, the democratic ideal. He wished to represent Lincoln, the man of the people and to do that he accentuated all that was rough and grotesque in his figure and bearing."

Weighing in on the transatlantic gift, Cox went on to say, "I think the question is whether Barnard's ideal is our ideal, and whether a statue of Lincoln that is to represent the country abroad should not more truly speak our thought than Barnard's expression of his ideal does."[53] Reasoning "that a successful public statue has to be both an inspiring symbol as well as a likeness of the individual,"[54] Cox favored the Saint-Gaudens, saying, "Saint-Gaudens has been remarkably successful in giving the dignity and gravity, necessary to monumental sculpture, to a modern figure without denying the homeliness of the man. . . . As for the face of Lincoln, Saint-Gaudens's tendency made him show the dignity and beauty in Lincoln's face."

In the end, that is precisely what happened. After much behind-the-scenes work, professional men belonging to groups such as Manhattan's Century Association, influential members of the United States Senate, and artists collectively produced enough pressure on the American Peace Centenary Committee to support Robert Lincoln's appeals. A duplicate of the Saint-Gaudens, which had been promised well before the war, would go to London. "The statue, by Mr. Saint-Gaudens," Robert Lincoln wrote, "is the best and most pleasing."

But all was not lost for Barnard's maligned statue. The city fathers
of Manchester, England, graciously accepted the statue. It was a fitting choice, given that Lincoln, during the Civil War, had corres-
ponded with Manchester's labor leaders of the textile industry.
Manchester had erected a statue of labor leader John Bright, and now
they had a Lincoln statue to join him. It was also home to some of
England's greatest sculptors, Matthew Nobel, William Theed, and a
host of other names more familiar in the United Kingdom than in the
United States. During the American Civil War, locals had offered a
clear support for Lincoln and his policies, as "local mill workers at
the expense of their livelihood, participated in the boycott of Confederate cotton, while simultaneously, Londoners sought to aid and comfort the Rebels."[55] Lincoln was deeply moved by their actions,
writing, "I know and deeply deplore the sufferings which the work-
ingmen at Manchester . . . are called to endure in this crisis."[56]

Charles Taft was happy to provide the Barnard statue at no cost to
Manchester. Dedication speeches delivered at the 1919 Manchester
Lincoln unveiling extolled the Anglo-American Alliance and the re-
sults of the combined victory in the Great War. The next day the
Manchester Guardian reported, "London, in possessing Saint-
Gaudens' statue will have Lincoln, the President; Manchester has
Lincoln, the Man—and in the great rugged head of the new statue it
has something to touch the spirit of the children of future generations
like the Great Stone face of another American's imagining."[57]

For the next sixteen years, Barnard struggled with physical illness
and continuing financial distress, trying to complete an odd assortment of projects, including *Lincoln in Thought*. Eventually, John D.
Rockefeller Jr. evicted him from his home and studio at Washington
Heights. In 1938 Barnard died of a heart attack and was laid out in
the studio where he had labored for thirty years, his tools resting on
his casket.

In his eulogy, Connie Greenway of All Souls Universalist Church
told his congregation, "To me, and to countless others, Barnard lives
in our hearts. He lives in the marbles and bronzes his hands shaped
into men. . . . George Grey Barnard has joined the Immortals."[58]

On this chilly early April morning, our pilgrimage group arrives at
Lytle Park an hour ahead of the Lincoln presenters. Daffodils, tulips,
and pansies in full bloom counter the overcast sky. The colors of the

flowers offset nicely the warm tone of the bronze Lincoln statue. My purpose of the early arrival is to get the students engaged with the sculpture now that they know the story and spend some time together with them talking about Barnard's work. On the bus ride last night we watched the film *Abe Lincoln in Illinois*, starring Raymond Massey. Even though the film was produced in 1939, it sets a kind of tone that will provide additional context to the story be it myth or reality. For really, isn't this so much of what studying Lincoln is all about? Throughout the film one can hear strains of the song, "Old Abe Lincoln Out of the Wilderness." That song, juxtaposed with Barnard's interpretation, seems fitting.

I give the students and the adults some time to take in the sculpture from all angles, making sure that they walk around it several times. When I see they are done I ask them to sit facing the statue on the benches in the park. From my satchel, I pull out my copy of William Howard Russell's *My Diary North and South*, an account of the Englishman's time here during the Civil War. Given all the discussion about Lincoln's appearance by those who knew him, I figured we could get closer to the truth if we heard from someone who might provide a more impartial judgment.

Drawn designer and college sweatshirt hoods pulled close, fleece vests, and parkas protect everyone from the chill. The group listens as I read Russell's words standing in the shadow of the "Hobo-Democrat."

Russell visited the White House on March 27, 1861, at the invitation of Frederick Seward, assistant secretary of state and son of William Seward, Lincoln's secretary of state. After entering the White House Russell reported,

> Soon afterwards there entered, with a shambling, loose irregular, almost unsteady gait, a tall, lank, lean man, considerably over six feet in height, with stooping shoulders, long pendulous arms, terminating in hands of extraordinary dimensions, which, however, were far exceeded in proportion by his feet. He was dressed in an ill-fitting, wrinkled suit of black, which put one in mind of an undertaker's uniform at a funeral; round his neck a rope of black silk was knotted in a large bulb, with flying ends projecting beyond the collar of his coat; his turned-down shirt collar disclosed a sinewy, muscular yellow neck, and above that, nestling in a great black mass of hair, bristling and compact like a ruff of mourning pins, rose the strange quaint face and head covered

with its thatch of wild republican hair, of President Lincoln. The impression produced by the size of his extremities, and by his flapping and wide-projecting ears, may be removed by the appearance of kindliness, sagacity, and the awkward bonhomie of his face; the mouth is absolutely prodigious . . . the lips are only kept in order by two deep furrows from the nostril to the chin; the nose itself—a prominent organ—stands out from the face, with an inquiring anxious air, as though it were sniffing some good thing in the wind; the eyes dark, full, and deeply set, are penetrating, but full of an expression which almost amounts to tenderness; and above them projects the shaggy brow, running into the small hard frontal space, the development which can scarcely be estimated accurately, owing to the irregular flocks of thick hair carelessly brushed across it. . . . A person who met Mr. Lincoln in the street would not take him to be what is called a "gentleman"; and indeed, since I came to the United States, I have heard more disparaging allusions made by to him on that account than what I could have expected among simple republicans, where all should be equals; but at the same time, it would not be possible for the most indifferent observer to pass him on the street without notice.[59]

Against these words and in front of this statue, Ruckstull's attack falls flat. Yet one always has to return to the same place with Lincoln. It is always a matter of interpretation. The students look intently at the sculpture, and then I ask them what they think about Russell's observation and what Ruckstull claimed. "Mr. Percoco," Rachel pipes up, "Lincoln kind of looks like a normal guy, and someone you can relate to." Chelsea, a lock of her light brown hair cutting across her forehead, nods in agreement, adding, "I know it is kind of simple, but I think there is a message here. Much of Lincoln's life was dedicated towards fighting for democracy, so naturally this kind of statue of him would be a perfect symbol. I mean, look at the imperfections of Lincoln, such as his disheveled appearance. Everyday people can understand this Lincoln. Isn't democracy meant to be accessible to everyone?"

Walt Whitman would have concurred. In his 1857 poem, "The Eighteenth Presidency!" he calls for a "Redeemer President of these states to emerge from the "real West, the log hut, the clearing, the woods, the prairie, the hillside."[60] His words proved prophetic.

Looking at Barnard's Lincoln, I am struck how both Barnard and Manship differed in their approaches to sculpt him. Manship's *Hoosier Youth* reflects a young, somewhat handsome Lincoln, which at one level has little historical integrity, since Manship did not use the Volk life mask. In spite of Barnard's homely-looking Lincoln, in Manship I find a greater sense of Lincoln reality. This reality though does challenge one's preexisting image of Lincoln and what Lincoln has come to mean. It does not bear the dignity or nobility of the dignified statesman with which most Americans are familiar. But most Americans are also unaware that Lincoln spoke with a high-pitched nasal twang that irritated the political establishment of the East. Actors Gregory Peck and Raymond Massey gave him a bass voice in their respective interpretations. In the intervening years Americans themselves have constructed their own identity of Lincoln, and that construct has been established by Hollywood, the Walt Disney Company, and Daniel Chester French's majestic figure of Lincoln seated in the Lincoln Memorial. Culturally, we can't possibly fathom how Barnard's Lincoln could be *our* Lincoln.

I wonder what Lincoln would have thought of this image. His self-deprecating humor has become the stuff of legend. One account has an accuser telling Lincoln he was two-faced. Lincoln retorted, "If I had another face, do you think I would wear this one?"[61] Lincoln scholar and iconographer Harold Holzer argues, "the homely, unusually tall Lincoln looked rather funny just as he was." Holzer reports that one comic biographer of the era pitched the following line: "His head is shaped something like a ruta-bago, and his complexion is that of a Saratoga trunk. His hands and feet are plenty large enough, and in society he has the air of having too many of them."[62] Shortly before his death, in a letter to his fellow Republican Thurlow Weed, Lincoln wrote, "Everyone likes a compliment."[63] We will never know whether Lincoln would view Barnard's sculpture as "the animal himself," as Volk said, or whether he would see it as a compliment. Given Lincoln's demeanor, it is fun, though, to speculate how he would view this Lincoln.

I find myself strangely drawn to this statue with a kind of tenderness. Yet I think the right call was made in sending the duplicate cast of the Saint-Gaudens Lincoln to London. I have seen that, too, and in that particular space Barnard's Lincoln would have looked very out of place. Lincoln the Statesman is to be preferred on the international stage as our exportable image for another nation's capital. I recognize my own contradictory position, because I, too, can relate to the views of Tarbell and Markham. There is something of great value with Barnard's sculpture. The tale of competing perspectives is a dynamic part of the Lincoln story that continues to play out.

I recall a conversation I had with Harold Holzer while we both sat relaxed in his Lincoln ephemera–dotted office at the Metropolitan Museum of Art, in which we discussed the 1917 imbroglio and the current trend of public art. "As important as it is as a reflection of one artist's perception of Lincoln," he told me,

> George Grey Barnard's sculpture has even more to teach us about the tremendous power of memory and public art. The controversy that has swirled around the image since its unveiling demonstrates how seriously Americans once took their monumental statuary—and their sixteenth president. It is hard to imagine such a dust-up about a statue today—yet time and again, in my own city of New York and elsewhere, audiences continue to cheer, protest, and mock public art when it disturbs them. Inevitably, this brings us to the purpose of monumental art in terms of public memory. Such work is meant to awe us, surely—but also can achieve high marks by shocking us, and disturbing us. It can't be denied that here Barnard succeeded tremendously. It is a tribute to his eye for provocative work, his sincerely considered image of Lincoln as an eternally simple man, and his audience's own deeply embedded image of Lincoln, that this work has remained so strongly etched in the public mind for so long. Barnard succeeded in showing one aspect of a man of infinite variety. In the narrow area in which he focused, he produced a masterpiece.

For a few minutes we sit still just as motionless as the statue, thinking and looking, only to have our reverie pierced by the sounds of a caravan of cars pulling up alongside Lytle Park. The caravan includes vehicles from across the nation, each one sporting a Lincolnesque license plate. Several read "OLD ABE" and "HNST ABE." Another says "NH ABE" while another reads, "NO 1 ABE." Behind each wheel sits a Lincoln presenter. My students laugh and giggle, Rachel's singular laugh carrying over the others. Our trip documentarian, Jeff, finds this an ideal opportunity to capture the moment on his video camera. Within five minutes this end of Lytle Park fills with about fifty Lincolns, several Mary Lincolns, and members of my group. Organized chaos now replaces solitude and reflection. Scholarship, kitsch, hamminess, public memory, living history, and camp are all rolled into one. Great revelry abounds as my students and the Lincolns connect enjoying being in the presence of one another.

Author, Applied History students, and members of the Association of Abraham Lincoln Presenters at Barnard's *Lincoln* (author)

Plenty of smiles go around too, punctuated with lots of laughter, and numerous photo opportunities. Brilliant, warm sunshine, cracking through the clouds only adds to the festive atmosphere. To whoever will take one the Lincolns distribute business cards. Some are very colorful and detailed, such as Homer "Abe" Sewell's from Jasper, Georgia, which includes a profile photograph of him in costume with an American flag as the background, several phone numbers, his web site and email address, and a list of awards he has received. Gerald Bestrom from Alto, Michigan, has an equally creative card and drives a "Rolling White House," his recreational vehicle festooned with a variety of Lincoln images and slogans. Formerly he drove a rolling log cabin, but that vehicle burned at an ALP meeting several years earlier.

Affixed to each Lincoln's lapel is a clear plastic name tag that reads Fred "Abe" Priebe, Chester "Abe" Damron, Jim "Abe" Rubin, and the like. Each Lincoln refers to each other as "Abe" so and so. The Lincolns also bring with them their own following, including spouses, children, and grandchildren. Even good friends tag along with them for fun.

I overhear some of my students talking with each other, discussing which Lincoln is the best. They settle on Pete Raymond from Wooster, Ohio. His accurate size and demeanor strike them as most presidential. They are quick to point out that the Lincoln presenters come in all shapes and sizes. No matter their height and weight, they are more interested in the essence of the man.

Some of the discussion focuses on Lincoln's trademark hat. "Lincoln wore two kinds of hats," Stanley Wernz explains. "One made of silk and the other made from beaver for rainy days. You see, Lincoln was a man of many hats." He draws a laugh. Taking a cue from Brad, some of the students pose for pictures wearing borrowed stovepipe hats.

Why have people been impersonating Lincoln since the 1920s? The tales of these committed folks are no less extraordinary than the life of the man they portray. Just as much as Lincoln held a deep commitment to preserving the Union these folks have an equally deep commitment to bring to life Lincoln and his message. Most of them portray Lincoln at school, community, or church programs. Max and Donna Daniels, of Wheaton, Illinois, have portrayed the

Lincolns for twenty years. In an average year they give 220 perform-
ances, seventy this past February alone. Ralph Borror, of Holland,
Ohio, grew his beard to antagonize his employer and soon found people calling him "Abe." After a bit of research on Lincoln's life he was
hooked. "I did not choose to be Abe," he claims, "I think Lincoln
chose me." "I was coaxed into portraying Lincoln," Steve Wood of
Claremont, New Hampshire, tells me, "for a re-creation of one of the
Lincoln-Douglas Debates in 1995." Wood was of the right build and
shape but had a handlebar mustache, sideburns, and a beard. After
making some facial adjustments, he thought the resemblance "a little
scary." In Wood's early Lincoln years he mostly marched in parades.
"But gradually," he continues, "began to acquire more period-correct
items of clothing and to read and study about Lincoln's life." Wood's
wife Sharon, a kindergarten teacher and librarian turned storyteller,
joined her husband in his effort to bring Lincoln to life. "Being Mrs.
Lincoln allows me to continue teaching and telling stories—Abraham
and Mary's stories of their lives together," she offers.

Our time with Barnard's Lincoln has come to an end. After posing
for a group photo with the "Abes" in front of Barnard's Lincoln, we
board the bus and drive off. Heading out onto the Interstate I chat
with Tom, a man I call my parent emeritus. His daughter Jessie took
Applied History three years ago, and since then Tom has come on
every field trip or excursion. We talk about Barnard's Lincoln. Leaning back against the reclining seat, Tom says, "My reaction to the
sculpture was consistent with what I consider Lincoln's greatest
strengths as a politician and a man and those traits have always endeared President Lincoln to me. I believe Barnard's Lincoln should
have been erected in Parliament Square in London," he says firmly.
"I think the United States missed an opportunity to generate a discussion about Lincoln's incredible ability to ignore social convention
and appearance on any side of an issue. His strong moral compass
guided him, allowing him to become an enduring and beloved leader.
Hobo-democracy concerns say much more about the American detractors than Lincoln's appearance or leadership." I am reminded of
what Holzer shared with me, "that's what makes the discussion of
Lincoln art so endlessly fascinating. We're not meant to agree unani-
mously—and thanks to the powerful visions and consummate talent
of the great sculptors who portrayed Lincoln, we don't."

Barnard's Lincoln is unique among Lincoln statues. He is neither the Great Emancipator nor the celebrated statesman. He just *is*. Visitors today can visit Lytle Park and look at Lincoln the man in a much different way than from visitors to Chicago who look at Saint-Gaudens's version of Lincoln the man. In some ways these two statues are the flip sides of the same coin. Barnard's Lincoln is the more accessible of the two. In Cincinnati Lincoln is literally more down to earth as evidenced by Barnard's placement of the sculpture on the low, natural granite boulder. There is nothing ostentatious or pretentious about Barnard's figure, and the rumpled, misshapen figure isn't necessarily the statesman we have come to admire. Barnard's Lincoln seems a bit naïve and vulnerable, very much human. After all, part of the Lincoln story is that of a man who, as the song says, "came out of the wilderness," and in a way that represents our nation on its collective journey through history.

The *Standing Lincoln* (author)

4

Contemplative Statesmanship

Augustus Saint-Gaudens's *Standing Lincoln* (1887), Chicago, Illinois

CHICAGO HAS AN ENERGETIC SKYLINE—the Sears Tower, the Wrigley Building, the Tribune Building, and other architectural gems rise into view off Interstate 80 as I leave rural Illinois behind. The architectural signatures of Louis Sullivan, Frank Lloyd Wright, Daniel H. Burnham, and Ludwig Mies van der Rohe find a home here. To celebrate my arrival in the Windy City, I slip a Frank Sinatra CD into my stereo and sing along with Old Blue Eyes, "My Kind of Town" and "Chicago," anthems to America's third-largest city.

Carl Sandburg's poem "Bronzes," his ode to Chicago's sculptural vitality, skips through my mind as I move through downtown. In particular, I think about his line to Augustus Saint-Gaudens's *Standing Lincoln*, the object of this leg of my quest:

> I cross Lincoln Park on a winter night when the snow is falling.
> Lincoln in bronze stands among the white lines of snow,
> His bronze forehead meeting soft echoes of the newsies
> Crying forty thousand men are dead along the
> Yser, his bronze ears listening to the mumbled roar
> of the city at his bronze feet.

The poem reflects a younger but no less vibrant city during the First World War. It was an ode to that war. Sandburg uses Lincoln imagery as a metaphor for the loss of life on the Western Front, carnage with which Lincoln, as the commander in chief, was all too familiar. In more recent memory, the rock band Chicago, in its popular hit song "Saturday in the Park," allude to a bronze man telling stories, an equally fitting tribute to the power of sculpture, as well as working as an allegory to the democratic spirit, people gathering and celebrating on July 4.

Riding his steed and with the American flag held aloft in his right hand, Civil War General John Logan, also sculpted by Saint-Gaudens, appears on a small knoll. Recently cleaned, the bronze statue glistens in the sun. Nearby, behind a line of trees, sits another Saint-Gaudens Lincoln, installed in 1926, many years after the sculptor's death. One Chicago newspaper dubbed the statue "The Lonely Lincoln," seated alone in a chair inside a sprawling plaza. It's a mediocre sculpture at best. Saint-Gaudens, as he battled the cancer that would eventually kill him, produced works of less merit near the end of his life. The *Seated Lincoln* is one of these. It would have been better for the sculptor and the city to have left Lincoln standing, alone, leaving the 1887 masterpiece to inspire. This Lincoln reflects the Whitmanesque Lincoln—Lincoln, the poet of democracy.

Saint-Gaudens was obsessed with Abraham Lincoln in the autumn of 1883, when he hurried east to Chicago by train from Helena, Montana. As the wheels of the Pullman coach made their syncopated music over the rails, three friends passed the time by playing cards, smoking, laughing, and enjoying one another's company. It was a three-day journey alone from Helena to Saint Paul, Minnesota, the hometown of the youngest of the three, the twenty-four-year-old architect Cass Gilbert. Augustus Saint-Gaudens, the senior member of the group, a rising star on the American artistic landscape, was anxious for his next commission, a heroic statue of Abraham Lincoln—a prize commission indeed, particularly for an energetic and ambitious artist. Two years earlier, his career as America's premier civic sculptor was launched with the unveiling of his tribute to Admiral David Glasgow Farragut in New York City's Madison Square Park. The third member of this trio, thirty-year-old Stanford White, had collaborated with Saint-Gaudens on the *Farragut*. He had designed the unusual pedestal, an exedra, which permitted visitors to sit within the confines of the monumental space and commune with the hero. The *Farragut* electrified the art world. It reshaped how Americans would commemorate their heroes and was hailed by critics and the public alike. One commentator, writing in the June 1881 issue of *Scribners*, said, "In modeling severe, broad yet minute in finish . . . full of dignity and reserved force—Saint Gaudens' bronze Farragut might also be called the work of some new Donatello."[1] A new bar was raised significantly for all subsequent public sculptures erected between 1881 and World

War I. The powerful collaboration of Saint-Gaudens and White elevated monuments to a new level of sophistication, opening a new age in public and civic memorialization.

Gus, as he was known by his close friends, was very congenial, a spirited fellow. An enthusiastic joiner of a variety of men's social clubs of the age, he drew people to him with his magnetic charisma and was a devoted friend. But now the normally gregarious Saint-Gaudens, sporting red hair, moustache, and beard—a genetic link to his Irish and French heritage—had become somewhat reticent. Just as he was singularly focused and involved with his art, he was transfixed by the physical landscape and breadth of the American continent, this having been his first trip west. Looking out the windows at the mountains and vast prairie, he drank in what he saw.

When the train pulled in to Saint Paul's Union Depot, Saint-Gaudens decided to push on to Chicago, declining an invitation to spend time at Gilbert's home. Years later, Gilbert remarked to the London *Times*,

> He told me in strict confidence that he was hurrying on to Chicago to close a contract with the committee there for a statue of Lincoln which should, he hoped, be the greatest work that had come to him. He said that he was absolutely absorbed in the thought of it, that he could think of nothing else, and that this journey from New York across the continent and back had given him a volume of impressions. He had never before realized the vastness and extent of the country; he had never before seen the Western men among whom Lincoln had passed his youth and early manhood, and he was going forward to the work with a great deal of responsibility. He was never satisfied with his own work. His passion for perfection drove him relentlessly to infinite pains and almost endless study not only of the superficial features of his subject, but yet more deeply into the study of the character, the life, the emotions and the very soul of the man whose features he so marvelously portrayed.

On November 11, 1883, Saint-Gaudens signed a handwritten, five-page, double-sided contract with the Chicago Committee, which had been given the charge by means of the will of Chicago resident Eli Bates. A self-made man whose fortune at the time of his death was more than $500,000, Bates yearned to be remembered for giving a Lincoln to Chicago. From his estate, $40,000 had been set aside to secure the erection of a suitable memorial to Lincoln. Bates, an amputee, believed that he, like Lincoln, had surmounted substantial obstacles and overcome incredible odds to achieve the level of success he attained. The site for the sculpture was to be Lincoln Park, renamed in 1865 after Lincoln's assassination. Bates enjoyed relaxing in the park and decided his tribute to Lincoln should be in the open, accessible to all. In the 1880s the location of the park remained bucolic, adorned with many trees and paths and well buffeted by the offshore breezes of nearby Lake Michigan.

At first Saint-Gaudens had been encouraged to enter a competition for the statue, but because of a perceived snub for a Boston statue to Senator Charles Sumner, Saint-Gaudens made a decision never again to enter a competition. The Lincoln committee must have liked his proposal and ideas, awarding the contract outright to him. The statue was to be no smaller than eleven feet from head to toe and was to be cast of the best statuary bronze. Like all sculptors of the day, Saint-Gaudens was to assume all related costs, including the foundry casting, as well as to make arrangements for the pedestal and accompanying setting. The contract was for $30,000 and was signed, "without restriction as to design, and with ample allowance of time."[2] The remaining $10,000 was to be used for a suitable nearby fountain, for which the sculptor also received the commission. Saint-Gaudens embraced the project, hoping to make it the greatest work that had come to him.

We can actually trace the evolution of the statue, particularly with regard to the pose, by looking at archival images of the clay maquettes and models used to develop it. Initially, these images show a freestanding figure in various attitudes. In one, Lincoln holds a sheet of paper, perhaps a speech, while in another his arms are crossed. For a time Saint-Gaudens even toyed with the idea of a seated Lincoln. He finally settled on his vision and called it *Abraham Lincoln: The Man.*

In 1885, at the suggestion of a friend, the lawyer Charles Beaman, Saint-Gaudens moved part of his studio operation from New York City to a rundown tavern and barn called Huggins Folly, off the beaten path in Cornish, New Hampshire. The structure was situated on a hill overlooking the Connecticut River and well within view of Mount Ascutney across the river in Vermont. Beaman told him, "There you will find the land of Lincoln-shaped men."[3] What initially was a temporary move turned, by 1900, into permanency as the Cornish Studio became part of the Saint-Gaudens enterprise. The sculptor named the estate Aspet, in homage to his father's home in the French Pyrenees. Around the sculptor would develop the Cornish Colony, the first such collection of noteworthy artists and writers, including such greats as painter Maxfield Parrish and poet Percy MacKaye, to emerge in the United States.

Shortly after moving to New Hampshire, Beaman's prophecy was fulfilled as six-foot-four-inch Langdon Morse, a resident of nearby Windsor, Vermont, agreed to serve as the model. From 1885 to 1887, with the help of assistants Philip Martiny and Frederick William MacMonnies, who would in time make their own unique contributions to American sculpture, the Lincoln project moved forward in the converted barn-studio. Like other artists, Saint-Gaudens wrestled for the true Lincoln, seeking the man, not the myth. He did not want to create a droll railsplitter. He was fastidious about modeling clothing. Details always drove his work. To secure the proper effect, complete with scuffs, fabric wrinkles, and creases, Saint-Gaudens ordered Morse to tramp through the meadow next to his Cornish studio in his Lincoln costume.

During the process Saint-Gaudens arranged for a local photographer, G. E. Knowlton, to take exacting photographs of the modeling process. This undertaking allowed the sculptor to work out anatomical details in a much more specific manner. "From the first Mr. Knowlton would make a full standing picture of Mr. Morse. Then the position another day would be shifted in order to carry out study for further analysis still later in the studio, but always standing, of course. After many months, perhaps running into the years, the accepted pose had been secured in detail and ensemble. We will say that first the shoulders were portrayed; then shifted then more or less and rephotographed; the same process was worked with the arms; the hands, the feet; the knees, singly and together; the thighs; the ankles; in other words, every section of the man's anatomy was pictured, and when the parts had been selected from the pictures, placed and replaced, they were moulded and modeled together and after long and toilsome, yet pleasant sittings, the body of Mr. Morse had been transferred into the wonderful statue."[4] Through a special arrangement, sculptor and photographer agreed not to share the knowledge of their collaboration with anyone except those involved with the project. In an odd twist of fate, Knowlton moved from Vermont to Sycamore, Illinois, presumably taking his singular photographs with him. To this day they probably are locked away in some trunk in some attic, waiting to be rediscovered and brought fully to the light of historical inquiry shedding a much better understanding of just how *Standing Lincoln* was crafted.

In the winter of 1886, through a mere accident, the well-connected Richard Watson Gilder, editor, publisher, and New York literary giant, stumbled upon what would become a boon for Lincoln sculptors. "Gilder, a strong supporter of the project, happened to drop in on his artist-friend Wyatt Eaton, who lived in South Washington Square. On the table in the library Gilder saw a mask of Abraham Lincoln and a cast of his hands. Astonished—for he had not been aware of their existence—he asked Eaton where they came from." The mask and casts had been made by Chicago sculptor Leonard Volk, in 1860, the face cast in Volk's studio in March, the hands cast in Lincoln's home in Springfield in June—the right hand a bit larger than the left, swollen, since Lincoln had spent the preceding evening shaking hands with hundreds of visitors to his house upon learning that he had secured the Republican nomination for the presidency—and had fallen into the possession of Wyatt.

With great energy, Gilder went to work organizing a committee. This thirty-three-member committee raised the necessary funds and purchased the Volk mask and hands. Saint-Gaudens supervised the bronze casting. Duplicate casts in bronze or plaster were made for each donor. The original plaster casts were eventually given to the Smithsonian Institution. They would well serve future Lincoln sculptors and are an important ingredient in understanding how sculptors have been able to capture Lincoln.

Some time after Saint-Gaudens gained possession of the Volk life mask, Gilder dropped by the studio to see how he was making out. The following conversation took place between them, as recalled by the editor:

Gilder: "What do you think of Lincoln?"
Saint-Gaudens: "I take him to be a good man, a benevolent, kind man, called upon to take a great executive office."
Gilder: "But how about a prophet, a poet, a dreamer called upon to take a great executive office?"
Saint-Gaudens: (begging the question): "What else shall I read of his?"

Augustus Saint-Gaudens

Saint-Gaudens with full scale clay model of the *Standing Lincoln* (Saint-Gaudens National Historic Site, National Park Service)

Early clay sketch of the *Standing Lincoln* (Saint-Gaudens National Historic Site, National Park Service)

Top: Dedication of the *Standing Lincoln*, October 22, 1887 (private collection). Bottom: The *Standing Lincoln* (author)

Saint-Gaudens immersed himself in reading Lincoln's writings and available works about the president. On another visit to the studio, the sculptor solicited Gilder's opinion about his work in progress, to which "Gilder urged his friend to lower the head still further to give 'that contemplative look which is so fine and characteristic of Lincoln.' Here we can see a touch of Saint-Gaudens' genius, as he was willing to listen to the advice of others in an effort to achieve distinction. This would become one of his hallmarks, an ability to always seek to do the best, sometimes prolonging projects, even if it infuriated clients."[5]

Like other sculptors who found success modeling Lincoln's image, it was the skillful combination of a careful study of the Volk mask with close inspection of Mathew Brady and Alexander Gardner photographs taken of Lincoln during the Civil War that enabled Saint-Gaudens to depict his figure so well.

Where Saint-Gaudens and White's collaboration departed from other Lincoln statues, getting it right in Chicago was in the use of the presidential chair as balanced against the pensive figure. The chair creates the needed interior volume. Lorado Taft, ever the astute student of sculpture, said,

> Before the chair stands the gaunt figure with bowed head, as though lost in thought or preparing to address a multitude. The foot is well advanced; the left hand grasps the lapel of the coat in a familiar gesture. The right hand is behind the back, affording an agreeable but inconspicuous counter-balance to the droop of the head. . . . The bent left arm gives interest to the lengthy front and at the same time suggests an arrested movement of the hand to the brow, thus reinforcing the idea of concentration of mind. But it is the expression. Of that strange, almost grotesquely plain, yet beautiful face, crowned with tumbled locks, which arrests and holds the gaze. In it is revealed the massive but many sided personality of Lincoln with a correctness and a serene adequacy. . . . This gnarled form has a profound grace which a profound master has apprehended and made visible."[6]

The chair, in part, makes the monument work. As one approaches the statue, Lincoln appears to be rising from the symbolic chair of state. The chair provides a sense of monumental quality to the work from a great distance. Nearing the figures, the chair of state appears to recede as the posture and position of Lincoln's head and face grabs your attention. As one Saint-Gaudens biographer has put it, "Saint-Gaudens has done more than make Lincoln not ugly. There is strength and beauty here, and an austere beauty." Years later, Saint-Gaudens confided to one of his nieces, "I never thought of Lincoln as ugly."[7]

It is not clear whether Saint-Gaudens intended for his sculpture to suggest that Lincoln was about to speak. Lincoln spoke publicly little more than one hundred times. He did not like speaking extemporaneously and was generally opposed to giving public addresses. When speaking he tended to be nervous, his voice moving from that of a tenor to that in a falsetto range. But his voice did resonate with those who heard him as it reflected a presence of integrity and truth. As a younger politician, Lincoln was a good stump speaker and debater, but not necessarily a great orator, as the Saint-Gaudens figure would imply. For the major addresses he gave while president, Lincoln always held in his hands his carefully thought out and highly edited written remarks. While the pose of *Standing Lincoln* is striking, the subject does not hold a speech in his hands. Oddly, archival images of Saint-Gaudens's early clay sketches have Lincoln holding a piece of foolscap. The implication of the final pose plays on a prevailing myth that was well entrenched in America at the time that Saint-Gaudens crafted his masterpiece—namely, that Lincoln was a great orator. It was the words that were great, not necessarily the presentation. Ultimately, the genius of the statue is that it works with many subtle and nuanced interpretations.

In the case of *Standing Lincoln*, Saint-Gaudens would fulfill his contractual obligations on time—three years from signing the contract to delivery of the sculpture.

Fame and popularity added to growing base of work, which he often pursued while singing opera as he labored in his studio, the "Serenade" from Mozart's *Don Giovanni* being one of his favorites.[8] During the time Saint-Gaudens worked on the Lincoln additional contracts poured in, including those for two of his other great works, the Robert Gould Shaw and 54th Massachusetts Memorial in Boston and the enigmatic Adams Memorial, which adorns the grave of the American author and historian Henry Adams and his wife, Marian, on a small knoll in Rock Creek Church Cemetery in Washington, D.C.

Increasingly, Saint-Gaudens would struggle to meet his contractual obligations. The combination of a large business enterprise and his

tendency to perfectionism would delay projects and create great consternation with memorial committees. But in the case of the *Standing
Lincoln* none of this aggravation would become manifest. His career
was still at an early point. Surrounded by casts and models for other
contracts, including the *Shaw Memorial*, he finished his Lincoln in
his New York studio, before shipping the model off to the foundry
for casting. He invited an eager press to cover the completion of his
stage of the work.

October 22, 1887, a Saturday, proved to be a raw, rainy Chicago
day. In spite of the weather, a huge crowd assembled to witness the
ceremony, its festive mood breaking the gloomy atmosphere. Um-
brellas were ubiquitous. The *Chicago Tribune* reported the story in
full detail calling the ceremony "impressive" despite the weather.
Preceding the ceremonies, a military band played "a spirited prelude
of airs appropriate to the occasion, among them, 'My Old Kentucky
Home.'" Saint-Gaudens and his wife, Augusta, sat on a platform
filled with dignitaries and Lincoln's friends, including Lyman Trum-
bull and Leonard Swett.

Seated with the Saint-Gaudens on the dais was forty-four-year-old
Robert Lincoln, the president's sole surviving son. By 1887 he had
actively begun to protect his father's memory and legacy in the many
forms in which it manifested itself in America. For the rest of his
life he labored to ensure that his father's memory be lionized and
popularized. Saint-Gaudens had not failed him. In 1908, a year after
the sculptor's death, the younger Lincoln wrote a letter to the American Institute of Architects in Washington for a Saint-Gaudens retrospective, saying, "I am one of the many who most highly appreciate
the genius of Mr. Saint-Gaudens, and the great work that he has done
for Art; and particularly do I feel grateful to him for his work in per-
petuating the memory of my own father."[9]

At three o'clock, Chicago Mayor John A. Roche stepped up to the
podium, and the official ceremony commenced. The first remarks
linked benefactor Eli Bates to Lincoln, reflecting their journey from
poverty to self-made accomplishment. The sixty-two-year-old Leonard Swett, with whom Lincoln had traveled the Eighth Circuit
Court in Illinois, gave the keynote address. In particular, Swett addressed Lincoln's firm belief in the tenets of the Declaration of Independence that each American be able to take himself as far in life as
his or her natural ability would permit. Swett called Lincoln's belief

in the Declaration "his perfect standard of political truth" and as-
serted that Lincoln "believed in God as the Supreme Ruler of the
world," adding that Lincoln saw himself "as an instrument and leader
in the forces of freedom." Swett's speech also recalled the brutal end
of Lincoln's life, concluding, "Let us hope that after 'life's fitful fever'
he sleeps well. Let us hope that on the eventful night of the four-
teenth of April, A.D. 1865, when his spirit first left the earth and
crossed the great divide between here and hereafter, the angel at the
gate met him with a smile and said, 'well done thou good and faithful
servant, enter into the joy of thy Lord.'"[10]

Lincoln, accompanied by his son, Abraham Lincoln II, then
stepped up to the platform and pulled the chord that drew aside the
flag that had draped the figure. The thunder of thirty-eight cannons
reverberated around the Lake Michigan shoreline. A hush fell over
the crowd, and then the band filled the air with patriotic music. According to the official report, *Ceremonies at the Unveiling of the
Statue of Abraham Lincoln*, "there were tears in the eyes of many
who had known Lincoln."

Lincoln had been dead only twenty-two years, but his reputation
and the esteem with which he was viewed by his countrymen was
very much alive. A year before, the city had been convulsed by the
Haymarket Bombing. Now the city was in a mood to celebrate something for which it could be proud.

Press accounts of the dedication poured in from around the country and were reported in the major papers of New York and Los
Angeles. All were filled with effusive praise. One account offered that
the statue was "a labor of love, on the part of the sculptor," while
another noted the statue, "proved that classic drapery is not indispensable to artistic effect in sculpture, nor theatrical accessories to
make the human form seem somewhat divine."

Mariana Griswold Van Rensselaer, the respected critic, enthusiastically weighed in on the Saint-Gaudens Lincoln in *Century Magazine*
in 1887. "Strange as it may seem," she wrote, "no previous monumental composition had furnished a precedent for this. The world
had had seated statues and standing statues in plenty; but a figure
thus recently risen from its seat is that rarest of things—a true novelty
in art. . . . The union of idealistic conception and realistic rendering
which it reveals is almost always found when modern art is at its very
best. But it also shows a union of perfect repose with strong dramatic

significance, and this union is characteristic when at its best. There as here it is secured by the same expedient,—by the choice of a moment which is not the one of most vigorous action but the one in which such action is immanent."[11]

Like other sculptors who dealt with Lincoln as subject matter, Saint-Gaudens would have his struggles. Lincoln's oddly shaped head, cockeyed face, and ungainly physique left many sculptors frustrated. His lanky arms and legs were almost always problematic for those who attempted to capture him in stone or bronze. And then there were the moral or spiritual dimensions of the man. The dean of nineteenth-century American sculpture, John Quincy Adams Ward, refused to take on such a task, claiming trying to capture the essence of Lincoln was too daunting. Lincoln's personal secretary, John G. Nicolay, offered both a unique promise and challenge to all artists:

> Lincoln's features were the despair of every artist who undertook his portrait. . . . They put into their pictures the large, rugged features, and strong prominent lines; they made measurements to obtain exact proportions; they "petrified" some single look, but the pictures remained hard and cold. . . . Graphic art was powerless before a face that moved through a thousand delicate gradations of line and contour, light and shade, sparkle of the eye and curve of the lip, in the long gamut of expression from grave to gay and back again . . . to that serious, far-away look with prophetic intuitions beheld the awful panorama of war, and heard the cry of oppression and suffering. There are many pictures of Lincoln; there is no portrait of him.[12]

Royal Cortissoz, art critic, and no stranger to the life of Lincoln, wrote convincingly in his 1908 retrospective of Saint-Gaudens's talent. "It is not simply that each one of [his] the monuments has certain specific artistic merits, lifting it to a high plane," he commented. "It is rather that in every one of his studies of historical subjects, Saint-Gaudens has somehow struck the one definitive note, has made his Lincoln . . . a type which the generations must revere and which no future statues can invalidate."[13]

An unintended consequence occurred with the unveiling of Saint-Gaudens's masterpiece. Ten years after the collapse of Reconstruction, white Americans began to view Lincoln differently, and this sculpture helped establish that sentiment. "Journey to Chicago," wrote Charles Henry Hart, "and kneel before the bronze statue by Augustus Saint-Gaudens. It is not Abraham Lincoln the liberator of slaves, but Abraham Lincoln the Saviour of the Union."[14] With that shift came violence; in 1887, seventy African Americans would be lynched in the United States.

A carpet of colors, lavender, pink, yellow and blue, the byproduct of verbenas, black-eyed Susans, lilies, and ornamental grass leads me from the street to Lincoln. The sweet floral fragrance from the air fills my nose and the gently drifting butterflies, more of nature's pleasures, adds to what has so far been a glorious morning. Lincoln is bathed in brilliant sunlight.

Children run, laugh, and play throughout the park and in the shadow of Lincoln. Two gardeners work the grounds, methodically removing debris and weeds from the flowerbeds. Sunrays play off the bronze just as the sculptor intended, casting facial shadows so necessary to create the right mood. The combined effort of Saint-Gaudens and White created a space that truly makes *Standing Lincoln* a monument that invites the visitor and admirer to participate with the sculpture, where one can engage actively in a kind of civic pilgrimage, walking the six steps up the expansive plaza to stand or sit at the feet of Lincoln. The president is raised on a separate granite altar, a kind of island, protected by White's curving bench. In this environment we are invited to contemplate on the life of Lincoln the man and engage in our own "mystic chords of memory." I wonder, as I do, whether the modern world can produce another Lincoln, someone who can provide a sense of compassionate yet firm leadership in times of travail while offering a fixed moral compass.

Saint-Gaudens's greatest works are psychological studies that engage the viewer to enter the action. As an artist, he actively seeks involving you. The space works exactly as the sculptor and architect intended. I approach the sculpture and ascend to the plaza. This is another step in my mythic pilgrimage. Here, a full eight hundred miles from home, I am at the feet of a kind of Holy Grail. Like fifteen-year-old George Gitt, who managed to position himself underneath the speaker's platform at Gettysburg on November 19, 1863, I am literally at the feet of my hero. My approach is reverent.

The spirit of the moment comes to a sudden end as I notice from the corner of my eye that someone had scrawled a green "X" on the granite pedestal; green paint had also been dripped on White's platform. My heart sinks. Why would anyone want to deface this statue and mar a space, a space that offered comfort and spiritual renewal? Someone, too, had spray-painted white graffiti at the point where the bronze meets the stone at the base of the statue. None of the graffiti was intelligible. The work of the vandals appeared to be for the sake of vandalism. Trash is strewn in places, while old newspapers and beer cans litter the area. I am saddened at the obvious facts of life in an American city.

Looking at Lincoln's face, I recall various remarks about his looks. Many of Lincoln's contemporaries commented that Lincoln's face bore the burden of the war. But this was not that Lincoln; this is Lincoln the Statesman. Walt Whitman observed Lincoln many times during his tenure as a nurse in Washington during the Civil War. "I see the President often," Whitman once wrote. "I think better of him than many do. He has conscience and homely shrewdness [that] conceals an enormous tenacity under his mild, gawky western manner." This is the strength, Whitman believed, that carried Lincoln and the nation for so long. Summarizing Lincoln's task, Whitman said, "The difficulties of his situation have been unprecedented in the history of statesmanship."[15]

This is the Saint-Gaudens Lincoln that stands in Chicago. The twelve-foot-tall statue on its seven-foot pedestal, dominating the space, yet complemented by White's sixty- by thirty-foot elliptical exedra. Lincoln is looking down, bearing a serious expression. His portrait is finely modeled and very natural. He appears to have just risen from the chair of state, which is placed strategically for volume and aesthetics behind him, suggesting perhaps an interior room or office. Lincoln's left hand grasps his left jacket lapel with a hint of tension. This gesture is reminiscent of the posture played out by Raymond Massey in the film *Abraham Lincoln of Illinois*. "When Mr. Lincoln rose up to speak," William Herndon, Lincoln's younger law partner and later biographer of sorts, confirmed this particular attitude of Lincoln's in 1887 saying, "he rose slowly—steadily—firmly . . . he frequently took hold with his left hand, his left thumb erect, of the left lapel of his coat, keeping his right hand free to gesture in order to . . . clinch an idea."[16] His right arm is behind him, his hand clenched.

Lincoln's left leg is forward of his torso, a stance he was apt to take before he was about to make a speech, and his foot extends over the base of the bronze. Suggesting forward motion are the wrinkles on his pants on the outside of his left knee. The fine modeling of details accentuates the piece. Lincoln's eyeglass lanyard rests against his vest, also wrinkled, which is buttoned but exposed by his open full-length coat, revealing the sculptor's penchant for realism. Lincoln's eyes are concealed by deep shadows that cross his craggy face. On the chair, Saint-Gaudens has modeled a fine bas-relief of an American eagle with laurels grasped in his claws.

The pose could reflect Lincoln at any point or moment in his presidency; this may be Lincoln issuing the Emancipation Proclamation, liberating black souls held in bondage, or perhaps it is Lincoln at Gettysburg, delivering America's version of Pericles' "Funeral Oration," or Lincoln of the Second Inaugural, what some call his Sermon on the Mount, the pastoral Lincoln, shepherding a hurting nation. Saint-Gaudens's bronze is not intended to convey a particular time. On White's exedra are inscribed the dates of Lincoln's life and his name, the only markings. On the ends of the exedra are carved wings with the inscription to Lincoln's right containing an excerpt from his Second Inaugural Address, "With malice toward none, with charity for all," evoking Lincoln's compassion. To Lincoln's left the chiseled words are from the conclusion of Lincoln's 1860 Cooper Union Address in New York City, "Let us have faith that might makes right, and in that faith let us to the end dare to do our duty as we understand it," eliciting Lincoln's firm belief in honor and well reasoned duty. Flanking the staircase are two bronze orbs. On one is etched the Gettysburg Address, on the other excerpts from Lincoln's August 22, 1862, reply to *New York Tribune* publisher and abolitionist Horace Greeley's editorial "The Prayer of Twenty Million," providing testimony to Lincoln's will and determination to preserve the Union foremost above the sensitive political issue of slavery. The selectively chosen Lincoln quotes resonate with a spiritual sense of the power of Lincoln the wordsmith.

Chicago sculptor and art critic Lorado Taft once said of this Lincoln, "Its majestic melancholy is beyond my power to describe. It has affected me and countless others more than any other statue has. It does not seem like bronze; there is something almost human, or—shall I say—superhuman about it. One stands before it and feels himself in the very presence of America's greatest soul."[17]

I bring years of Lincoln, Civil War, and racial memory to bear on my interpretations. At one level this could be the Lincoln, who in corresponding with Albert G. Hodges, in what he termed a "Little

Speech" that became a public letter, said, "I am naturally anti-slavery. If slavery is not wrong, nothing is wrong. I cannot remember when I did not so think, and feel." The duality of Lincoln's personal character in Saint-Gaudens, as I see it, is because of the intervening history that occurred since 1887.

Saint-Gaudens successfully addressed the sense of great resolve and heroic compassion internally in Lincoln. Daniel Chester French would echo the theme in his marble portrait of Lincoln. Here I find Saint-Gaudens's Lincoln thoughtful, engaged, purposeful, frozen in contemplation—the leader in action, thinking before doing.

The monumental arrangement is like the collaboration Saint-Gaudens and White did for client Henry Adams and the creation of the enigmatic Adams Memorial. There, too, an exedra invites people to sit, ponder, and muse and many did, including Eleanor Roosevelt. She would take herself out to the far fringes of Washington, D.C., to sit in front of the cloaked figure and contemplate life and its meaning. Saint-Gaudens's work has that kind of power.

Here in Chicago, in the midst of the great Pullman strike of 1894, activist and reformer Jane Addams sought solace with the *Standing Lincoln*:

> I recall a time of great perplexity in the summer of 1894, when Chicago was filled with federal troops sent there by the president of the United States, and their presence was resented by the governor of the state, that I walked the wearisome way from Hull-House to Lincoln Park . . . in order to look at and gain magnanimous counsel, if I might, from the marvelous Saint-Gaudens statue which had recently been placed at the entrance of the Park. Some of Lincoln's immortal words were cut into the stone at his feet, and ever did a distracted town more sorely need the healing of "with charity for all" than did Chicago at that moment, and the tolerance of the man who had won charity for those on both sides of "an irrepressible conflict."[18]

This visit of Addams is not without irony, for at the time of the Pullman strike Robert Lincoln, son of the figure from whom Addams sought wisdom as counsel for the Pullman Railroad Company, largely managed the site in George Pullman's absence.

The humidity is low, but the sun is hot. I sit in a shaded area of the exedra to be filled with the space and to contemplate all I have learned in my travels. Leaning back to rest, I remind myself how hard it is to truly encounter Lincoln. Bike riders pedal by. Mothers walk their infants and toddlers in strollers. Groups of people and couples holding hands all cross under the gaze of Lincoln. Some people stop and take notice; others hustle on without looking. Sparrows chirp and light in the small pools of water puddled on the platform, remnants of the sprinkling system, to catch a quick drink and then be off again. A dragonfly lazily swoops near Lincoln's left hand. Had he been real he would have brushed it away. It is not my intent this day to converse with anyone but Lincoln. I simply want to share the accomplishment of sculptor and architect.

For a few minutes I enjoy the private consultation with the president. Looking up at Lincoln again, I imagine the bronze saying, "The struggle of today is not altogether for today—it is for a vast future also." I feel a sense of understanding about all of life's struggles, though Lincoln was referring more specifically to the Civil War. Like others I claim Lincoln's words and place them, as a teacher, in a more personal context.

An older gentleman walks in front of the statue. He stops, looks at me, looks at Lincoln, then looks at me again. My solace is broken. Hesitatingly he ascends the steps. He walks first in front of the statue and then behind the pedestal. Then he sits next to me.

In fluent English, though with an accent, he reads the dates inscribed in Roman numerals on the curving surface of the exedra bench, "1809 to 1865." "Yes," I said, "Those were the years of Lincoln's life." "Oh, I see," he responds, crossing his knees and wiping his brow. I ask him where he is from, and he replies that he is from Shanghai, China, on his third visit to the United States.

Suddenly, as if he were a local tour guide, he begins to speak eloquently about Lincoln and the statue. "He's a great man," he says, a pensive look crossing his face. "The statue put up in 1887 is here for two reasons. One. Lincoln is a native of Illinois. Two. His liberation of the slaves is of magnificent significance in the United States so he is worth being commemorated." Without asking for it the universality of Lincoln has reached out and seized the moment. "This is the second time I come and visit this statue," he continues. "I think this statue is more open and wider than the Lincoln Memorial in Washington, D.C. There's a lot of meaning to this location. In China," he says enthusiastically, "Abraham Lincoln is well known. His contribution is written in English textbooks for middle school students."

Oblivious to our presence, a perspiring jogger runs up the steps around the pedestal, then exits.

In 1942, the United States Post Office issued a commemorative stamp recognizing the resistance movement against Japanese aggression in China. The blue five-cent stamp superimposed images of Lincoln and Dr. Sun Yat-sen, the founder and unifier of modern China, over a map of that nation. Beneath Lincoln's portrait are the last three lines of the Gettysburg Address, while beneath that of Sun are Chinese characters reflecting Sun's interpretation: "the people are to have, the people are to rule, and the people are to enjoy," which he called the "three principles of the people." On a visit to the United States, Sun had become impressed with Lincoln, whose portrait was the only picture on the wall of his house in Shanghai. It's the infusion of the words about liberty and equality in the Gettysburg Address that attracts attention in China. The Chinese Communists, too, under Mao Zedong, had their followers learn, verbatim, the Gettysburg Address because of its allusion to government "of the people, by the people, for the people"—a classic case of Lincoln's words being used to defend politically polar opposites.

I came to understand Lincoln's universal status while leading a delegation of history educators at an international education conference in Beijing. In opening remarks to my delegates and the Chinese history educators, I invoked a line from Lincoln's 1849 letter to Joseph Gillespie, "the better part of one's life consists of his friendships," hoping to engender a spirit of openness and collegiality. My choice of Lincoln as a guest ambassador paid off. With a copy of Alexander Gardner's November 1863 photograph taped to the front window of the delegation's bus, Lincoln went wherever we went. In my satchel I carried different kinds of Lincoln gifts—T-shirts, coffee mugs, and small portrait busts—to exchange with my Chinese counterparts, all labeled, "Made in China." At Peking Academy, a prestigious Beijing High School, I presented their principal with a Lincoln coffee mug. Gazing at the token of friendship, his eyes widened brightly, a big smile crossed his face, and he exclaimed, "Ah! Lincoln!" A chord had been struck. After presenting Lincoln gifts to my counterpart, the leader of the Chinese history education delegation told me that the two Americans that the Chinese people most admire are Martin Luther King Jr. and Abraham Lincoln because their values are universal.

But it was not until we visited Beijing High School No. 80 that I truly understood the global implications of Lincoln's life. Meeting in the history department office with the school's history faculty, I passed out Lincoln photographs and pencils I picked up at Gettysburg, Pennsylvania. Excitedly, one of the instructors pulled down a copy of the world history textbook. He flipped to page 93, where he proudly pointed to an illustration of Lincoln delivering the Gettysburg Address. It mattered not that the caption and text was written in Chinese; I recognized the image instantly. But as I turned the pages something else struck me. Here were pictures of Giuseppe Garibaldi, Otto von Bismarck, and Dr. Sun Yat-sen. Rather than have Lincoln stand alone within the singular context of the American Civil War experience, here Lincoln was set off within a broader context—the world. Lincoln here is viewed as part of something larger, as a unifier and preserver of harmony, two significant Chinese cultural norms traced back to Confucian thought. In understanding this, a kind of American myopia and hubris on my part came undone. Musing on the experience, I realized that I had had to travel to the other side of the planet to encounter a new Lincoln.

Back in Chicago, I tell my fellow visitor that I am traveling this summer and visiting Lincoln statues around the country to see what I can discover about Lincoln as well as myself. He tells me that he is sixty-three years old and a retired schoolteacher. For twenty-six years he taught middle school students history, mathematics, Russian, and English. His eyes brighten and his face lights up when I tell him that I, too, am a teacher. We talk about the differences and similarities between teaching in China and the United States. We discuss students and curriculum. My new friend tells me about his two sons and their wives living in the United States, one in Boston the other here in Chicago. He refuses to tell me his name when I ask, but otherwise speaks openly.

"There is a new philosophy in Chinese society," he says. "We can now travel abroad, and my sons can finish their education and work here. China is now a more open society." His words give me pause. Given Lincoln's search for fairness and equal opportunity for all, I wonder how much Lincoln has influenced the world at large with respect to these ideas. China is still, after all, a totalitarian state, and there seems to be a dichotomy between the words of my newfound friend and his homeland's political tenor. I let it remain a thought.

"My sons have been here for ten years now," he says. "The ordinary Chinese people have got to know America more and more. When I was in Boston I went everywhere," he says gesturing, his arms making a big circle. "I think you learn better when you see a site." He shares with me stories of his travels through Boston, to Lexington and Concord, the Longfellow House, along the Freedom Trail, of how he went to Philadelphia to see Independence Hall and the Liberty Bell.

I am glad that this gentleman from half a world away knows so much about our history, but I lament the fact there are so many Americans, who are adults, that have very little concept of significant developments in our nation's heritage. Secretly, I am embarrassed at my own lack of understanding Chinese history. Our national obsession with fame, idolatry, and money seems almost singularly to focus on sports figures and entertainers. I take some comfort in thinking that they will fade, but the legacy of Lincoln will not.

I ask whether he remembers seeing the Shaw Memorial along the Freedom Trail in Boston. "Across from the Massachusetts State House, the one with the gold dome," I remind him, "is a statue of a man on a horse leading his black troops toward combat." "Oh, yes," he exclaims, sucking in air as he speaks. "I saw that statue. It's so big." And with that he draws a rectangle in the air with his hands. "I enjoyed that statue very much. It's so vivid." I stop him with a smile and point to Lincoln. "Same sculptor," I say. He beams.

"You know," he says excitedly, "the whole history of the United States is very short, but I think it is great. Although we Chinese have five thousand years of written history, I still think the United States is great. We are two different cultures. Two different histories. Both are great. I think as a teacher of history," he says gently, "the total human experience of history is imaginative and remarkable. The more I visit the United States I respect it. I love the people of the United States." He places his hand on my arm. "I will do my best to learn the history of the United States not only by reading, but by visiting," he assures me.

Forty-five minutes have now elapsed. Where we are sitting, enjoying each other's company, once in shade, is now heated by the sun. Pulling off his Nike cap, he wipes perspiration off of his forehead. We are quiet, content in the moment. Lincoln has done more than his fair share of unification here between East and West.

"Will you pose with me for a picture in front of Lincoln?" I ask, seeing a friendly looking group of people walking by who might oblige my request. Again his face brightens. He springs up from the exedra and we pose for the picture, arms around each other in a kind of kinship. Looking directly into my face, he says, "I will now tell you my name." I beam. Houfu Xu formally introduces himself. We exchange phone numbers and addresses. Looking a bit sad, he says, "I have to continue my walk." With that we clasp hands and tell each other it has been an honor. Walking down the steps of White's exedra, he turns to me and says, "I think we will meet again." With that he is gone as quickly as he had appeared. In the moment I can't help but think again about Lincoln's letter to Gillespie.

Having been so caught up in the conversation with Xu, I return to my business at hand and take time to study the work of Saint-Gaudens, connecting with the sculptor's past.

He was born in Dublin in 1848. His father Bernard had moved from France several years earlier and married an Irishwoman, Mary McGinnis. Saint-Gaudens's parents immigrated to the United States when he was six months old, settling in New York City. Early in his life he displayed a talent for art, and his parents encouraged his skills by apprenticing him to a local cameo cutter, enrolling him at the age of sixteen in 1864 at the Cooper Union—the same institution where Lincoln in 1860 delivered a speech that some consider launched him on the road to the White House. There Saint-Gaudens took drawing classes, and then in 1868 went to study sculpture in Paris at the École des Beaux-Arts.

As a teenager, Saint-Gaudens experienced wartime New York City. He saw troops moving through the city on their way to Washington and then to the battlefront. He witnessed the savage Draft Riot of 1863. In a late 1890s conversation with his assistant James Earle Fraser, who would become a noted sculptor in his own right, Saint-Gaudens talked about his experience in 1861 when he saw the president-elect pass through New York City on his way to assume the presidency. Saint-Gaudens remembered, "Lincoln stood tall in the carriage, his dark uncovered head bent in contemplative acknowledgement of the waiting people, and the broadcloth of his black coat shone rich and silken in the sunlight."[19] Perhaps this is where the master sculptor drew inspiration for the gently bent head on "his" Lincoln. Saint-Gaudens would see Lincoln only one more time. On the occasion of Lincoln's assassination, in 1865, Saint-Gaudens wrote, in his *Reminiscences*, "Then came news of Lincoln's assassination. I recall father and mother weeping, as he read it to us in the morning at breakfast before starting for work. Later, after joining the interminable line that formed somewhere down Chatham Street and led off to the bier at the head of the staircase, I saw Lincoln lying in state in the City Hall, and I went back to the end of the line to look at him again. This completed my vision of the big man, though, the funeral, which I viewed from the roof of the old Wallack's Theatre on Broome Street, deepened the profound solemnity of my impression, as I noticed everyone uncover while the funeral car went by."[20] As the young artist matured, he would claim the mantle of creating civic masterpieces to the legacy of the Civil War, saying, "I have such respect and admiration for the heroes of the Civil War that I consider it my duty to help in any way to commemorate them in noble and dignified fashion worthy of their great service."[21] His Civil War pieces, including the tribute to Admiral Farragut (1881) for New York City's Madison Square Park, the Shaw Memorial (1897) for Boston, and the William Tecumseh Sherman Memorial (1903) located at the southern entrance to New York City's Central Park, are among his finest.

Saint-Gaudens is often cited as the leader of an American Renaissance in the visual arts, the period from 1880 through the early twentieth century marked by a great collaborative flourishing of the American visual arts. Writing in the November 1887 issue of *The Century* magazine, Mariana Griswold Van Rensselaer conceded, "The Lincoln monument for Chicago is the most important commemorative work that Mr. St. Gaudens has yet produced and may well remain the most important of his life. . . . In the architectural portion of his work Mr. St. Gaudens was assisted by Mr. Stanford White, and together they have given us a monument which is the most precious the country yet possesses; which is not only our best likeness of Abraham Lincoln, but our finest work of monumental art."[22] Saint-Gaudens provides a subject with profound psychological depth, and White's pedestal complements and does not compete with the bronze Lincoln.

Saint-Gaudens's sculpture is a complex work of art. So too, was the subject matter. One has to resist the temptation, when studying monuments and statues erected to Lincoln's memory, to elevate Lincoln's stature into the stratosphere of the gods. Lincoln was a masterful politician who seized almost absolute authority during a constitutional crisis. For Lincoln, preservation of the Union was paramount in his mind, and he was willing to use whatever means were at his disposal to satisfy that end. He used the political skills he honed on the Illinois prairie to his advantage in waging the Civil War. True, his efforts saved the nation, and he did preserve what he called, "the last best hope of earth," for future generations, but he remains a human being complete with contradictions. Historian Marc Bloch argues, "By curious paradox, through the very fact of their respect for the past, people come to reconstruct it as they considered it ought to have been."[23] So it goes with Mr. Lincoln, not only in the history books, but also in marble and bronze.

Looking at the bronze Lincoln, staring at his face, the visitor is a good fifteen to twenty feet from Lincoln's head. The obvious scale of the sculptor's approach is evidenced by this particular space. Here, Lincoln is of heroic proportions. In the museum in the basement of Ford's Theatre in Washington, on display are some artifacts from Lincoln's assassination, including the clothes he was wearing the night he was murdered. These clothes are dressed on a Lincoln mannequin that measures Lincoln's actual height. In observing this mannequin one also has to gaze upward at Lincoln to see his face. The sense of his actual physical monumentality is quite evident. One can see how Lincoln towered over people and dominated them with his size. It is obvious why people who met him almost always remarked on his height. That height is more than doubled by Saint-Gaudens in his figure, suggesting the psychological, heroic, and spiritual monumentality of the subject matter. It is clear that Saint-Gaudens, in 1883, was drawn to what was by then a growing mythology of Lincoln.

In the American mind, Lincoln has achieved godlike stature. But is that really fair? Lincoln was not infallible; he was a human being. And he was a very shrewd politician who could be Machiavellian when he needed to be. This is the same president who gave tacit approval to a prisoner-of-war policy that permitted thousands of Union prisoners of war to languish and die in wretched Southern camps and who suspended the right of habeas corpus, a power reserved to Congress by the Constitution, on more than one occasion. All of this remains murky.

Lincoln fully knew that he was stretching the powers of the Executive, but believed that he had no choice in waging the kind of war he did in an effort to save the United States from destruction. His use of power was not power for power's sake, but rather to be used to uphold the oath he had taken on March 4, 1861. A man driven all his life by duty, Lincoln was obligated to act as president in the manner he saw fit. Was justice sacrificed by expediency? Daniel Farber argues that at the time of Lincoln's decision to suspend the writ of habeas corpus it "seemed more like autocracy than constitutional democracy," and "although the constitutional issue can hardly be considered free from doubt, on balance Lincoln's use of habeas in areas of insurrection or actual war should be considered constitutionally appropriate."[24]

To Lincoln there was no alternative. And yet this same man visited wounded Confederate soldiers recovering in Union hospitals and offered numerous pardons to deserters, arguing his position and explaining his dilemma in a letter to leading New York Democrat Erastus Corning. "Must I shoot a simple-minded soldier boy who deserts, while I must not touch a hair of a wiley agitator who induces him to desert?" While numerous historians, even some of Lincoln's biggest boosters, have chided him over the POW issue and the suspension of habeas corpus, from their vantage point they bring to bear a certain kind of present-mindedness arguing a very difficult point with the hindsight of more than 140 years of Lincoln and Civil War memory to help shade their views.

In spite of seeming contradictions, pilgrims cannot help feel that in the shadow of Saint-Gaudens's *Standing Lincoln* that they are in the presence of a great man. Saint-Gaudens not only tells us how great Lincoln was, but the sculpture and its arrangement in the space ask the visitor to consider his life against that of Lincoln. F. Lauriston Bullard claims, "A great soul guided the fingers that moulded this statue. What we see in this bronze giant depends on what we are, but few there are who can resist the spell of triumphant achievement. Augustus Saint-Gaudens gave us the man whom we love as our comrade and friend, the statesman we revere as our leader. We turn away from his memorial accepting anew Abraham Lincoln's vision of what ought to be."[25]

Since it was unveiled, this Lincoln has resonated with people. Like all great works of art, it elicits a response reflective of the intensity of the subject matter. For our benefit, Saint-Gaudens masterfully harmonizes the real with the ideal. In 1920, Franklin K. Lane, the Canadian expatriate who embraced and adopted America as his homeland, serving as Woodrow Wilson's secretary of the interior, recorded in his personal journal, in a section titled "Lincoln's Eyes":

> I never pass through Chicago without visiting the statue of Lincoln by Saint-Gaudens and standing before it for a moment uncovered. It is to me all that America is, physically and spiritually. I look at those long arm and long legs, large hands and feet, and I think that they represent the physical strength of this country, its power and its youthful awkwardness. Then I look at the head and see qualities which have made the American—the strong chin, the noble brow, those sober and steadfast eyes. They were the eyes of one who saw with sympathy and interpreted the common sense. They were the eyes of earnest idealism limited and checked by the possible and the practicable. They were the eyes of a truly humble spirit, whose ambition was not a love for power but a desire to be supremely useful. They were the eyes of compassion and mercy and deep understanding. They saw far more than they looked at. They believed in far more than they saw. They loved men not for what they were but for what they might become. They were patient eyes, eyes that could wait and wait and live on in faith that right would win. They were the eyes which challenged the nobler things in men and brought out the hidden largeness. They were humorous eyes that saw things in their true proportions and in their real relationships. They looked through cant and pretense and the great and little vanities of great and little men. They were the eyes of an unflinching courage and an unfaltering faith rising out of a sincere dependence upon the Master of the Universe. To believe in Lincoln is to learn to look through Lincoln's eyes.[26]

The *Standing Lincoln* was restored and has been protected since 1989 by the Friends of Lincoln Park, an all-volunteer citizen group that maintains the 8,200-square-foot plaza, which includes the statue and the flower gardens. The spirit of Saint-Gaudens can rest easy. Unlike other significant Lincoln statues around the country, this Lincoln retains its luster and prominence, even if from time to time skateboarders use the exedra to practice their stunts.

It was a duplicate cast of the *Standing Lincoln*, given to England in 1920 as a gift of friendship from the Carnegie Endowment for International Peace and Robert Lincoln, that ended the brouhaha over Barnard's statue, as we saw in the previous chapter. This was the sculpture that most Americans thought would better represent President Abraham Lincoln on the international stage, as opposed to pre-presidential Lincoln sculpted for Cincinnati. The Saint-Gaudens stands in London, in Canning Enclosure, across the street from Parliament, facing the entrance to the north transept of Westminster Abbey. The ceremonies for this unveiling almost mirrored that of the Chicago dedication thirty-three years earlier. It rained, but a large crowd was on hand to witness the dedication. Cass Gilbert also was there for the ceremonies and reported the gathering "as representative a group as could have been gathered at any time or place in the world." Among those participating in the dedication were the Westminster Abbey boy's choir, American Boy Scouts, and an honor guard of fifteen Union veterans of the Civil War. Accepting the statue on behalf of his people and nation was Prime Minister David Lloyd George, a longtime admirer of Lincoln, who in delivering the keynote address said, "In his life he was a great American. He is no longer so. He is one of those giant figures, of whom there are very few in history, who lose their nationality in death. They are no longer Greek, or Hebrew, or English, or American; they belong to mankind."

Years after the sculpture was unveiled, in 1920, the Ford Motor Company ran a full-page magazine add combining images of the statue and a luxury automobile, the newly dubbed Lincoln. In the hand-drawn illustration, the automobile sits parked crisply in front of the statue. The word "masterpieces" is emblazoned at the top of the ad. Underneath the drawing at the foot of the page is the word "Lincoln." A small caption set above the sculpture reads, "Saint-Gauden's Lincoln, Lincoln Park, Chicago; greatest American portrait statue—A striking delineation of the simple nobility of Abraham Lincoln." Above the car are the words, "Those stalwart qualities of character which distinguish the leader are not attained easily, nor by chance. Only through faithful adherence to lofty principles can they be acquired." The commercial message is lost on no one.

Shortly after Saint-Gaudens lost his painful and debilitating fight with cancer, his friend and former assistant James Earle Fraser remembered fondly how the ever-reticent sculptor often refused to be cornered by visitors into explaining his work and his art. He preferred to let his work speak for itself. That embodied the core of his quiet philosophy. "You can do anything you please," he told Fraser. "It's the way it's done that makes a difference." This Lincoln does.

Lincoln of Gethsemane (author)

5

Lincoln of Gethsemane

Gutzon Borglum's *Seated Lincoln* (1911), Newark, New Jersey

ON OCTOBER 19, 1913, seventy-one-year-old Union veteran Osborn H. Oldroyd struck out on foot from Washington, D.C., to make a two-hundred-mile pilgrimage north to Newark, New Jersey. Wearing his faded blue woolen Union uniform and carrying a knapsack and camera, the aging veteran had one purpose in mind: to sit next to a new statue of his former commander in chief. Oldroyd had once served with the 20th Ohio Volunteer Infantry in the 1863 Vicksburg Campaign, and now he was the nation's largest collector of Lincoln memorabilia, holding well over a thousand documents, autographs, photographs, and artifacts. Oldroyd's treasures became the basis of the Lincoln Museum for Ford's Theatre in Washington. Among the prized possessions was Lincoln's office chair from Springfield, Illinois, a black locust rail that Lincoln was said to have split, and the Lincoln family cradle and Bible, from which, according to legend, Lincoln's mother read to him during his childhood.

Nine days later, after making a detour to see the site of George Washington's winter camp at Valley Forge, Oldroyd arrived in Newark. Not only did he pose for his own camera, but a photographer of the *Newark Evening News* also caught him lovingly gazing into the face of his hero. "Abraham Lincoln," Oldroyd wrote, "needs no marble shaft to perpetuate his name; his *words* are the most enduring monument, and will forever live in the hearts of the people."[1] It's true: people are more aware of Lincoln's words than of all the statues of him across the United States. We treat Lincoln's word as American gospel, venerating them as permanent and durable, much as these monuments petrify Lincoln's physical image.

As he looks at Lincoln in the *News* photograph, Oldroyd appears satisfied at the end of his journey and well pleased with the work of sculptor John Gutzon de la Mothe Borglum. Among the possessions of this aged fighting man was a photograph of Borglum's 1908 marble portrait bust of Lincoln, personally signed to Oldroyd by the sculptor. Borglum's rendering of Lincoln would attract all manner of persons from all stations in life, encompassing a cross-section of America.

Oldroyd's journey to Newark took days. My sojourn from my home in Northern Virginia takes only five hours. Circling the Capital Beltway, I am reminded of the circular ring of sixty-odd fortifications and gun batteries, interconnected by trenches, that protected the nation's capital from Confederate attack. At the time, Washington was the most fortified city in the world, more tightly secured than even in the post-9/11 era.

Four hours later, I leave the Garden State Parkway at Exit 145, just north of where it bisects Holy Sepulcher Cemetery, as highways are prone to do in the New York metropolitan area, and wind my way to downtown Newark. I find myself wondering if I can still make the kind of connection I made eighteen years ago with a student, one of the first to be exposed to my public sculpture quest.

Drew was my student twice in my early years of teaching. In ninth grade he was in my world history class, where, among other creative displays of his myriad talents, he performed an interpretive dance of Tchaikovsky's *1812 Overture*. Drew was in my class when I began my odyssey as a journeyman art historian. He was so intrigued with my blossoming interest, at the time, focused mostly on the work of sculptor Augustus Saint-Gaudens, that he read part of Burke Wilkinson's biography as he prepared for a wrestling match in the school gym.

As an eleventh grader in my American civilization class, Drew went with several other students on my first group pilgrimage to look at sculpture in Washington. On that early sculpture road trip in 1988 we visited Augustus Saint-Gaudens's Adams Memorial. Drew, fascinated with the seated figure but also being a teenager, rolled up a piece of paper and placed it in the figure's hand as if it were a cigarette.

I had not seen or talked with Drew for fifteen years, but I had recently bumped into one of his classmates, who informed me that he lived in northern New Jersey and worked in Manhattan. After an Internet search I made a phone call. His caller ID tipped off my surprise. "Jim. Jim Percoco," he shouted into the receiver with his familiar exuberance. "This is amazing. Perk! It's so good to hear from you!" It had been a long time since I had been called "Perk." My moniker had changed as I aged and became a permanent part of the West Springfield High School landscape. I was now Mr. P., but Perk sounded great and brought back a flood of memories.

After a few minutes of getting caught up, I asked Drew to join me on my Lincoln quest at the Borglum. He was more than up for it. As it turned out, he could easily catch the PATH in midtown Manhattan and meet me in Newark. Together we would visit Lincoln and then catch lunch at one of Newark's famous Portuguese fish restaurants. Before hanging up I assigned him a task: he is to read, before my visit, William Gienapp's concise but excellent *Abraham Lincoln and Civil War America* to provide our visit some context. Like the Drew I remembered, he took up the challenge with great zeal, confirmed by an email follow-up titled, "Gienapp Rocks!"

A cerulean sky complete with puffy cumulus clouds provides a perfect setting this beautiful late August day; there is not a trace of Newark's infamous pollution in the air. The rosary beads hanging from my rearview mirror gently dance, propelled by the motion of the car and the air conditioner. To avoid ludicrous parking fees, I nestle my car between an Amtrak van and a pickup truck in a reserved spot, hoping to avoid detection, just adjacent to Newark's art-deco Penn Station.

Ten minutes later my cell phone rings. "Hey, Perk, where are you?" Drew inquires. "I'm off the train." For a few minutes I have to drive around Penn Station, making my fair share of illegal U-turns. "I see you," Drew says. "Pull straight ahead into the bus exit lane." I do as commanded, wondering if the veteran Oldroyd encountered such obstacles on his journey. An older, more mature-looking Drew bounds down the sidewalk, still full of the teenage exuberance I remember. His business satchel slug across his shoulder and chest matches the rhythm of his motion. This time he is the one wearing a coat and tie, while in my shorts and golf shirt I'm the one casually dressed. I open the door and Drew jumps in. "Perk, it's so good to see you, man," he says, offering me a hearty handshake. "Do you know where you're going?" he asks. "Yeah, it's not too far from here," I reply as I gingerly pull out into the noon traffic.

Within five minutes we are on Market Street, making our way to the Borglum. In that five-minute span, we quickly reacquaint ourselves, picking up from where we left off so many years ago. I find a parking space only a block from Courthouse Square, in front of a ramshackle furniture store. I feed the meter with enough coins to give us plenty of time to spend with Lincoln.

As we cross the street, Lincoln looks ready for us. The burnished rich bronze tones of the sculpture glow in brilliant sunlight set off against the hue of the sky, providing for an ability to pick up details. For an instant I sense that Lincoln is bidding us to come forward and share time and space. If ever there were an image of an unscripted presidency, Borglum has captured it.

With me is a file folder of copied archival photographs of the sculpture including images of the dedication photographed by William F. Cone. Cone chronicled and captured life in Newark, with more than nine thousand photographs taken from 1895 to 1966. As we reach the curb, I pull one of Cone's panoramic shots of the dedication out and share it with Drew. "Wow! Look at that crowd!" he offers, staring at the image.

A century ago, it was a different scene. The plaza was ringed by nine- and ten-story buildings, department stores, and a Romanesque African American Anglican Church that cast its shadow across the plaza as the sun set. Behind the church was the eight-story Briderman Apartments, reminiscent of New York City's Flatiron Building. An offshoot of New York City, just across the bay, Newark was populated by Irish Catholic, German, Italian, and Jewish immigrants, among many other ethnic groups, who spent their free time shopping in this district. In 1910, the city's population was 347,000.

Newark today is a city of 123 square miles, one of the most segregated in the United States. In some of the public schools not a single white child attends class. Much as it was in 1911, the community today is ethnically mixed. Of the city's 267,000 residents, most are African American, Hispanic, and Portuguese. Eighty percent of the city's residents are off of the tax rolls, making Newark the poorest major city in the United States, even though it is the country's third-largest port.

Against this backdrop we are here to encounter Borglum's Lincoln. Of all the great Lincoln sculptors who created more than one statue to Lincoln, Borglum was the only one who got it right every time. But why this the second of three Lincolns that Borglum sculpted? This is not a magisterial statesman, but rather a human president trying to come to grips with a war that had ripped the nation in two.

Gutzon Borglum in front of his 1908 marble portrait bust of Abraham
Lincoln for the Rotunda of the United States Capitol (Borglum Archives)

Archival images of *Lincoln of Gethsemane*: African American youth as bootblack used on a Newark New Jersey Calendar and Newark "newsies" with Lincoln (Newark Public Library, Newark, New Jersey)

Dedication of *Lincoln of Gethsemane,* May 30, 1911 (Newark Public Library, Newark, New Jersey)

Author with *Lincoln of Gethsemane*

Borglum's Newark Lincoln was a radical departure from Lincoln sculptures up to this point. Lincoln is seated, but not in a chair of state, rather on a simple bench. Lincoln is close to the earth; there is no pedestal from which he can be knocked. Borglum's decisions make Lincoln more accessible, and in the intervening years people of all creeds and races have been photographed sitting next to the statue. One Newark newspaper quipped that the unique design was "ethically and artistically sane, as well as sculpturally satisfactory."

Drinking in what he observes, Drew says, "This is really an intimate sculpture. But its intimacy is different than that of the *Adams Memorial*. Borglum seems to convey the idea that Lincoln was a troubled soul dealing with the war. I dig this so much more having read Gienapp." My assignment has paid dividends. "You have to wonder," he adds, "if Lincoln questioned the price that he was paying." It's a good question, and one I had not considered.

"The Lincoln Memorial," Drew confides, "struck me as being silly when you took us there. I mean after all Lincoln was a regular guy elected by other regular guys. Borglum understood that Lincoln, even though he was a mythical figure, still needed to be accessible. Still, regular people don't get to be president. To be in this position, you have to stomach whatever comes along and take risks."

Like most sculptors of the age, Borglum saw Lincoln as larger than life and he competed for numerous major commissions. To garner a Lincoln commission a century ago was a major coup for a sculptor. A Lincoln commission secured and affirmed a reputation. "Lincoln is one of my hobbies," Borglum wrote to fellow sculptor Frank Ellwell after he had received the commission. "A pretty good sized one, I admit. But I am fond of big hobbies."[2]

Borglum consumed life and his work with so much passion that it often led to controversy. "Gutzon was for war, all sorts of war, six wars at a time," claimed Supreme Court Chief Justice Felix Frankfurter. "People weren't wrong; they were crooked. People didn't disagree with him; they cheated him. He was a powerful fellow with his jutting forehead, and he talked with his hands."[3] Photographs of the man show a brooding, enigmatic personality, with smoldering dark eyes. His gaze pierces even in the present. He never thought he was wrong, and he never doubted that he was the most talented sculptor alive. Reading through his papers, one gets the feeling he felt he was bigger than his subject matter.

During his fiery, ambitious career, each one of the Lincolns that Borglum sculpted is different and unique, reflecting the shades and nuances of Lincoln's life and legacy. The first Lincoln, sculpted in 1908, was purchased by Eugene Meyer Jr. and given to the people of the United States. The ten-ton marble portrait bust now resides in the Rotunda of the U.S. Capitol. Robert Lincoln, on seeing the sculpture for the first time, remarked, "I never expected to see father again."[4] The heroic marble head of a beardless, rugged Lincoln sprouts forth from the rock, a reflection of Lincoln's emerging from America's native soil.

Borglum also sculpted the four monumental presidential portraits at Mount Rushmore in South Dakota, completed in 1941. There Lincoln, like his companions George Washington, Thomas Jefferson, and Theodore Roosevelt, springs from the mountainside surveying the Black Hills, the sculptor once more using solid earth as a metaphor for greatness, this time depicting a strong Lincoln, a man in control.

One thing remains constant in all of Borglum's Lincolns: the sentiments he brought to bear on his work. "I do not believe there ever was a grotesque Lincoln," he said. "You will find written in his face literally all the complexity of his great nature."[5]

Borglum, the son of immigrant Danish Mormon pioneers, grew up in the heyday of the frontier American West and was drawn to the region's great natural beauty and diverse expanse. Animals fascinated him and were the subjects of his early works, as well as Indians. While attending college in Kansas, his artistic skills attracted attention. In 1890, Borglum moved to Paris, where he studied painting. Yet, more and more, Borglum was fascinated with sculpture. In Europe he saw and studied great works. In 1891, Borglum submitted a piece to the *Los Angeles Times* describing his enthusiasms. "The ability to represent form is what has placed them so high in sculpture. They have reached a point not far behind the best antiquities, if not equal to them," he wrote. "Paris is the home of the greatest living sculptors." For a period he enrolled in the École de Beaux Arts and the Academie Julian, where he worked and studied under master sculptor Jean Antoine Mercie. Borglum spent time with Rodin, who, he believed, brought sculpture to a new level. In 1893 he returned to the United States in time to have some work displayed at the World's Columbian Exposition in Chicago. By that time he was a committed sculptor with a particular confident presence, always promoting himself, his work, and his vision.

Borglum lived in an America overshadowed by the life and tragic death of Abraham Lincoln. The Lincoln he came to know was the venerated Lincoln, the great martyr who led the nation through a fratricidal conflict. By the time he reached adulthood, the sculptor worshiped the sixteenth president, naming his only son in Lincoln's honor. Borglum's affinity for Lincoln bordered on obsession. Yet he was also an anti-Semite and a xenophobe, seemingly unaware of the glaring contradiction. He once said, "Jews refuse to enter the mainstream of civilization, to become producing members of the world community. They do not share or create, but choose instead to clannishly hold onto their old ways and with mere money buy and sell the efforts of others." This is a strange sentiment, given that the man who helped launch his career as a Lincoln sculptor, Eugene Meyer Jr., was Jewish.

Despite his affinity for Lincoln, Borglum manifested an American enigma: a country constructing a national image of greatness, aspiring to and believing that it had secured high republican and democratic ideals through equality, while denying all people of color and other "outsiders" a place at the table. In 1915, the United Daughters of the Confederacy offered him the commission to sculpt a huge monumental tribute to the Confederacy on the side of Stone Mountain, near Atlanta. That same year he joined the Ku Klux Klan. During his lifetime Borglum never saw the incongruity between honoring a man who came to embody and personify American ideals and having a personal antipathy for blacks and newly arrived immigrants from Eastern and Southern Europe. Neither did most Americans. Ironically, within a short time after Borglum's Lincoln was dedicated, immigrants and African Americans would find a deep and abiding affinity for the sculptor's work.

An enthusiast by nature, Borglum was impulsive and threw himself with great energy into his many projects and interests. In addition to his work as a sculptor, he was a painter, political crusader, social critic, journeyman aviator, city planner, and sportsman. He met with presidents from Theodore Roosevelt to Franklin Roosevelt, and they admired his art and his work ethic. His place in the American art world of the first half of the twentieth century provided him with unprecedented access to the White House. Along the way he would manage to impress most and infuriate one president, Calvin Coolidge. During his work on Mount Rushmore, envisioned as his shrine to democracy, he asked Coolidge to write the words for a huge entablature he planned to carve into the mountain adjacent to the four presidential portraits. Borglum did not like what Coolidge wrote. He rewrote it and released his words to the press, implying that his prose was what the president meant to write. Coolidge later said that the two thousand miles between his Northampton, Massachusetts, home and South Dakota "is as close as I want to be to Mr. Borglum."[6]

He named his Stamford, Connecticut, studio, "Borgland," appropriately defining his empire and will to reign supreme in the world of American public sculpture. Along with his openly self-aggrandizing style, Borglum possessed an equally patriotic sentimental side, which he combined with a unique kind of realism. If you look carefully at his work you can pick it up. The North Carolina Monument on the battlefield of Gettysburg in particular drips with this realistic yet romantic emotionalism. This realism would come to play in his Newark Lincoln.

In 1915, four years after the Newark Lincoln was dedicated, delivering the Lincoln Centennial Association Address in Springfield, Illinois, Borglum described an artist as "simply a man whose heart beats a little quicker than those of the rest of you. It is because he gathers a little more of the struggle, of pathos, of sweetness, of desires, that come to man during twenty-four hours; and he must express it, he must write it, he must sing it, he must paint it, he must model it." The purpose of art, he added, was to "drop a plumb line into the depths of life, to find thereby the great emotions that are common to all mankind, and to express them so that all mankind will understand the expression."[7]

Here in Newark, this vision and philosophy is embodied in the Lincoln sitting before us. Unlike other seated sculptures of Lincoln, visitors can sit on the simple bench right next to Lincoln and look into his face. This is not the superhero American statesman; rather, it is a man struggling painfully with leadership of a nation during a time of great tragedy and sadness. Of the more than one hundred and thirty photographs of Lincoln, all posed, one has to look deeply into Lincoln's face and interpret his emotions. Unlike Lyndon Johnson, also fatigued by a divisive war, there are no photographs of Lincoln actively bearing the burdens he carried. In sculpture, Borglum has been able to convey that suffering.

Borglum liked to think that Lincoln was simply a man of the people, a man with whom ordinary folk can connect. He captured President Lincoln alone and in contemplation. He based his concept on his understanding of Lincoln's daily evening habit to visit the War Office next to the White House to read telegraphed dispatches from the field. As the Civil War dragged on Lincoln often found little news from the front to cheer. In the wake of receiving the casualty report from the December 13, 1862, Battle of Fredericksburg, where eighteen thousand Union soldiers had been killed or wounded, Lincoln commented, "If there is a worse place than hell, I am in it."[8] In such moments he would take himself out to a bench on the White House grounds and silently sit there. Lincoln's personal secretary, John Hay, often recalled such scenes in his memoirs. Borglum described his *Seated Lincoln* this way: "Lincoln often wandered into the Garden of Gethsemane and always alone." The metaphor is fitting, given that many contemporary Americans viewed Lincoln's assassination on Good Friday, April 14, 1865, as tantamount to Christ's crucifixion.

"The Lincoln I have endeavored to portray is not thinking about himself or of anything that will be of advantage to himself," Borglum offered. "His mind is engrossed with the vast responsibilities that have weighed him down. He alone realized their magnitude; he alone knew the strength he must have to support them and hold himself erect."[9]

Situated at the top of five short tiers of granite steps, Borglum's nine-foot bronze Lincoln faces east, a forlorn and weary look on his face. His right hand rests gently on the bench, palm flush with the surface, and seems to bid someone to sit next to him and visit. There is a slight tension in the torso. Lincoln shifts to the right with his left hand resting on his right leg just above his kneecap. The weight is borne by the right shoulder and arm. His silk stovepipe sits on the bench. The folds in the coat and other drapery around the figure are highly realistic. The right foot moves forward. If this Lincoln stood, he would be fourteen feet tall. Borglum got Lincoln's legs right, too. Lincoln's long legs proved vexing for sculptors, particularly those who wanted to depict Lincoln seated. In real life, when Lincoln sat, his bent legs often appeared to the observer to reach his chin. His right hand is two times larger than an average adult's. Lincoln's wrinkled, exposed vest even has the right amount of tension between the buttons and the fabric, which holds the vest snuggly towards his body. A small detail—the left corner of Lincoln's coattail bent over the left side of the bench—demonstrates Borglum's attention to the everyday. His face bears a weary look. Even from behind the sculpture resonates. Through Lincoln's overcoat you can feel the tension of the back muscles.

Unlike other Lincolns I have seen on my road trips, there are no words of Lincoln to read or ponder. If one understands the life of Lincoln, words are not necessary. Nothing but silence and space is needed to complement Borglum's Lincoln. In the silence we feel Lincoln, and knowing his story, we understand. Compositionally, Borglum's Lincoln is very much a human being.

The *Christian Science Monitor* praised the style and natural pose of the figure, reporting, "the result was that Mr. Borglum produced that marvelous figure of Lincoln, seated on a bench in all his awkwardness and with the familiar stove-pipe hat beside him, while the rest of the bench was vacant, so that the public might come and sit alongside of him." The *Monitor* rhetorically queried whether such a scene might have literally taken place to which they answered their own question, "He [Borglum] knew that such an act was within the realm of probability; he felt that it was assuredly in consonance with the humanity and the compassion of Lincoln. Therefore he was safe in idealizing and symbolizing."

Newark remains a symbol of the long, hot summer of 1967, when race riots erupted there and in other troubled urban areas of the nation. Mostly white National Guardsman who had been called into the city to restore order killed forty people in July 1967. Much of the rioting took place in the Central Ward section of the city along Springfield Avenue. Borglum's Lincoln, close to the center of where the riots took place, remained untouched, a mute witness.

Attempting to move beyond its past, today Newark sprouts new life as it undergoes steady and serious economic and physical revitalization. The world headquarters of Prudential Insurance Company now finds its home here. MBNA has built several large complexes throughout the city and seeks no tax relief. New crisp and clean architecture dots the urban landscape. Just as Lincoln oversaw the creeping urban blight of the last century, today he over-looks Newark's reconstruction, something he was unable to do with the nation.

Amos Van Horn, a Civil War veteran who survived serious combat wounds, made a fortune after the war operating a furniture store in Newark. He left to the city funds for a number of civic sculptures. The 1893 Chicago World's Columbian Exposition, showcasing works of a great many public sculptors, inspired Newark and other large cities in the late nineteenth century to embellish their public spaces. When Van Horn died in 1908 he left to the city $50,000 to erect monuments to George Washington and Abraham Lincoln.

By the time a committee in Newark had been organized to secure a sculptor for the Lincoln project, Borglum had achieved some recognition for his Lincoln portrait bust in the U.S. Capitol. With his ego unchecked, Borglum refused to enter any competition for commissions, saying, "Bidding for statues of such importance as a general, a president, or any great character in history was impossible for men of [his position] to take up work by the competitive method."¹⁰ Fortuitously for Borglum, the executor of the Van Horn estate, Ralph E. Lum, a Newark attorney, was a good friend. Lum's influence and a small model of *Seated Lincoln* helped persuade the Lincoln Monument Committee to award the coveted commission in 1909 to Borglum.

For his first sculpture of Lincoln, Borglum lovingly studied and took exacting measurements of Leonard Volk's life mask of the subject. For two years he immersed himself in Lincoln and the project. He read all that he could about the president; he studied Lincoln memorabilia and sought the advice of those who could offer perspective and insight about Lincoln. Writing in 1910 for *Everybody's Magazine* in an article titled "The Beauty of Lincoln," he compared Lincoln's life mask to the life mask of George Washington taken by the visiting French sculptor Jean Antoine Houdon, believing that "Houdon leaves us utterly uninterested." He added, "I . . . took the life mask, learned it by heart, measured it in every possible way—for it is infallible." Borglum's goal was to get to the man behind the mask. "No mask," he said, "will satisfy *us*; we want to see what we care for; *we* want to feel the private conscience that became public conduct." Having measured the Volk life mask in every possible way and "learned it by heart," he claimed, "His face was large in its simple masses. His head was normal in size; his forehead high, regular and ideal in shape. His brow bushed and projected like a cliff. His eyebrows were very strong. His mouth was not coarse or heavy. His right side was determined, developed, ancient. The left side was immature, plain, and physically not impressive."[11]

With the $25,000 contract secured, Borglum went to work. The contract covered the sculptor's work, time, materials, and casting. The small profit Borglum made was of little concern. He was more interested in securing a great artist's reputation.

Completing the modeling in his New York City studio at 166 East 38th Street, on whose walls hung an assortment of small plaster gargoyles he designed for the Cathedral of Saint John the Divine and several of his Western-scene canvases, Borglum made several small clay models and then enlarged the image along the way. His vast collection of Lincoln photographs was used to help shape his figure, though he determined that only five or six really captured Lincoln's essence. Through careful study of his Lincoln photographs Borglum believed that Lincoln recognized that the right side of his face provided the best view of the man. Borglum thought Lincoln honest but also an excellent actor who possessed great mobility and expressiveness.

As the project unfolded, Borglum decided to have the Gorham Manufacturing Company of Providence, Rhode Island, cast the sculpture all in one piece. This increased his cost by 40 percent, but he bore the additional expense and time needed to complete the work for artistic reasons. By casting the sculpture in one piece, no seams would be visible where sculptured works are typically joined.

Borglum also covered additional expenses in preparing the site at Market and Springfield Streets. All sculptors worry about the arrangement of their work with regard to the site. A good sculpture can often fail if the siting is not harmonious with the environs. Borglum wanted to take no such chances, and when he did not like the level the city of Newark had provided for his statue he made the necessary changes.

The dedication ceremony of Borglum's Lincoln in Newark on a hot Memorial Day, May 30, 1911, was not unlike that of similar unveilings of public sculpture in the United States. It was a spectacle. Close to 35,000 people crammed into the plaza in front of architect Cass Gilbert's 1906 imposing Essex County Court House. Adjacent streets and sidewalks picked up the overflow of a veritable sea of humanity. Flags, banners, and buntings draped the courthouse. Clever folks secured bird's-eye seats for the ceremony on the rooftop. According to Borglum's design, the *Seated Lincoln* was also draped in flags and bunting. The event, organized by Lincoln Post 11 of the Grand Army of the Republic, included a huge parade. Six thousand soldiers, including aging Civil War veterans, marched past the wooden dedication platform. Military bands played stirring music. The sound of hoofbeats against the pavement could be heard as mounted cavalry made their way along the parade route. The *Newark Evening Star* reported that the city enjoyed "a degree of patriotic fervor and enthusiasm almost without precedent." Among those in the crowd were the "new" Americans, immigrants and people of immigrant stock. For them, witnessing the dedication was a way to feel connected to their new home and to Lincoln; a Lincoln that the sculptor insisted was a man of the people.

Borglum arrived the morning of the dedication via a ferry ride across the Hudson River to Jersey City. In an open carriage with Theodore Roosevelt and Ralph E. Lum, the sculptor enjoyed the procession to the ceremony. Though three years removed from his tenure in the White House, Roosevelt remained a formidable and potent figure on the American political scene. Along the way an adoring crowd cheered. The late spring heat and hot sun beat down on the anxious congregation waiting in front of and around the Court House as the time for the unveiling neared.

An invocation offered by Reverend William H. Morgan, pastor of the Central Methodist Episcopal Church at 11:00 a.m. opened the proceedings. In his prayer he asked that the sculpture "perpetuate the memory of Abraham Lincoln and remind Americans of the qualities he possessed and of the work he achieved, and that it might serve to stimulate a desire on the part of everyone to pattern themselves on his character and ideals."

Following the invocation, the assembled crowd heard a dramatic reading of Walt Whitman's tribute to the fallen chief of state, "O Captain! My Captain!" Those lucky enough to receive a program could follow the verse. The crowd remained deeply silent.

When the poem was finished, Lum, representing the executors of the estate of Amos Van Horn, rose to deliver a few remarks. "May this memorial of him who is perhaps most near to the heart of our nation, be forever a reminder to posterity of the lasting debt owed to Lincoln and to all who helped in his life's work," Lum said. The crowd remained silent. Lum pulled the chord and the flags dramatically parted, bringing Lincoln into view. Ecstatic applause erupted and echoed across the plaza. "The exclamation of admiration on the part of those who were close enough to appreciate the beauty of the modeling mingled with the exultant shouts of the thousands who only knew the formal unveiling had been effected," one account reminisced. The forty-seven-year-old sculptor's work was a success.

Gratefully receiving the statue was Mahlon Pitney, chancellor of New Jersey and a future justice of the United States Supreme Court. Pitney, too, extolled the virtues of Lincoln and the work of the artist, saying, "the lines upon the face deepen, the pensive look comes into the cavernous eyes; the rapt spirit, oblivious of the wearied frame, searches for the proper solution . . . but the face manifests a serene confidence in the ultimate triumph of the cause to which his life is dedicated."

Roosevelt then moved center stage. Speaking in his loud reedy voice, audible only to those within one hundred feet or so of the platform, Roosevelt spoke lovingly about the subject. "You have done it," he said. "you have commemorated here in fit form one of the two greatest statesman that this country has ever had, one of that very limited number of great men whose greatness is for all the world and for all ages."

Addressing the question of the Civil War forty-six years after it was concluded, Roosevelt continued, "There never was a great cause more absolutely embodied in a great man than the cause of union and freedom. The cause of order and liberty, the greatest cause was embodied in Abraham Lincoln, and now I speak in no momentary fervor, but as expressing what I am sure will be the absolute verdict of history." Speaking directly to the Union veterans gathered at the dedication of their commander in chief, Roosevelt said, "the war in which you men here today were victorious was the greatest war for justice, and was the most just of all wars that the world has seen since the day that history dawned."[12]

As he spoke, parents close in hoisted their children up to get a better glimpse of the former president and perhaps secure a handclasp when his remarks were finished. Roosevelt cheerfully obliged. With the speech concluded, he received the brightly colored, elaborately lettered ornamental sheepskin deed for the statue in behalf of the Lincoln Post of the Grand Army of the Republic. The post then turned the deed over to Newark's mayor, Jacob Haussling, who promised that the city would never move the statue. The exercise concluded as the band struck up "Marching Through Georgia," a favorite tune among Union veterans.

A story of sorts has emerged from the dedication. Allegedly Roosevelt inspected Borglum's work from all sides and then exclaimed, "This doesn't look like a monument at all!" Borglum took this as the most fitting and greatest compliment his work received. His simplicity of presentation made it a grand work of civic sculpture. "So far as sculpture permits," he mused, "I have tried to give to posterity, in a true, unstudied picture of this great human being, a glimpse of possibly the best loved man in our national history as he might sit . . . free from the artifice which art too often falsely clothes our great characters, and thereby fails to give that personal note of manner, attitude and movement—the only means an artist has of conveying the soul of a man."[13]

The next day, Borglum wrote a letter of thanks to Roosevelt. "The story has just come to me," he wrote, "that an old lady climbed onto the seat and embraced the figure, and had to be taken away by a policeman. And one of my workmen last night, moving through the crowd about the statue, heard a mother tell her children that Lincoln was sitting down on a bench so that he could tell children stories. These are the first sproutings of the folk lore that will build around that bronze. It makes me very happy to have my statue provoke such emotions."[14]

A week after the dedication, Borglum received a letter from seventy-six-year-old William O. Stoddard, Lincoln's third secretary behind Hay and Nicolay. Unable to attend the unveiling, Borglum sent Stoddard a copy of the memorial presentation exercises and a photograph of the statue. Stoddard replied, "I wish to thank you heartily for the fine art and excellent judgment which you exhibited in your work. I have seen other attempts at portraiture and sculpture which were really harmful to ones who knew Mr. Lincoln as I did. No other man now living knew him as well."[15]

It also rained in Newark on May 31, 1911. Despite the soaking, a crowd collected around the statue, admiring Borglum's handiwork. It did not take long for the soul of *Seated Lincoln* to resonate with the people. The event was even noticed by the immigrant press. In 1913, an issue of the Italian-language newspaper *Il Progresso Italiano-American* featured an article that praised the monument and its attitude of accessibility: "This Lincoln is not towering and dominating the masses from a pedestal." The journalist was quick to make note that the bench on which Lincoln sat was shaped "like one of those stone benches commonly found in our Italian public gardens." With regard to children and the statue, the author duly noted the enjoyment of youngsters playing on Lincoln, reporting that one young girl was seen embracing the figure of Lincoln, kissing him and stroking his face, saying, "Hello, old man." Editorializing further, the article concluded "that to expose the figure of Lincoln to the innocent play of children is not a crime of lese majesté, and that the artist that created such an original work had fully understood the American soul."

Borglum was pleased that the statue attracted children. By 1915, letters poured in to Newark newspapers complaining about children climbing on the statue. Some individuals urged greater police protection, to which Borglum responded, "children should not be prevented from playing around the statue and sitting on the bench, etc. It should be quite possible for the police to see that these children behave themselves in an orderly manner, without depriving them of the educational and patriotic inspiration which a daily contact with this lifelike representation of America's greatest citizen is calculated to afford them."[16]

Robert Lincoln, less charmed, concluded that it was "used as a playground by the hoodlum children of the neighborhood."[17] Somehow the junior Lincoln's sentiments ring hollow in face of the evidence. He seems to have missed the point of the sculptor's intent. The real Lincoln would have been glad to have children clamber and climb all over him. Lincoln often overlooked the child-play and shenanigans throughout the White House of his own rambunctious children, Willie and Tad. To the consternation of many, he refused to admonish them, once telling a reporter friend, Noah Brooks, "Let him run, there's time enough yet for him to learn his letters and get poky."[18]

Numerous photographs taken since the dedication serve as witness to the power and attraction of the statue. Many include children. Some are casual snapshots, while others are formally posed. The people who congregate with Lincoln include men and women, young and old, black and white. In October 1911, black musicians, members of the A. C. Fletcher Social and Athletic Club, dressed in their Sunday best and with an assortment of musical instruments, crowd in and around Lincoln in a dignified pose. A more recent photograph shows a lone black saxophonist, complete with portable stereo, serenading Lincoln. On the cover of the August 1912 issue of *The Masses*, a socialist monthly magazine, two black children, one sitting on Lincoln's knee, gaze up at the president. A 1921 calendar shows an African American boy giving Lincoln's boots a shoeshine. Two women mug with the statue in 1939, while numerous photographs show groups of Newark schoolchildren posed with Lincoln, having fun. The cover of the February 8, 1930, issue of *Collier's* shows a small black child comfortably nestled in the crook of Lincoln's left arm. A poignant image from 1951 captures baseball great Jackie Robinson laying a wreath at the statue as part of a Lincoln Day Pilgrimage Ceremony. Even Lincoln impersonators have paid their homage.

"You were really onto something, Perk," Drew says, "hooking us with public sculpture to teach history. The accessibility is great with this statue, and proves that public art is important. It's too bad that people just whiz by this and other statues every day and fail to hear their messages or learn their stories."

"So," I ask, "are you going to bring your children down and pose them here?"

"Yeah," he replies, smiling.

Poets were quick to seize upon the sculpture's imagery. In "One of Our Presidents," Wendell Phillips Stafford observed children and foreigners comforted by and admiring Lincoln.

> Eight at a time swarming upon him there,
> All clinging to him—riding upon his knees,
> Cuddling between his arms, clasping his neck,
> Perched on his shoulders, even on his head;
> And one small, play-stained hand I saw reach up
> And laid most softly on the kind bronze lips
> As if it claimed them. They were children—
> Of foreigners we call them, but not so
> They call themselves; for what we asked of one,
> A restless, dark-eyed girl, who this man was,
> She answered straight, "One of our Presidents."
> "Let all the winds of hell blow in our sails,"
> I thought, "thank God, thank God, the ship rides true!"

Stephen Meader, reflecting on the African American experience, composed "Their Lincoln":

> And the calm and kindly eyes
> Seem, in them, again to see
> All the hope of youth that lies
> In the child race he set free.

Borglum's Lincoln found success in other ways, too. The Prang Company secured the exclusive rights to sell two special images of the new statue. A twenty-four-inch by thirty-two-inch copper photogravure in sepia cost $2.00. For $15.00 one could purchase a twenty-nine-inch by forty-inch bromide enlargement in sepia. Each image was autographed by Gutzon Borglum. A 1912 Prang Company brochure claimed, "No picture could be more appropriate for schoolroom decoration or for the home than this beautiful photogravure reproduction of the famous bronze statue of Abraham Lincoln modeled by Gutzon Borglum and unveiled in front of the City Hall of Newark, New Jersey, a short time ago. Mr. Borglum's statue is regarded as the greatest statue of Lincoln in existence and one of the really great statues of the world." The poem "Lincoln, The Man of the People" by Edwin Marklam completed the reverse of the brochure. In 1924, you could purchase for $625.00 from Bamberger's Department Store small bronze reductions of the statue measuring twenty-three inches high and twenty-eight inches long, while a pair of smaller bookends cost $10.00.

Lincoln holds an interesting place in New Jersey history. Among his connections is the Newark story related to Lincoln's trademark stovepipe hat, manufactured by a machine invented by Seth Boyden, a resident of Newark, who also has a statue in Newark. In the presidential elections of 1860 and 1864, Lincoln failed to carry New Jersey and the city of Newark. Many New York financers and Wall Street investors had their fortunes tied up in cotton production and thus slavery. During the Civil War, New York City and New Jersey were hotbeds of Southern sympathy. But a state that did not have any affinity for Lincoln managed to raise three other sculptures to Lincoln's memory, all of them erected during the heyday of Lincoln memorialization, residents and politicians of the Garden State seeming to have put the past behind them. Maybe it was Lincoln who had the last laugh.

Today no one is here but us to offer Lincoln any solace. Like others who have visited, we too must leave. So Lincoln will, in the end, remain alone. He must have felt that kind of loneliness as president, even with people coming and going to see him at either the White House or the Anderson Cottage on the grounds of the Old Soldiers' Home, where Lincoln lived in the summers of 1862, 1863, and 1864. In the end he was always the one alone bearing the burden of Civil War on his shoulders. No children are at play, most likely satisfying Lincoln's oldest son. It is silent. Charred, crushed cigarette butts and foil gum wrappers, dingy human refuse littering the ground in front of the bench, are his only companions. I kick some of the butts aside. Like so much of American public art, Borglum's Lincoln seems forgotten. Our great works of public sculpture are at the mercy not only of the elements, but also of people, many of whom are probably unaware of the significance and power of the monuments they do not really mean to desecrate.

Lincoln had a fondness for Shakespeare, *Richard II* in particular. To visitors who stopped by the White House or the cottage at the Old Soldiers' Home, Lincoln would often recite his favorite line from the bard, the lament of the deposed king: "For God's sake, let us sit upon the ground and tell sad stories of the death of kings." David Herbert Donald observes, "As an often lonely leader, he found it easy to identify with Shakespeare's heroes; he could sympathize with their fears and understand their anxieties."[19] A beguiling connection between two great men several centuries removed from each other resonates with Borglum's interpretation. I wonder if this was Lincoln's favorite line because he secretly foresaw his own death.

Sad stories about the Lincoln White House years crowd my mind sitting with Lincoln. Upon the first personal loss of the war he endured, the death of his twenty-one-year-old surrogate son, Elmer Ellsworth, an inconsolable Lincoln wrote his parents in Illinois from the White House, "in the untimely loss of your noble son, our affliction here, is scarcely less than your own. . . . My acquaintance with him began less than two years ago; yet . . . it was as intimate as the disparity of our ages, and my engrossing engagements, would permit. . . . [He was] my young friend, and your brave and early fallen child." Lincoln signed the letter, "Sincerely your friend in a common affliction—A. Lincoln."[20] Ellsworth was not the only good friend Lincoln would lose during the war. Six months later, in October 1861, his close friend Edward "Ned" Baker was killed in the debacle at Ball's Bluff, Virginia. The White House was also plunged into grief when Mary lost two half-brothers who fought for the Confederacy. The Lincolns remained as personally touched by the war as many Americans, who also bore loved ones in the field. And there was the death of Willie.

Here, Lincoln's conversation with members of Congress, including Speaker of the House of Representatives Schuyler Colfax, skips through my collective memory. The day after the bloodletting on May 2, 1864, at the Battle of the Wilderness, Lincoln was wracked with guilt. "My God! My God!" Lincoln lamented to one congressman. "Twenty thousand souls sent to their final account in one day! I cannot bear it! I cannot bear it!" Colfax found him agitated and pacing and recalled Lincoln saying, "Why do we suffer reverses after reverses! Couldn't we have avoided this terrible war! Was it not forced upon us! Is it never to end!" Borglum's Lincoln looks as if he is bearing the entire loss of the 625,000 Americans killed during the war.

There are days at school when I feel fatigued and stressed, particularly when my job forces me to contend on occasion with whiny, self-absorbed students and irritable, bullying parents in an atmosphere dominated by a culture of strict teacher accountability. Then I think about what Lincoln endured, and I am able to move on.

In the end Lincoln got it right, and that remains important. The war preserved the Union and liberated the slaves. Modern critics who charge that Lincoln had no feelings or care for those lost on the battlefield or in hospital tents cannot imagine the feelings of guilt Lincoln endured knowing his policies bore the fruits of carnage and the terrible by-products of war.

But the obverse is that Lincoln did endure despite his deep sensitivity; thus the mysterious Lincoln is also evident in Borglum's creation. The man who was moved to ask his good friend Ward Lamon Hill to sing the mournful ballad, "Twenty Years Ago" on the battlefield at Antietam managed to work almost every day and get the job done. In spite of losing close friends like Ellsworth or Baker, he was always back at work, did not let his grief trap him or the nation, and ran the war to its eventual conclusion. This contradiction plays itself out here in Newark. Borglum's Lincoln, wrestling with the carnage of the war, somehow manages to invite innocent little children to pose with him.

Some military historians claim Lincoln possessed a particular bond with men serving in the field and that his moral courage suffused with pain elevated him in stature among Union soldiers. "His identification with the wounded and suffering," argues one, "is an unspoken invocation of shared humanity, making it easy for the common soldier to identify with a Commander-in-Chief immersed in his own warborne agony."[21]

A look up at his careworn face elicits a sense of the emotional burden he bears. It resonates throughout his body. A haunting quality echoes between the real Lincoln and Borglum's bronze. But is Borglum's Lincoln of the common man a true reflection of our common ideals? Clearly, Borglum's work as art aspires to high ideals, yet its history has shown that it attracts those from every strata of our society. Why? Perhaps because through its artistic merit, the sculptor has discovered a way to embrace the humanity found in and amongst the greatest and the lowliest among us. Anyone who chooses to can sit and be photographed and become part of the collective whole.

Yet I must take issue with one thing. Most sculptors sign their works in small letters in unobtrusive places, generally along the bronze seam near where the metal meets the stone pedestal. In huge letters across the top of the bench to Lincoln's right is Borglum's name. For such a contemplative work of art, the sculptor should have reined in his ego and placed his signature somewhere in an inconspicuous spot, as did Ball, Manship, Barnard, and Saint-Gaudens.

Yet, like Osborn Oldroyd, a modern sojourner can still draw inspiration and learn from this most human of Lincoln sculptures. Great works of art force the serious viewer to evaluate their life in its presence. Here a visitor can sense the struggle of daily living, juxtaposed with the life of the man who bore the burden of America's most serious crisis and felt pain and loss at a deeply visceral level. Solace can be discovered in that experience, giving one a reason to pause and consider one's own life within the context of Lincoln's.

Lincoln the Mystic (David B. Wiegers)

6

Lincoln the Mystic

James Earle Fraser's *Lincoln* (1930), Jersey City, New Jersey

ON FEBRUARY 12, 2006, forty-plus inches of snow blanketed Jersey City, New Jersey. An intrepid band of twelve people emerged from the blizzard. Led by Jersey City natives Dennis Doran, wearing a Lincoln stovepipe hat, and Guy Catrillo, the frozen contingent had one purpose in mind: to maintain the seventy-six-year tradition of placing a wreath at the city's beloved statue, James Earle Fraser's *Lincoln the Mystic*.

The band waded through the knee-deep powder to the base of the monument. Covered and crusted in snow, shivering in the cold, they used a broom to wipe the drifting snow from Lincoln's head and shoulders, revealing the shawl that Lincoln was fond of wearing. The ceremony took place without fail, as it had every Lincoln's Birthday at noon since 1931. Doran read the Gettysburg Address. The group sang the "Battle Hymn of the Republic," recited the Pledge of Allegiance, and laid the wreath at Lincoln's snow-covered feet.

There was still one more ritual to complete in an effort to keep the ancestral chain of honoring Lincoln in motion. Since 1865, or 1866, or 1867, depending on who you talk with or what newspaper account you read, Jersey City has been honoring Lincoln with what has become the city's singular gala event, the Lincoln Association of Jersey City's annual dinner. Under normal circumstances, two to three hundred dignitaries and guests pack the Casino in the Park, Jersey City's answer to Manhattan's Tavern on the Green, as they have been doing since the dinner was moved there in the mid-1960s. This night that tradition would continue in somewhat less ornate settings—a private residence—but the dinner would be held nonetheless. The formal gala would have to wait, but Lincoln's memory could not.

One of the most challenging aspects of my Lincoln sculpture odyssey has been trying to figure out where the monuments end and the real man begins. This is a most difficult nut to crack in the world of Lincoln iconography and Lincoln studies. Thus, it made sense as I headed north, once more along the I-95 corridor, to listen to Joseph Campbell and his postulations about the "Power of Myth." I slipped the audio CD into my player and listened to Campbell and Bill Moyers wax philosophical about humanity's narrative and the need and power of myth in those narratives.

At first blush Jersey City, New Jersey, and Abraham Lincoln may seem incongruous, but he did come through the town on four occasions. Jersey City was once the nation's second-largest rail terminal behind Chicago. To cross America by rail and get to New York City, you had to get off the train in Jersey City, passing through the mammoth main terminal, and take a ferry across the Hudson River.

In 1860, Lincoln crossed the Hudson on his way to deliver his Cooper Union Address. He made the same journey on his way to his inaugural, where he addressed the crowd that met him at the rail depot on February 21, 1861. On that occasion the president-elect, standing on the platform of the last railroad car, after being introduced by New Jersey attorney general William L. Dayton, graciously thanked those in the crowd for their welcome and said,

> Ladies and gentlemen of the State of New Jersey, I shall only thank you briefly for this very kind and cordial reception—not as given to me individually, but as to the representative of the chief magistracy of this great nation. I cannot make any speech now to you, as I shall be met frequently to-day in the same manner as you have received me here, and therefore, have not the strength to address you at length. I am here before you care-worn, for little else than to greet you, and to say farewell. You have done me the very high honor to present your reception of me through your own great man—a man with whom it is an honor to be associated anywhere—a man with whom no state could be poor. His remarks of welcome, though brief, deserve an hour's well-considered reply; but time and the obligations before me render it necessary for me to close my remarks—allow me to bid you a kind and grateful farewell.

The crowd roared its approval. Many handkerchiefs were waved in his direction in addition to the thunderous applause. But as the crush of the joyous throngs surged forward to shake his hands, Lincoln ducked back inside the car. Cries of "Lincoln, Lincoln," eventually enticed the president-elect to reemerge where with his typical genial self-effacing humor he said, "There appears to be a desire to see more of me, and I can only say that from my position, especially when I look around the gallery (bowing to the ladies), I feel that I have decidedly the best of the bargain and in this matter I am for no compromises here."[1] The audience applauded and howled with much laughter. It was the only time he would speak in Jersey City.

In 1862, in order to reach West Point and consult with retired army general Winfield Scott, he passed through again. The last time his train berthed in Jersey City was on April 24, 1865, when his body was being returned for burial in Springfield, Illinois. The crowd that greeted him in triumph four years earlier was plunged, like the rest of the nation, into deep grief. From that moment on, Jersey City has honored Lincoln's memory.

Some historians have trouble with Lincoln the myth, while others view it as part of the whole. For the debunkers, these Lincoln monuments and memorials invite a kind of popular celebration inconsistent with the man himself. This begs the question, Who is Lincoln, really? And perhaps even more provocatively "Whose is Lincoln?" Clearly there is a tension between the memorial edifices in marble and bronze and the factual Lincoln. But, like Lisa Simpson, the philosophical member of television's most popular cartoon family, I think most Americans prefer the myth. Perhaps the reason we buy into myths is that we are still a relatively young nation and need this kind of collective memory to engage more directly with our past. As a nation that practices no state-endorsed religion, we have managed to create one, a civil religion where Lincoln emerges as one of our venerated saints. While I acknowledge we need to understand a more fully human Lincoln, like all our past leaders, as much as we can, the naysayers need to be careful that they not undermine the value of the narrative. These sculptures provide a kind of physical narrative on our landscape, yet they ask us to rise to a certain challenge. We have similarly mythologized Martin Luther King Jr. to the point of such sanitization that we really miss the great challenge of his life.

Even Doran, who affectionately, as only someone native from New Jersey can, call Lincoln, "the guy," explained in an interview with the *New York Times* that one of the Lincoln Association's goals "is to stop the silly caricatures of Lincoln—you know, you get the white sale at the department store and they have Lincoln wearing all these funny costumes. It's degrading to the guy."

I have pored over biography after biography and assorted historical analyses of Lincoln and weighed what each author has offered about him, and I have concluded that irrespective of the man, people bring their biases full well into play when they confront Lincoln. Once, at a PTA event, the father of a student approached me. He was an army colonel from Alabama. Walking up close to me, he said, "Lincoln was a real dictator, no different from Hitler. His policies abused the South. He oppressed Southerners and he full well violated the Constitution." At the time I was taken aback. This preemptive strike was several years before I began my pursuit of Lincoln in earnest, and it was only when I got home and looked in our bedroom mirror that I realized that what had stirred the colonel's ire: a T-shirt I had picked up the previous summer on a family trip west in Springfield, Illinois, celebrating the Land of Lincoln, with Old Abe's visage squarely in the center of the shirt.

There was a lesson to be learned here. The present always imposes its values on those who have gone before them. Subjective interpretation will always remain a step ahead of truth. Lincoln sculptures invite interpretation and reengagement in a different way from a book or film; monuments, in their own way, are a form of popular culture, one that predates television and other modern diversions. That's why they appeal to me.

New Jersey, a Democratic stronghold with great ties to the cotton kingdom of the South in the elections of 1860 and 1864, voted against Lincoln. Still, Lincoln felt ties to the state, if only because during the Civil War, Lincoln's eldest son, Robert, nearly lost his life inside Jersey City's rail depot. While standing on the platform, he recalled, "there was some crowding, and I happened to be pressed by it against the car body while waiting my turn. In this situation the train began to move, and by the motion I was twisted off my feet, and dropped somewhat, with feet downward, into the open space, and was personally helpless, when my coat collar was vigorously seized and I was quickly pulled up and out to a secure footing on the platform."[2] By a strange twist of fate, the man who saved Lincoln was Edwin Booth, America's foremost actor of the mid-nineteenth century and the brother of John Wilkes Booth.

James Earle Fraser with full size Lincoln plaster model in his Westport, Connecticut studio (National Cowboy and Western Heritage Museum, Oklahoma City, Oklahoma)

Lincoln the Mystic, before restoration (author)

Lincoln the Mystic, after restoration (David B. Wiegers)

New Jersey has reciprocated Lincoln's esteem by erecting four monuments in his honor. And now, on this bright summer day, I am standing in Jersey City's beautiful but weary-worn Bay View Cemetery looking at the grave of Walter Scott Tully. It is a cemetery that looks like *it* needs a cemetery. Tully's body in 1935 would have crossed under a single entrance for what was then New York Bay Cemetery and Bay View Cemetery. Today the decorative granite arch, erected in 1902, still stands flanked by two smaller pedestrian archways connected to the same larger archway—on the left side it reads "NY Bay Cemetery 1850," on the other side "Bay View Cemetery 1884." The central transom is held together by a keystone and crowned with a decorative marker denoting 1902. The black wrought-iron gate, however, is now closed and locked shut. Beyond the gate, the avenue, shaded by a canopy provided by the trees on either side of the roadway, remains quiet.

There is a Grand Army of the Republic plot in Bay View Cemetery named for Gilliam Van Houten, the commander of the 21st New Jersey Volunteers, killed at the Battle of Chancellorsville in May 1863. Four cannon barrels planted in the ground, breech ends sticking up, mark off the plot, which holds the remains of forty-four Union soldiers and sailors from New Jersey. They are buried beneath vintage Civil War–era marble military markers—the kind found in national cemeteries, faded, hard to read, covered with bird droppings. Two markers lean against each other as if supporting a wounded comrade.

Tully, a member of this post and a state commander of the New Jersey branch of the Grand Army, is buried separately from his comrades, roughly twenty-five yards inside the fence beyond the traffic of Garfield Avenue. Unlike the graves of his brothers in arms, his is not military, but a dark gray rectangle with a domed top etched with poppies.

Part of my quest is to connect some lines between Lincoln, Tully, and Jersey City that have been tugging at me. Tully, a first sergeant in Company B of the 11th New York Cavalry, had been assigned in 1862 to provide protection to Lincoln in Washington. After the war he settled near Jersey City and lived until the age of ninety-two.

Tully was proud of his service in the presidential protection detail. Eighteen months before his death, he granted a lengthy interview to the *Newark Ledger*. He claimed to have been Lincoln's chief body-guard, but that may be a bit of a stretch, since it was principally Company A of the regiment that guarded Lincoln on his route to and from the White House to the grounds of the Old Soldiers' Home four miles from downtown Washington.

The story relates that "it was a thoroughly human Lincoln who questioned the youthful Tully as to the gossip of Washington and the camps, and who went to bat for the Union soldiers when profiteering contractors sold shoddy material or raised prices so high that they were a hardship on the soldiers." One evening, seated around a campfire on the White House grounds, one of Tully's comrades tried putting on a pair of socks he had just drawn from the quartermaster. The socks immediately fell apart. The soldier exploded into a stream of violent profanity, expressing his disdain for quartermasters and contractors who provided such items to the troops. The next day, when Tully called on Lincoln to see if the president was to go riding that day, Lincoln asked him, "What was all that swearing I heard down in the camp last night?" Tully told Lincoln the story. Lincoln personally intervened in the matter, ordering the quartermaster to trace the shoddy socks to their source. The manufacturer was then punished for defrauding the government. Through this and other such episodes, the soldiers learned to speak loudly when Lincoln was casually in their presence, finding to their delight that Lincoln would take such matters into his own hands.

Tully's home in nearby Hillside had a relic of the war of which he was most proud. It was a new sash presented to him by the first lady. Whenever Lincoln went for a ride, those in the escort detail were required to wear a red ceremonial sash. Tully accidentally tore his original sash, snagging it on a White House kitchen chair one day while waiting for the president. "Mrs. Lincoln came into the room," Tully reminisced, "and told me she was sorry it had happened. I told her I could sew it and forgot the incident." Three days later Mrs. Lincoln presented him with a new silk sash as a replacement.

Dennis Doran, casually dressed in a forest-green golf shirt and cargo pants, has joined me. As we walk through Bay View, the accumulation of dead, dried leaves crackles beneath our feet. The sound of summer cicadas punctuates the air. "Why are all old beautiful cemeteries overrun with debris?" I wonder aloud. "That's because most old cemeteries no longer have burials so there's no money flowing in to help with maintenance," Doran offers.

A former newspaper reporter turned freelance historian and historic preservation advocate who restores old homes and then serves as their landlord, Doran has clung as fiercely to his Jersey City heritage as he has to Lincoln's memory. In 2006 he received an Excellence in Preservation Award given by the Jersey City Landmarks Conservancy. In 1998 he served as president of the Jersey City Lincoln Association, organized shortly after Lincoln's assassination, the oldest consecutively meeting Lincoln group in the United States. It was formed by local Lincoln boosters in a predominately Irish Catholic, Democratic town as a reaction to Lincoln's murder. Veterans helped organize these groups, which became national.

In June 1865, these boosters organized an outdoor Lincoln Memorial Service, now the site of Lincoln High School, which was formerly Bonnell Woods Park. It was well attended, and the association eventually became a prominent Jersey City civic group. This led to an annual formal dinner on February 12, where members gathered to discuss all things Lincoln-related, some of them dressed in period clothing. They put aside all acrimony in honor of Lincoln, fully agreeing with the words of the guest speaker, Homer Hoch, a U.S. Representative from Kansas:

> There is no new thing to be said of Lincoln. There is no new thing to be said of the mountains, or of the sea, or of the stars. The years may go their way, but the same old mountains lift their granite shoulders above the drifting clouds, the same mysterious seas beat upon the shore, and the same silent stars keep holy vigil above a tired world. But to mountains and seas and stars men turn forever in unwearied homage. And thus with Lincoln. For he was a mountain in grandeur; he was sea of mystic holiness; he was star in steadfast purity of purpose and of service. And he abides.

Attendance at this dinner has a certain cachet, and speakers over the course of the years have ranged from CBS commentator Charles Osgood to Lincoln scholar Harold Holzer, Rhode Island Supreme Court Chief Justice Frank Williams, and cartoonist Bill Mauldin, whose image of a grieving Lincoln statue in the Lincoln Memorial in the wake of President John F. Kennedy's assassination struck a chord with Americans. General William T. Sherman offered up the toast at the 1890 gathering. Former President William Howard Taft, no stranger to honoring Lincoln's public memory, addressed the association in 1917, and in 1991, Roy Innis, the executive director of the Congress of Racial Equality, addressed the gathering.

These dinner addresses have become classics of a "usable past," and like the man himself, who can be quoted on all sides of all issues, the various topics of the keynote speaker have reflected the tenor of the times projecting how Lincoln would have seen or addressed them. Many of them have been keenly ironic, addressing a variety of issues such as North-South reunification, justification for American imperialism in the late 1890s, and support for immigration quotas.

It was at its particularly enthusiastic sixty-first annual meeting in 1926 that the association called for $100,000 to raise a fitting monumental tribute erected to Lincoln's honor. Civic leaders from both Jersey City and Hudson County deemed the time opportune to join the ranks of other American cities to honor Lincoln with a statue. At the close of the meeting, outgoing president Howard Cruse moved "that the Association call upon the Hudson County Park Commission to set aside a site at the entrance to County West Side Park for Lincoln monument" and "that the Park Commissioners be asked upon to call upon the public to raise funds by popular subscription for the erection of suitable monument." Cruse was selected chairman of the memorial fund-raising drive and played a singular role in the deliberate selection of the site.

The Lincoln Highway, one of the first cross-country automobile roads, officially starts in New York City's Times Square. At the entrance to what is now called Lincoln Park, the Lincoln Highway turns west as it makes its way to its western terminus, San Francisco. At an equally enthusiastic and well-attended fund-raising kickoff rally at the Bergen Lyceum, where the inclement May weather did not dampen spirits, Cruse passionately argued, "No city in the country has such an ideal site for a Lincoln memorial as has Jersey City. Located at the start of the Lincoln Highway that links State after State, from the Atlantic to the Pacific, a fitting memorial to the martyr President will make the most splendid advertisement that Jersey City and Hudson County ever had." Ironically, the same night the Association voted to spearhead a drive to raise the needed money for the monument, the Association also voted to prohibit female membership.

Raising the needed funds to contract for such a sculpture proved relatively easy in the years before the Depression. Association members sold public subscriptions for twenty-five cents apiece. Other civic groups, such as the local Kiwanis Club, contributed as well. Local blue-collar workers also kicked in an additional $2,500 through the subscription program, while schoolchildren raised the final $3,500 in nickels, dimes, and pennies.

To sculpt their Lincoln, Organizers turned to fifty-year-old James Earle Fraser, who had an outstanding sculpture pedigree and oeuvre and who, the *New York Times* reported, "lived for his work, quietly, almost humbly, as though it was nothing at all to make the rush of history or the glow of a human soul emerge in stone and bronze."

By 1926, Fraser's works were widely known. His catalogue of public monuments in the United States makes him one of the most prolific sculptors this nation has produced. His first significant public monument commission was in 1917 for an inspiring statue of Alexander Hamilton that stands on the steps of the Treasury Department Building in Washington. From 1917 until his death Fraser consistently had major projects under his direction. Jefferson City, Missouri; Cleveland, Ohio; the United States Military Academy at West Point; New York City; Niagara Falls, New York; and Chicago all have important public monuments sculpted by Fraser. Washington is home to more than thirty works by Fraser, more than any other sculptor.

At seventeen he sculpted what would become an iconic American image, *The End of the Trail*, depicting an utterly defeated American Indian warrior slumped over on his equally worn pony. The idea was to depict the American Indian both metaphorically and literally at the end of the trail. In 1895, while studying at the École des Beaux Arts, the American Art Association in Paris awarded Fraser $1,000 for *The End of the Trail*. His work also attracted an important mentor, the great American sculptor Augustus Saint-Gaudens, who invited him to work in his studios. "The opportunity was a greater boon than the prize award," Fraser recalled. "I had stood in long study before the heroic Lincoln in Chicago, the Farragut in New York and the Adams Memorial in Washington—and now I was to know the creator of those masterpieces." Several days after Fraser received an invitation from Saint-Gaudens to visit him in his Paris studio, he gleefully called on him. Bringing with him a model of *The End of the Trail*, he anxiously awaited Saint-Gaudens's criticism. "My heart was high," Fraser recalled, "when he looked at my spent Indian brave on his pony and said, 'You haven't done a man. You've done a race.'" By the end of the visit Fraser agreed to become one of his assistants.

Fraser was also a skilled numismatist, having designed, in 1913, the buffalo nickel, which depicted an American bison on one side and a moving portrait of a Plains Indian on the reverse side. The buffalo nickel, replaced by the Jefferson nickel in 1938, is considered one of the finest coins ever minted in the United States. "In designing it," said Fraser, "my object was to achieve a coin which would be truly American, [and] that could not be confused with the currency of any other country. I made sure therefore to use none of the attributes which other nations had used in the past. And in my search for symbols, I found no motif within the boundaries of the United States so distinctive as the American buffalo or bison." These were the nickels the Jersey City schoolchildren collected to help pay for the statue.

American Indian and frontier themes were germane to Fraser's nature. He was born in 1876, the year of the fateful Battle of the Little Big Horn, on the Minnesota frontier. For much of his childhood he enjoyed Indian playmates while his father, Thomas Alexander Fraser, a mechanical engineer for the Chicago, Milwaukee Railroad, worked in the Dakota territories. For ten years he lived on a ranch in the small community of Mitchell in what is now South Dakota, while at other times with his family he lived on the "right-of-way . . . sleeping on the floor of a box car, covered by painted Indian buffalo skins." The unpretentious Fraser loved to tell stories, particularly about his youth. Near the end of his life he wrote a letter to an admiring youngster,

A long time ago, when I was a small boy, younger than you are, I lived in the Indian country of Dakota, in the land that belonged to the Indians, and I saw them in their villages, crossing the prairies on their hunting expeditions. Often they stopped beside our ranch house; and camped and traded rabbits and other game for chickens. They seemed very happy until the order came to place them on reservations. One group after another was surrounded by soldiers and herded beyond the Missouri River. I realized that they were always being sent further West, and I often heard my father say that the Indians would some day be pushed into the Pacific Ocean and I think that accounted for my sympathetic feeling for them."[3]

Fraser often spoke of "seeing whitened buffalo bones showing through the snow, the waterfowl, the running jackrabbits and badgers and gophers," and the "antics of his pet antelope." He met trappers, learned how to make arrows from his Sioux friends, and knew the sting of Great Plains blizzards. The West left an enduring mark on his heart and art.

During these years on the prairie, Fraser began to dabble in sculpture, modeling animals and figures using soft chalkstone found in a quarry near his home. His interest in natural subjects and statuary blossomed while he lived in Minneapolis for a time. In 1891 he enrolled in the Art Institute of Chicago, earnestly pursuing serious work as a professional sculptor. This decision did not rest well with the elder Fraser, who carefully advised his son that he "might have many hungry moments, as art was not the most paying work to be selected, particularly if one did not reach the top." Holding firm and with a wry sense of humor that would mark him all his life, Fraser responded that "it would be no worse to be a poor artist than an incompetent mechanic, cab driver, or any other profession." Fraser's father relented.

After working with Saint-Gaudens for several years in Paris, Fraser moved to Aspet, the Saint-Gaudens home and studio in Cornish, New Hampshire. There he assisted in a number of projects, laboring on the William T. Sherman monument, designing one of the large barn studios, and becoming an active member of the Cornish Art Colony that grew up around Saint-Gaudens. Eventually Fraser struck out on his own and set up his own studio at 3 MacDougal Alley, in the Greenwich Village section of Manhattan. Several other important American artists, painters, and sculptors became neighbors with Fraser, most notably fellow sculptor Daniel Chester French and painter George de Forest Brush.

Like his mentor Saint-Gaudens, Fraser believed very much in the training of young artists in a supportive academic instructional environment. In 1906 he began instruction at the Arts Student League in New York, an institution established in part by Saint-Gaudens working his way up to director, leaving in 1911. Here he rekindled a Chicago childhood acquaintance with one of his pupils, Laura Gardin, who would excel and become a fine sculptor herself. Thirteen years his junior, she married Fraser in 1913 after a long engagement. Gardin descended from a long line of Virginians and counted Mary Ball,

George Washington's mother, in her lineage. One admirer of Laura wrote lovingly, "Mrs. Fraser was a woman of great charm of manner, with a modesty and an interest in people that made her a great favorite with new neighbors [in Westport, Connecticut] from the very beginning."

With a burgeoning business of important and highly placed clientele, steady work, and an attractive wife and soulmate by his side, Fraser sought larger quarters. The small village of Westport, Connecticut, fifty-five miles from New York City along the northern shore of Long Island Sound, caught Fraser's eye in 1914. Until his death, Fraser was a beloved member of the community.

In many ways, Fraser was Westport's first daily New York City commuter, beginning a pattern for numerous residents that continues to this day. Laura would drive her husband each and every morning from the Coleytown section north of Westport's center, chugging along the "dusty road to the rude, little railroad depot" and then pick him up in the evening retracing her route. The couple and their automobile caused quite a stir in the community of 3,500 residents in 1914. Six years before the advent of the flapper and a woman's right to vote, a young woman was seen seated behind the wheel of an automobile, an equally unusual site, of which there were "fewer than half a dozen" in Westport. The Frasers purchased the Morehouse Coley House, on North Road, a colonial-era home, which they upgraded. Most of the community's artists lived within walking distance of town or the small trolley line that served the village. "It became not an unusual site" wrote one local, "to see men in knickers and tweed cap (trademark of an artist at that time) walking along Main Street in the direction of the post office." Hence, the need for the Frasers to purchase an automobile. While they were having a large double-sized studio erected across the street from their home, Fraser continued to work at the MacDougal Alley workplace.

Inspired by the architecture of Florence, Italy, Fraser designed his Westport studio to reflect a heavy Tuscan stone appearance supported by massive pillars. From 1914 until his death in 1953, both husband and wife entertained clients and worked prodigious hours in a facility that would see its fair share of great heroic sculpture, and a plethora of a galaxy of greats, parade through its doors. By 1953, Fraser had created an audacious monument to General George S. Patton for West Point; the Treasury Department's delicately arrogant Alexander Hamilton; Hamilton's political rival Thomas Jefferson for the steps of the Missouri State House in Jefferson City; a pair of tributes to Meriwether Lewis and William Clark to complement Jefferson's presence in Jefferson City as well as above the portal to the Central Park Avenue entrance to the American Museum of Natural History; and a massive marble, mirthful-looking Benjamin Franklin for Philadelphia's Franklin Institute. There were many other important commissions from individual clients to federal government commissions. American heroes and international dignitaries visited Fraser in Westport for sittings and consultations.

Fraser designed the headstone for President William Howard Taft and the sarcophagus of Robert Lincoln, both of which are located in Arlington National Cemetery. Adding to the atmosphere of their home and studio, the Frasers prided themselves in their spunky pair of black cocker spaniels, Victory and Commando. All who encountered Fraser, from fellow artists to patrons, were "impressed by his talent, his industry, and his fair-mindedness [which] have won him a high place in the esteem of his colleagues."[4]

By the time Fraser secured the Jersey City Lincoln commission, he was no stranger to presidential portraiture. During his life he sculpted three images of Theodore Roosevelt, one from life in 1906 that served as the model for the other two, at the age of thirty, when his cancer-stricken friend Saint-Gaudens could not complete the commission. Roosevelt, an admirer and good friend of Saint-Gaudens, looked Fraser over pretty sharply when he arrived at the White House to begin work. He had expected someone much older. "However," he told Fraser in his distinctive voice, "if Saint-Gaudens says you can do it I guess you can." That portrait, considered the best sculptural likeness of Roosevelt, was placed in the Senate Chamber of the United States Capitol, and with it he and Roosevelt became fast friends.

Fraser dabbled in the early 1920s with a seated figure of Lincoln. At one point the Sulgrave Institute of America, an American-Anglo League of friendship, considered Fraser to create a suitable Lincoln statue as a token of good relations between the United States and the United Kingdom. On March 24, 1922, Fraser replied to the organization's chairman, John A. Stewart, writing, "I am working at present on a Lincoln Statue which might interest you. I will be glad to furnish photographs of it if you wish them. It is a thought I have had in mind for some time, and I believe a little different from any statue of Lincoln which has been produced."[5] For whatever reason, the Sulgrave Institute passed as duplicate casts of the Saint-Gaudens statue in Chicago and the George Grey Barnard figure from Cincinnati were presented to the British people. Irrespective, Fraser's Lincoln statue is indeed different if simply for the fact that Lincoln is beardless, yet the sculptor insisted that this was an interpretation of President Lincoln.[6]

Fraser's Lincoln is a thoughtful portrait of Lincoln, seated on a boulder, lost in either meditation or deep thought, contemplation. It is possible that the sculptor drew inspiration for seating Lincoln on a boulder from Saint-Gaudens's Adams Memorial, which Fraser had admired before he undertook his tutelage under his master. The clean-shaven, hair-tousled, bow-tied Lincoln sits with his head slightly drooped, shoulders rounded a bit, his familiar coat open, beneath it his closed vest. His hands rest together, the right hand lying on top of the left, with his forearms supported by his thighs. Lincoln's long legs are bent and spread somewhat apart cradling his hands. There is an air of pensiveness and quiet tension in the piece mixed with a touch of serenity, almost as if Lincoln has finished breathing a sigh and is now centered in calm repose of mind and heart.

This attitude is universal and consistent with those in human history who seek truth and with great leaders who pull from the depths of not so much organized religion but rather from the true benevolence of their nature a singular kind of tradition, in which clarity emerges from stillness. Standing before *Lincoln the Mystic* one might imagine Lincoln thinking, "thy will be done versus my will be done," and like the true mystic embracing the void and silence fully. That is their way. Here it would appear Lincoln could commune easily in silence with either a Buddhist or Trappist monk.

Fraser's Lincoln invokes Lincoln's "Meditation on the Divine Will," a private, spiritual reflection he wrote in 1862 between the death of his twelve-year-old-son Willie and the Battle of Antietam. Not discovered until after his death, the meditation reveals Lincoln's wrestling with and consideration of the role of an infinite power in the affairs of humanity so often thrust into tragic circumstances, arguing that "the will of God prevails . . . that God wills this contest, and wills that it shall not end yet."

The feeling expressed by the pose accentuates more fully the quote etched on the wall of the exedra, a kind of bench designed by the collaborating architect, that permits the viewer to sit and encounter Lincoln; "With Malice Toward None" as part of the design, we can fully appreciate Lincoln's sense of forgiveness toward the South.

If we accept Tully's stories of encounters with Lincoln as true, then Fraser's monument reflects as well the noteworthy kindness often reported by others regarding Lincoln's treatment of them. Lincoln's gentle gray eyes, often deepened by the circles beneath them, generated a kind of tenderness that endeared him to many people, particularly during his presidency. In a war that ripped the country apart, Lincoln was able to treat people kindly, particularly when they were hurting. Out of his deep reservoir of compassion emerged a strength and resilience with great power during a time when kindness was sold very short. It was this power that touched many people during his lifetime that continues to resonate today. Those who prefer to focus on Lincoln's political wiliness, consistently pointing out that he, too, was a mortal made with clay feet, equally deny him the fullness of his humanity through a prism that dismisses his virtues.

The fifty-foot, sweeping, red granite semicircular exedra, with the statue raised on a platform in the center, was designed by architect Albert Randolph Ross. The exedra is flanked by two abutment walls upon which are etched the last lines of the Gettysburg Address on one side and the last line from the Cooper Union Address on the other. An anniversary bronze tablet placed by the Lincoln Association of Jersey City honors the schoolchildren and their contributions.

The face of this bronze Lincoln, a young and soulful man, was never meant to have a beard. Fraser, working with the Volk life mask, wanted to portray Lincoln with a more vigorous visage. "It will be a smooth-faced Lincoln," said Cruse. "Lincoln lived 56 years, and for 53 years as far as I have been able to discover, wore no beard," Cruse erroneously insisted. "The face is taken from a life mask of Lincoln," Cruse continued, "which was made just after his first inauguration, and shortly after he made his only visit to New Jersey." Howard Cruse may have been the consummate fund-raiser, but he was sorely in need of a history lesson.

In one way this figure is perfect for Jersey City today. It is a city trying to revive itself coming to terms with boarded-up shops, hundreds of stacked multicolored and rusting container carriers alongside the New Jersey Turnpike, and a disheveled cemetery while boasting a vibrant and bustling riverside of new development and up-scale office and government buildings, restaurants, and businesses.

Lincoln Association trustee Guy Catrillo, a Jersey City planning aide whose other heroes include Mother Teresa, Albert Einstein, and Martin Luther King Jr., met me in his seventh-floor office in one of those newer buildings, complete with a pristine view of the Hudson and downtown Manhattan. "If you could talk to Lincoln today, he would be dismayed about the gang situation," he sighs. "He would be upset with the different kind of slavery in gang membership. There are those in Jersey City who live with a 'gangsta' mentality—young people who give up their family, community, and education and become the 'dog' of the O.G.—Older Gangsta—he's the new slave master—it is a renewed kind of new voluntary enslavement." The recently restored figure was even more recently spray-painted.

Still, Catrillo is optimistic. "We are trying to turn the gang problem around," he says. "There is a junior ROTC program just started at Lincoln High—the Lincoln Association of Jersey City has made their color guard the official one for the statue."

I think that Lincoln would be pleased, noting the connection with the perseverance tied to his nature and recalling the photograph that appeared in the *New Jersey Journal* showing the statue flanked by two Boy Scouts, one white and one black, standing at attention after a wreath had been placed at Lincoln's feet.

Lincoln High School, erected in 1917, with an architectural style reminiscent of a temple of learning, complete with decorative entab-latures on its tan sandstone facade, is also part and parcel of Jersey City's public memory affection of Abraham Lincoln. For sixty years athletes of the Lincoln High School Lions would emerge from the locker room and rub the head of the statue of the Railsplitter for good luck before games and contests. Students who joined the school fra-ternity would make their pledge by kissing Lincoln. The small bronze statue, placed on the top of a rectangular marble pedestal, was remi-niscent of heroic public sculptures that depict Lincoln as a youth, dressed in a linsey wool shirt and frontier breeches, "seated on a log intently studying," having laid down his ax in preference to intellec-tual over manual labor. In 1994, the tradition came to a grinding and unexpected stop as the statue, which sat proudly for six decades in the main foyer of the school entrance, was stolen. A gift to the school, the statue, "made possible by the members of the graduating classes of the school from the beginning of 1916," was sculpted by a Lincoln High graduate, Archimedes A. Giacomantonio. In 1983, a result of the shift in Lincoln memory and meaning that continued to evolve, a bronze plaque was affixed to the marble pedestal reading, "Abraham Lincoln—The Great Emancipator," making the sculpture more accessible to the school's large African American population.

For ten years the whereabouts of the much beloved statue was a mystery. Then 1976 Lincoln High graduate and star football player Brian Smith, a Jersey City police detective who "had rubbed Lincoln's head hundreds of times and kissed it to become a member of Kappa Beta Epsilon," reopened the case, which had gone cold. For Smith, an African American, it was a matter of family as well. His mother and four sons were graduates of Lincoln High School. In December 2003, Smith received a tip from Manhattan antique dealer and Jersey City property owner Jack Shaoul, in whose possession the statue had landed. For three years, including multiple contacts with the school and the FBI, Shaoul tried to get the sculpture back to its proper home, to no avail. Shaoul purchased the piece from what he described as a "thief in a pickup truck" for $5,500. Placing Lincoln in the front of his shop proved fortuitous. Several days later the shop was visited by Phillip Schiavo, "the grandson of the owner of the foundry" where *Railsplitter* was cast. Schiavo related the tale to Shaoul, who, rather than sell it for a sumptuous profit of $30,000 to $40,000, roused the Lincoln in himself and let the better angels of his nature take control. Speaking to a reporter for the *Jersey Journal*, Shaoul said, "I have four children in school. In my house you move something around my kids miss it. This property has to go back to the kids. I am part of the community. I want to give it back."

The statue was reinstalled in February 2004, and today the small bronze talisman is back in place where it rightfully belongs. "Tradition," said a satisfied Smith after the recovery "is not just in your heart and soul. Tradition is what you see, what you can touch. What you can use to further tomorrow."[7]

The Lincoln Association of Jersey City reflects Catrillo's and Smith's hope and optimism as well continuing its long-standing tradition of meeting head-on civic obstacles raised by an urban environment, never letting wars or economic depressions impede their annual honor to Lincoln. For Doran, it is about something in Jersey City's makeup. "You can't go wrong with honoring Lincoln," he says.

"And we are very civic minded folk. Given the condition of Jersey City with all its ups and downs—it's a tough town—Lincoln can serve as an inspiration."

"Lincoln helps give us a fundamental sense of community, and this helps the town cope," he adds emphatically. "The statue reflects Lincoln deep in thought, and this kind of resonates with people who live here—it is one of the great things we have in Jersey City. We can say, 'Look at this! We are proud of our association with Lincoln. It's the one thing we can be proud of.'"

As if to underscore the history of the degree of seriousness with which Jersey City brings to its homage to Lincoln, an apocryphal tale connects the Lincoln Association directly with the last time Lincoln came through their city—in a coffin.

An undertaker by the name of Bunnell, attached to the Union Army in Washington, allegedly helped to embalm Lincoln's body after his assassination. Years later, the Bunnell Funeral Home opened in Jersey City. Through successive generations, the Bunnell family clung to their role in the Lincoln narrative and erected a Lincoln shrine inside their funeral home.

By 1969, the Lincoln Association admitted women into the group, and Dorothy Nicoll Bunnell, the wife of Milton Bunnell, the great-grandson of the undertaker, was elected president. A very blue-blood type, she became a self-appointed Grand Dame of the Association. Only she could address the invitations in the proper gold lettering calligraphy, only she could organize the meetings. She brought a certain woman's touch to the group, to be sure, organizing the meetings with class and dignity, adding some pomp and pageantry to the proceedings. This continued well past her term as president expired. At the time, the Jersey City Public Library owned a very heavy bronze bust of Lincoln. Each year, until she closed the family business, Mrs. Bunnell would dispatch a hearse with a complement of pallbearers down to the library to retrieve the bust and bring it to the dining hall, where it would be set up as a centerpiece on the dais. Now the Bunnell Funeral Home is gone, as is its shrine to Lincoln, and the bust which Mrs. Bunnell so lovingly fetched for the annual gala.

Some have argued that Fraser's sculpture shows Lincoln as he appeared when he first visited Jersey City on his way to New York City in early 1860 to deliver the Cooper Union Address. But that counters Fraser's argument, and one must conclude that Fraser deliberately and for reasons that to this day are not completely clear depicted a beardless President Lincoln. On one occasion, Lincoln's personal secretary, John Hay, told the sculptor that "during the early days of the Civil War, when things were new to the chief magistrate and when his problems and burdens were multiplying so rapidly, the President formed the habit of going at sunset to an eminence over-looking the national capitol, and there, seated on a rock, in solitude and meditation, he fortified his faith that 'right makes might,' held communion with the Eternal, and found the strength to bear his bur-dens and the wisdom to solve his problems."[8] The problem with this statement is that it would appear that the scene Hay recreated in his mind may have taken place out at the Old Soldiers' Home, so it could not have been during the first days of his administration. But Walter Tully, who was invited to place a wreath at Lincoln's feet on Flag Day in 1930, when the sculpture was unveiled, supported Hay's assertion. "When I saw it for the first time, I was startled," he claimed. "I've seen that before," he told the chairman of the unveiling committee. "That pose is exactly like the time when I saw Mr. Lincoln sit down in Rock Creek Park, north of Washington. He sat there, very thought-ful, and though it's nearly 70 years ago, I can recall the expression and pose."

The sculpture cost $75,000 and was copyrighted by Fraser. Pre-viously sculptors did not copyright their works, but as organizations sought to raise money they often ordered smaller versions to sell as fund-raisers. Artists saw this as an additional way to increase their coffers as well as to protect their design.

Under Cruse's direction, the subscription drive was well sustained, beginning with a $100 check presented on the evening the associa-tion resolved to erect the monuments. Frank D. Miner asked Cruse if he could have the privilege of making the first donation. "I'd be tickled to death," replied Cruse, to which Miner responded "All right, here you are." It was registered as "Subscription Number 1 for the Lincoln Memorial Statue." A local newspaper article reported the story, offering, "the committee [yet to be formed] will probably be ready to receive subscriptions at an early date, but if there are others who would like to get their subscriptions in among the first—no one can take away Mr. Miner's credit for being No. 1—doubtless Mr. Cruse would be willing to accept the subscriptions for the time being." Cruse took the lead more than just symbolically. He signed the initial contract for the sculpture for $35,000 with Fraser and an additional $25,000 for the granite, paying out of his own pocket when only $18,000 had been raised.[9]

Almost three years later in December 1928, ground was broken at one of the city's most graceful and commanding sites, the entrance to the 273-acre West Side Park, soon to be renamed Lincoln Park. On Memorial Day 1929 the cornerstone was laid. Placed into the cornerstone was a copper box, manufactured by Jersey City's Ringle and Sons, whose content included speeches of Lincoln; the menu of the Lincoln Association's 1929 annual banquet; a copy of the *New York Herald Tribune* from February 10, 1929, with a facsimile of Lincoln's letter of May 25, 1861, to the father and mother of Colonel Elmer Ellsworth, with pictures of Ellsworth and photos of Lincoln's cabinet members; a copy of the March 5, 1929, *New York Herald* covering the inauguration of Herbert Hoover; statements from Jersey City civic organizations such as the Young Men's and Young Women's Christian Association, various business and banks, Lincoln Pennies minted in 1928; a medal made from a captured German artillery piece from the First World War; a list of all the public and parochial schools from Jersey City; a small metal plate inscribed with the Lord's Prayer; and copies of various newspaper articles from Hudson County newspapers. A formal ceremony was held for the laying of the cornerstone, presided over by Robert J. Rendell, followed by an invocation and the presentation of the ceremonial trowel to Mayor Hague, who sealed the cornerstone off after it had been laid by Cruse. Delivering the oration was A. Harry Moore, former governor of New Jersey, followed by brief remarks by Spanish American War and Civil War veterans.

Seventeen months later, Jersey City received its Lincoln statue. Among the three thousand people assembled on that 1930 Flag Day stood a young J. Owen Grundy, a distant relative of Lincoln's and the future historian of Jersey City and of the Hudson County Historical Society. He recalled that it "was a bright, sunny spring day, with blue skies and beautiful white clouds floating overhead. A cool welcome breeze caught the many flags and kept the red, white, and blue colors rippling above the vast audience." Echoing the sentiments of the city's residents and the subsequent fund-raising drive, including the $3,500 dollars chipped in by schoolchildren and the $2,500 provided by local factory workers, Grundy remembered, "This was truly a people's tribute to a 'Man of the People' and the vast outpouring of the populace that June day . . . bore testimony to the widespread enthusiasm."

After a flurry of opening remarks and an invocation, the moment the assembled crowd had waited for took place. Dr. Frank O. Cole, a Union veteran and the commander of the Van Houten Post of the Grand Army of the Republic, tugged at the cord attached to the veil. "As the great cloth covering fell away, it revealed what experts have proclaimed as one of the finest and most magnificent memorials in bronze to Abraham Lincoln to be found anywhere." It was then that a bent and wrinkled Tully placed the wreath at Lincoln's feet as the police band played John Phillip Sousa's anthem, "Stars and Stripes Forever." For Grundy it was a magical and historical moment, and chills went up and down his youthful spine.

After Cruse formally presented the statue to the city, John Wesley Hill, chancellor of Lincoln Memorial University in Harrogate, Tennessee, gave the keynote address. In his remarks, Hill declared, "Only the spirit of Abraham Lincoln, his devotion to liberty, will bring the new birth of freedom for which he worked." Turning and speaking to the statue, Hill continued, "Oh, Lincoln thou should be living at this hour. We are selfish men, raise us up to virtue again." It was Hill who dubbed Fraser's statue "Lincoln the Mystic." The name and Lincoln's memory have endured.

Years later, Fraser gave Grundy an autographed photograph of the sculptor standing in front of the completed statue in his Westport studio. The ten-foot figure of Lincoln dwarfed its creator. The inscription signed beneath the photograph signaled Fraser's psychic connection to the project, writing, "Dear Mr. Grundy, it gives me great pleasure to autograph this print of my statue of Lincoln for someone who so appreciates the wonderful qualities of the Great Emancipator." In the same frame that hung for years on Grundy's Jersey City home wall, Fraser included an excerpt from a poem penned by his good friend, the Pulitzer Prize–winning poet Edward Arlington Robinson, which Fraser described as the finest summing up of the Emancipator's character rendered in words:

> Elemental when he died,
> As he was ancient at his birth

The saddest among kings of
Earth,
Bowed with a galling crown, this
man
Met rancor with a cryptic mirth,
Laconic—and Olympian.

For the seventy-fifth anniversary of the statue, the city and Hudson County, working with the Save Outdoor Sculpture project of the Smithsonian Institution, gave Lincoln a much-needed cleaning. The first time I visited the statue on an early sculpture foray I chatted with some homeless men in the park, in whose living room the "Green Man," as they affectionately called him, sat. Then the corrosion, pitting, staining, and layers of bird droppings gave the sculpture an appearance beyond repair. The pedestal was equally in sorry shape, badly stained by the sculpture's metallic runoff, and the park entrance was in need of serious cleaning and sprucing up.

The cleaning touched off a controversy that roils to this day. Many members of the Lincoln Association were in favor of the restoration project, while a fair number of them were outraged at the results. For some, the clean Lincoln has taken away some richness of the neighborhood.

Charlie Markey, a professor of political science and a member of the Lincoln Association for a decade, says, "The restoration is an abomination. It looks like it was covered in Hershey chocolate." Others thought it a paint job gone bad. Catrillo, for his part, has mixed emotions: "I know the restoration had to be done. It was the right thing to do, but the tarnished Lincoln had the war-torn sadness and grief that Lincoln endured during the Civil War. The statue had more character the way it looked before it was restored. It seemed as if Lincoln was really, really tired and the corrosion added to that effect."

Then, leaning back in his chair, Catrillo adds, "That sculpture has a magical quality—it is superb. It has something often lost in modern art—feeling and expression. Fraser captured the mood of Lincoln. I think, to myself, 'You, Guy, have something lost in modern politics—feeling and expression.' In the hippie days, people used to sit around him and drink and smoke pot when they did not care about Lincoln. In the late 1970s some ignorant people covered him in toilet paper.

And now that the park is cleaned up kids play touch football in the field behind the statue."

Doran regards the restoration as an aesthetic necessity, telling me, "That is the way it is supposed to look. The original photos show it with the bronze hue, not covered in green crud like it is in decay."

We relate to monuments that we live near no matter their condition, and we become conditioned to them. They help us identify ourselves. Joseph Campbell would understand a need for this kind of narrative theme in our lives. Yet, in spite of its charm, allure, and deep sensitivity, Fraser's statue remains historically incorrect. That poses a problem, particularly since all parties concerned claim the image is Lincoln as president.

As I pursued Fraser and his Lincoln, I cut my way sixty miles from Jersey City to Westport, Connecticut, to see if I can find Fraser's house and what remains of his studio. After some effort and a few wrong guesses at direction, I did find the place. Fraser and his wife are buried not too far inside the cemetery gate, up on a little knoll that overlooks the gatehouse. In death as in life, the "most famous unknown sculptor," as he was once called, remained unpretentious to the end, his final resting place marked by a simple and small rectangular pink granite stone, flush to the ground that reads,

James Earle Fraser
November 4, 1876–October 11, 1953
Beloved Husband of
Laura Gardin Fraser

Laura rests to the right of her husband, marked by a similar stone and epitaph.

In a newspaper interview at the time of its dedication, Fraser noted, "I particularly wanted to make a sympathetic and human study of Lincoln. There are so many 'President Lincolns,' and I hoped that I might create something that would give an idea of his outdoor personality. . . . I have learned that he did much of his thinking outdoors. . . . His many-sided genius always astonishes me, and when I remember that he accomplished all he did before he was fifty-six years of age, and consider the remarkable qualities of his writings, I am amazed."[10]

I return to Jersey City to complete one more task before returning to Virginia. The teacher in my driver's seat is tugging again. A story about a nine-year-old boy, Christopher Monte, from Hillsborough, New Jersey, caught my attention a few years earlier when I ran across an article in a Springfield, Illinois, newspaper about the dedication of John McClarey's statue *Lincoln the Surveyor* in New Salem, Illinois. Reading the article about Chris reminded me of me, and I connected with him. I contacted Monte's parents Anthony and Gail, asking them if they would be willing to let me interview their young Lincoln buff at Fraser's statue. They made the fifty-mile drive north from central New Jersey to meet me today and engage in conversation with me, Lincoln, and Chris. It had been three years since their family, at Chris's insistence, made a Lincoln road trip of their own to Illinois. Now twelve, Chris has boned up for our meeting by reading, as had Drew for our visit with Borglum's statue, William Gienapp's *Abraham Lincoln and Civil War America*.

Chris is dressed casually, ready for a day at the beach or the park. Besides his infatuation with skateboarding and Lincoln, Chris, like many boys his age, also enjoys playing baseball, football, and basketball. Like me, I think, Lincoln would be struck and pleased with the young man's sense of purpose and eager motivation. He regales me all that he has learned in a few short years about the life of Lincoln and why Lincoln is important to him. We converse as we walk around the lower edge of the three steps that lead to the platform, in the shadow of our hero. I ask Chris to look at the statue and tell me what he sees.

"The expression on his face," he tells me earnestly, "is sad. It makes me feel like he took the whole war upon himself and to see the war won and ended." Then he stops and in a serious voice reminds me, "It was a big job." To that he adds, "It's not what I thought it would look like at all. I thought he would be standing up. And he is sitting on a rock and not a chair."

We look at Lincoln's face, and I ask him what is missing. "He doesn't have a beard," he replies, knowing he has hit the mark. I explain that even though this is President Lincoln, the sculptor decided to leave the famous beard off in an effort to capture the more spiritual, contemplative side of the man.

Anthony, joining in for the first time, points out how well the sculpture looks against the azure sky, and Gail points out the large size of Lincoln's hands. We walk up the steps, and I ask Chris if he can identify the purpose of the semicircular wall. "I think it is a bench," he replies, again somehow knowing he has provided the correct answer. The American and black POW flags hoisted to the top of the flagpole directly behind the statue flap slightly in the soft breeze, recalling Grundy's impression of the dedication.

I tell the three of them that the sculpture has recently been restored and pull out a photograph Catrillo gave me of the statue before it was cleaned, as well as a Lincoln Association poster depicting the corroded figure. Chris looks back and forth between the statue and the photographs. "Hmmm," he says, "It's a little bit too clean. It's better when it's a little dirty—that shows you it's been here for a while. That makes it look more real."

For a few minutes I send Chris on a mission. There are stars that encircle the granite base on which the statue rests, and I ask Chris to count them. Cheerfully he walks around and we can audibly hear, "One, two, three," until he reaches "thirty-six."

"Do you have any idea of why thirty-six stars are on the pedestal?" I ask.

"I think it is because there were thirty-six states in the Union during the war," he once more answers correctly.

"I think Lincoln was a really nice guy," Chris says. "He liked his troops and they liked him. I feel sorry that he lost his sons, though. And he was a really good leader."

"Okay," I say, "why do you think he was a good leader?"

"Well, with his cabinet officers, he won the war. Most people think the war was always about slavery. It wasn't just that, it was also about the Union and keeping it together."

"Chris also learned some new vocabulary terms," Anthony informs me. "Go ahead, Chris," he encourages, "tell Jim some new words you learned from reading Gienapp."

"Well," Chris says proudly, his brown eyes sparkling, "I now know what 'chagrin' means and that Lincoln and his wife were sometimes 'estranged.'"

"Hey, that's great," I reply, and, taking a cue, I move to a discussion of the word *malice* found on the back of the exedra, as part of the inscription from the Second Inaugural. "I think it means not to hate," Chris says.

"You are right," I tell him. "So what does that make you think about Lincoln?"

"I think he did not want to punish the South and be mean to them," he replies. "He thought no more bloodletting would be necessary."

"How might that relate to this statue?"

Chris says, "It looks like Lincoln did not want any more people to die."

The forty-five-minute conversation has flown by in our outdoor classroom. The breeze has picked up considerably, and the flags behind Lincoln are snapping smartly in unison.

Before we part company, Gail pulls from their car a large frame in which she has lovingly matted photographs of their Lincoln pilgrimage and the newspaper story that featured Chris. Proudly, Chris and his Mom point out the different images identifying their locations in Springfield.

I chuckle to myself when I read the text box quote pulled from the article from Chris: "It's amazing! I can't believe I'm actually here." I have very well known that feeling during the course of my life, and my fondest hope for Chris is that he, too, will continue to have such life-changing encounters.

Going from Lincoln statue to Lincoln statue has been an eye-opening experience for me. At each sculpture I learn something new about Lincoln and our cultural memory. It boggles my mind how one man has been able to reach out and touch so many people in so many different and unusual ways.

Dan Weinberg, the owner of the Abraham Lincoln Book Shop in Chicago, once told me about a poll conducted in the former Soviet Union on who the citizenry thought were the top one hundred most influential people in history. First on the list, not surprisingly, were Marx, Engels, and Lenin. Number 35 was a tie between Jesus and Khrushchev. Number 36 was Abraham Lincoln, whose talk of freedom, liberty, and antislavery reverberates with people all over the world. In 1998 a statue of Lincoln was dedicated in Moscow at the Russian State Library for Foreign Literature. People everywhere can connect with him. He remains timeless, enigmatic, and much beloved.

IN THIS TEMPLE
AS IN THE HEARTS OF THE PEOPLE
FOR WHOM HE SAVED THE UNION
THE MEMORY OF ABRAHAM LINCOLN
IS ENSHRINED FOREVER

Daniel Chester French and Henry Bacon inside the Temple Chamber of
the Lincoln Memorial prior to dedication in 1922 (Library of Congress)

7

A Lincoln for the Masses

Daniel Chester French's *Seated Lincoln* (1922), Washington, D.C.

IN 1966, THE NOBEL PRIZE–WINNING WRITER John Steinbeck visited President Lyndon Baines Johnson in the White House. With him was his nineteen-year-old son John Steinbeck Jr., wearing his United States Army dress uniform. Before they called on the president, the Steinbecks walked up the steps of the Lincoln Memorial. The nation was once again divided over a war—this time in faraway Vietnam. Thanking Johnson for the Oval Office visit, Steinbeck wrote the president about his son's experience in the shadow of Lincoln. "He stood for a long time," Steinbeck said, "looking up at that huge and quiet figure and then he said, 'Oh Lord, we had better be great.'"[1] Countless other visitors since the memorial was dedicated in 1922 have stood at the feet of Abraham Lincoln and pondered the meaning of Lincoln's life, and their own.

The Lincoln Memorial remains the greatest public space in America, the ultimate destination monument. It is unlikely that the two men most responsible for the memorial's design imagined that, like the man whose memory they honored, the Lincoln Memorial would become a place of historical significance. Seated there in his flag-draped chair of state, protected by architect Henry Bacon's magnificent neoclassical temple, Daniel Chester French's *Lincoln* has witnessed history: civil rights rallies, protests against the Vietnam War, prayer vigils for a host of causes, assorted concerts, and celebrations for both Republican and Democratic Party presidential inaugurals. On June 8, 1968, the hearse carrying the body of slain U.S. Senator Robert F. Kennedy paused before Lincoln for four minutes at the request of his widow Ethel, while a choir assembled on the steps of the Memorial sang "The Battle Hymn of the Republic."

From there the motorcade moved onto Arlington National Cemetery, where Kennedy was laid to rest in Section 45 several yards from the grave of another murdered president, his brother John.

As with Lincoln before him, a train had carried Robert Kennedy to his final resting place, chugging slowly south over many hours from New York City to Washington. As a ten year-old boy who was becoming increasingly aware of the world around him, I watched the funeral on national television. Two weeks later, the popular folk singer Dion would release his biggest single, "Abraham, Martin, and John," an ode to Lincoln, Martin Luther King Jr., John F. Kennedy and Robert Kennedy, visionaries who offered hope for the future, all gunned down in senseless acts of violence.

Hollywood filmmakers have used the Lincoln Memorial as a movie set, while each year on the Fourth of July thousands gather on its steps to watch the capital's fireworks display. In 1983, the summer I proposed to my wife, Gina, we took in the patriotic spectacle holding hands with thousands of others in Lincoln's presence. French and Bacon's timeless collaboration has a singular power that cuts across time and space, in the way of the best memorials and monuments since the Seven Wonders of the World.

The first time I trekked into Washington with students on a monument adventure was in 1988. Listening to composer John Williams's "Star Wars Theme" on my car stereo, as we crossed the Memorial Bridge over the Potomac River, Bacon's shrine loomed larger and larger, as if keeping pace with the crescendo of the music. This night I returned to the Memorial to meet with three graduate students who had just completed taking my spring semester course, "Abraham Lincoln and His Legacy" at American University. In the intervening years, I have come to see students, no matter their age, as simply that, "students." I like to teach, period.

Alyce, LauraBeth, and Steve have agreed to meet me at the base of the Memorial at 6:30 p.m. It is an unseasonably cool early summer evening. I park near the Department of the Interior building and cross Constitution Avenue between 19th and 20th Streets, just east of the Vietnam Veterans Memorial. Ambling along the walkway that parallels one of the few remaining open green spaces on the Mall, I find organizational kickball and softball teams, complete in a variety of corporate or government agency logo-imprinted silk screen colored uniforms, warming up. An equally colorful array of ice coolers populates the sidelines. The "clank" of an aluminum bat driving a softball and the "thwacks" of softballs smacking into the leather of softball mitts punctuate the air, joined by the piercing sounds of aircraft departing Reagan National Airport.

The sounds of the jets remind me how much I love flying into Washington at night. Approaching Reagan from the north and west, approximating the flow of the Potomac and looking out the left side of the aircraft, one sees the two-mile expanse of the Mall lit up. The monuments, the White House, the buildings of the Smithsonian, and the Capitol look from the air like a miniature toy village set up by some giant.

Since Henry Bacon Drive and Circle are now blocked off by Jersey barriers to prevent a terrorist truck bomb attack on the Memorial, the closed street is now a makeshift plaza for pedestrian traffic. All manner of people congregate at the foot of the steps that lead to architect Henry Bacon's temple and sculptor Daniel Chester French's seated figure of Lincoln. Indian women in saris, veiled Muslim women, Asians, African Americans, tourists from Europe, the world's people come to this statue, carved by Italian American craftsmen.

A seated group of forty-four teenagers, neatly clad in gray T-shirts, black nylon sweatpants, and baseball hats, contrast nicely with the white marble steps. They pose for a photograph halfway up the staircase. These at-risk kids are part of the Fort Gordon, Georgia, Youth Challenge Academy. Ken Jones, their adult leader, explains that this program offers young people a second chance at life. Lincoln, ever a proponent of the notion of a fair chance at life, would approve. Under much-needed adult supervision, these boys and girls learn basic life skills such as how to write a check and balance a checkbook, self-discipline, and respect for all people. They learn the relationship between good citizenship skills and a successful life. Being captured for posterity in a photograph in the shadow of America's greatest democratic citizen makes sense. Finished, they march off in unison. Their experience reminds me of a piece that ran in the *Boston Herald* during World War II: "Thousands of our men in uniform, stopping in Washington for a few hours, rather indifferently climbed the steps of the memorial and then, having stood silently before the fatherly Lincoln and communed as it were, with him, came down the steps, their shoulders straight, their heads high, and their eyes shining." Once more the marble Lincoln has silently imparted his wisdom to the faithful.

Arriving out our predetermined location, the base of the plaza across from the Reflecting Pool, I meet my former students. Alyce, twenty-eight, biked in two miles from her home near Lincoln Park, not far from Thomas Ball's Emancipation Monument. Steve, twenty-seven, sports a T-shirt celebrating the first Battle of the Beltway series of interleague baseball games between the Washington Nationals and the Baltimore Orioles. Both he and LauraBeth, twenty-three, have come in on the Metro. I wear my favorite Lincoln T-shirt, the white pen and ink silkscreen design by Thomas Trimborn.

Before making our ascent, we are caught in a pop-up summer rain, always a danger in Washington. LauraBeth snaps open an umbrella, but it's not big enough to cover all of us. We sprint to a protected position of the South Wall, beneath one of the two decorative tripods that flank the staircase, and huddle. Five minutes later the pesky clouds subside and the sun shines.

Eighty-four years of human traffic, pollution, and acid rain have taken their toll on the marble. Since 1959, the sesquicentennial of Lincoln's birth, when the National Park Service began keeping a count, it is estimated that well over 100 million people have made the trek from Henry Bacon Drive up the staircase of the Memorial. Climbing the worn marble steps of the Lincoln Memorial, which in places have eroded into uneven yet smoothly defined depressions, is no easy task. The climb is steep and exerting, especially when the steps are wet. Visitors are often winded by the time they reach the top. Bacon may have made this a deliberate part of his design, providing a sense of struggle and exhaustion upon reaching Lincoln so that one might empathize with him.

A National Park Service sign reading "Quiet. Respect Please," greets us as we reach the chamber, but the chamber is hardly silent, since hundreds of people talking makes for an unintelligible buzz in the cavernous hall.

The central chamber that contains the statue is sixty feet wide by seventy-four feet deep. Flanking the central chamber are two side chambers, each thirty-eight feet wide and sixty-three feet deep, separated from the central chamber by four fifty-foot Indiana limestone Ionic columns on each side. Inside the south chamber, etched in the limestone walls and flanked by a pair of sculpted American eagles, is the text of the Gettysburg Address. Across in the north chamber are the words of the Second Inaugural Address. The Lincoln Memorial marks the greatest collaboration in America between sculptor, architect, and space.

Catching our breath and standing off to the right of the statue, we begin conversing with respect to the Memorial as a place not only of memory for Lincoln but also for the nation's collective memory.

As if on cue, Alyce says, "My mother once interviewed Marian Anderson." The opera diva performed there after she was turned away from singing at the Daughters of the American Revolution Constitution Hall because she was black. The controversy only deepened when First Lady Eleanor Roosevelt resigned her membership in the Daughters to show solidarity with Anderson, creating a firestorm. In this atmosphere the African American community and civil rights leaders organized a skillful and crafty response to the snub, using the Memorial both physically and metaphorically for the first time by arranging to have Anderson sing at the Memorial on Easter Sunday, 1939.

LauraBeth remarks on how people have appropriated Lincoln, as with the civil rights movement and the whole nonviolent cause. "Yeah," says Steve, who is African American, "but I'd like to know more about that Oscar Chapman dude."

Chapman, a native Virginian, from the conservative southeastern corner of the commonwealth, served as President Franklin Roosevelt's assistant secretary of the interior. It was forty-two-year-old Chapman's brainchild to hold the Anderson concert at the Lincoln Memorial when the District of Columbia refused to let Anderson sing in a city school auditorium after the initial rebuff by the DAR. A frustrated Walter White, head of the National Association for the Advancement of Colored People, met with Chapman, who asked, "How about the Lincoln Memorial?" "That would be terrific," White replied, "but how do we get permission?" Taking his signal, Chapman called on his boss, Harold Ickes. A past president of the Chicago branch of the NAACP, Ickes telephoned Roosevelt at the White House to gauge the president's response. Roosevelt, generally tepid in matters of race in an effort to protect his New Deal coalition, which numbered key Southern Democrats in the Senate, agreed to listen. Ickes concluded, "I didn't want to do this without notifying you." Chapman held his breath, thinking to himself, "Oh God. He's afraid of what will happen to his budget." But quite audibly he heard Roosevelt's distinctive voice, "Harold!" he said sympathetically, "That's a wonderful idea. You tell Oscar she can sing from the top of the Washington Monument if she wants to."[2]

Thirty-three years earlier, as an eighth-grade student in Omega, Virginia, Chapman received a different kind of education when he learned firsthand the complexities of American idealism. His fellow students selected him to purchase a picture for their school. With five dollars in his pocket, Oscar and his cousin headed over to the nearby town of South Boston. They were attracted to a "fine-looking man, in a fine-looking frame." After they made their selection, the storekeeper queried, "Are you sure you want that one?" The boys affirmed their decision.

"Well, you know," the storekeeper continued, "that's Abraham Lincoln. Do you know anything about Abraham Lincoln?" "He was President of the United States," Oscar responded. *McGuffey's Reader*, Chapman later claimed, had only two sentences about Lincoln, but it did mention that fact. The storekeeper wrapped it up, and Chapman and his cousin went back to Omega and hung it on their schoolroom wall. The next day, when Chapman's teacher arrived at school, she was horrified. That night, at a special session of the school board held at the school, Chapman returned to the scene of his crime. There, through the window, he witnessed board members removing the picture from the wall. "They chucked it over the wood box, and put it in the wood box bent," he recalled. After they filed out, a distressed Chapman climbed through the window into his classroom, retrieved the picture, straightened it out, and hung it back up. The next day, his teacher returned to school to find the damaged Lincoln portrait hanging from the wall. The school board expelled Chapman. Years later, in the *Washington Daily News*, columnist Raymond Clapper wrote, "Bewildered by the angry feelings aroused in the school board, Oscar began to ask questions. From that time he has taken the side of tolerance in every showdown that has come his way."

On Easter Sunday, April 9, 1939, a tightly packed integrated audience of 75,000 gathered around the Memorial and along the Reflecting Pool. Guests seated on the landing included members of the Supreme Court, some members of Congress, and Secretary Ickes. Anderson dramatically appeared from the recesses of the chamber in the shadow of Lincoln's statue. Chapman and Arizona Representative Isabella Greenway, a good friend of Eleanor Roosevelt's, escorted her down to the landing, where the microphones and speakers were set up. Anderson opened with a subtly altered rendition of "America, the Beautiful,"—"My country 'tis of thee, Sweet land of liberty. To thee we sing."

The following day, civil rights activist Mary McLeod Bethune wrote to Charles H. Houston, law professor at Howard University, capturing for the African American community the essence of the historical significance of the moment: "We are on the right track. Through the Marian Anderson protest concert we made our triumphant entry into the democratic spirit of American life."

The concert was a seminal event in civil rights history and memory. Our coming together at this time and place would not have been possible without the efforts of people like Anderson and Chapman. I think how far we have come since that day, recalling the variety of people gathered around the base of the Memorial's staircase posing for pictures.

Walking around the chamber, we continue our discussion. There is plenty of food for thought regarding how French depicted Lincoln and what the textbooks say about him. "It depends on your perspective," offers Alyce. "Textbooks gloss over history and don't offer balanced viewpoints. Some Southerners still vilify Lincoln." For Steve it's a matter of topic coverage. "Look at it this way: when you come here you want to remember Lincoln for the good he did and not look at the negative. But I agree with Alyce," he says. "Textbooks don't do a very balanced job. They only skim the surface, and they are selective. People don't want to deal with the negative. I mean, there are a lot of good things to talk about with Lincoln, so why bring up civil liberties?" Looking around, Steve adds, "Would most of these people rather know that Lincoln suspended habeas corpus, or that he won the Civil War?"

"So," I ask, "do you think if I went up to random tourists here and asked them if they knew that Lincoln limited civil liberties during the Civil War, they would be able to articulate a response?"

"Probably not," Steve replies. Alyce and LauraBeth nod in agreement.

In the back of my mind I once more hear the bell of "presentism" ringing—that odd proclivity of the present moment and reality that

easily passes judgment on those who have trod before us. It's hard
not to avoid this when researching and teaching history, given the
biases and points of view we bring to bear to our investigations and
queries whatever they be. Hubris also plays a role, as does collective
memory. We visit the Lincoln Memorial now with a century and a
half of Lincoln memory in the national experience.

In this the age of the cult of celebrity, information saturation, and
full disclosure, Lincoln would not stand a chance. His lanky frame,
his odd face with its prominent mole, and his high-pitched voice
would be fodder for pundits and media critics. Yet this remains
somehow part of his charm. There is an affinity for Lincoln among
not only Americans but also people all across the globe precisely because he was "one of us," yet literally made it to the top. Deep down,
people like Lincoln because they can relate to him in some way and
at some level. Even though he sits nineteen feet away from visitors
inside his memorial, we all can touch him and tap into his reality
because at some level we identify with him. Debunkers have tried
mightily to chip away at his essence. A National Park ranger and interpreter at Lincoln Home National Historic Site once told me that
she has grown weary of people visiting the only home Lincoln ever
owned and being more interested in his troubled marriage than anything else. Lincoln has been put on the couch and psychoanalyzed,
and his sexuality has recently come into question, too. Those who
have secured fame, for whatever reason, live under a microscope.
The media likes to expose people's warts, which people seem to find
entertaining.

Yet Lincoln endures. He remains important to us in the crazy mix
that has become American life at the beginning of the twenty-first
century. We could not live without his presence. The American people, burdened with a cynicism of modern American politics, have a
collective wistful hope that another Lincoln is possible among us.

For fun, we walk to the back on Lincoln's left to look at his head.
One of the many "myths" that circulate about French's sculpture is
that the back of Lincoln's head represents Robert E. Lee looking
back across the Potomac at his home, Arlington House. Straining our
neck and eyes, each of us tries to envision Lee's profile in the waves
of Lincoln's hair, but it is a stretch, to say the least. The records of
the Memorial's construction and the statue's creation are very complete, and nothing indicates that this story is remotely accurate.

Daniel Chester French in his Chesterwood Studio in Stockbridge,
Massachusetts (Archives of American Art)

Lincoln Memorial dedication, May 30, 1922 (Library of Congress)

Marian Anderson at the Lincoln Memorial, 1939 (Thomas D. McAvoy/Stringer, Time & Life Pictures/Getty Images)

National shrines and historic sites are replete with myths, such as the one that the Battle of Gettysburg was fought over shoes. Most historians acknowledge that the battle had more complex causes, but it makes for a great story. While looking for the nonexistent profile of Lee, I point out the modest signature of the sculptor. Looking at Lincoln's profile, I am also reminded of my first visit to French's home and workshop, also designed by Bacon.

Clambering between shelves, holding French's models and maquettes, and exploring the curatorial storage facilities of Chesterwood, in the bucolic Berkshire Mountains of Massachusetts, I came across a forty-two-inch plaster version of Lincoln's head resting on a small dolly. Kneeling next to it, I was just slightly larger than the head. French made the plaster head so he could wheel it out in his studio to show visitors the heroic scale of his work.

On that same visit I was stunned when I walked into French's studio. Standing there was the original seven-foot model of the Lincoln statue. Looking at it, I suddenly realized how French pulled off the enormous project so successfully. Creating sculpture is very labor-intensive. A statue is born in a process encapsulated by the artist's brain and environment. That process comes to life for visitors here, one of only two historical sites in the nation that pays homage to both the sculptor and the process. Inside the thirty- by thirty-foot studio, with its massive thirty-foot ceilings, natural north light streams in through the ceiling window, providing optimal and uniform working light that does not cast hard shadows. Inside the studio stand ropes and pulleys gracefully draped from wall to wall that were used to lift and move projects and the ladders used to climb up heroic casts and models. It is easy to imagine the mustachioed French, sporting his customary bow tie and a smock, diligently at work with his assistants.

French, like Thomas Ball, had no formal academic training. He wanted to be an engineer, but after failing at MIT he returned to Concord, Massachusetts, where he learned to sculpt under the direction of Abigail May Alcott, sister of author Louisa May Alcott. Legend has it that he first tried his hand at carving turnips, impressing Alcott. In 1875, at the age of twenty-five, French sculpted another American icon, *The Minute Man*. Dedicated in Concord near the battleground on the centennial of the "shot heard round the world," the sculpture drew wide acclaim. His lifework was bookended by two national symbols that helped shape American identity.

Laboring on the Lincoln project from 1915 to 1919, French made two maquettes, one of Lincoln standing and one of him seated. With his standing figure he originally conceived Lincoln holding a sheet of paper. When he and Bacon settled on a seated figure, the next problem to solve was the kind of chair to use. An initial composition depicted Lincoln seated in a parlor chair. He got the details ironed out on the working three-foot model, adjusting the legs to get their position right, and incorporated an American flag draped over a larger chair of state. Initially he envisioned a twelve-foot-high statue. Using a twelve-foot model and enlarged photographs inside the chamber of the nearly completed temple, French and Bacon realized they had a dilemma on their hands. At twelve feet, the statue would have been dwarfed by the interior space of the chamber. To insure spatial and visual success, French and Bacon concluded that the figure needed to be nineteen feet high, for which a bronze casting would have been cost-prohibitive. As they always had, working so well in tandem, sculptor and architect settled on the use of marble. For purposes of volume the statue had to be large, not only to fill the space in the chamber but also so that the sculpture would seem to grow in size as a viewer ascended the staircase. This was accomplished by creating the massive flag-draped chair in which Lincoln sits with his arms extended out, resting on the arms of the seat of state.

French and Bacon were a team in the best sense of the word, collaborating on a number of previous projects. This was their second memorial to Lincoln, the first being a less successful 1909 monument to him unveiled on the grounds of the Nebraska State House in Lincoln. They admired each other, respected each other's work, and had a certain ease in each other's presence. Once Bacon secured the endorsement of the Lincoln Memorial Commission in 1912, there was no one but French who he would consider for creating the central statue and focal point of the Memorial.

Ironically, or perhaps symbolically, the seated Lincoln consists of twenty-eight separate two-ton blocks of Georgia marble atop a pedestal of pink Tennessee marble. (French could have used Indiana marble, after all.) When finished, French shipped the final plaster model to the Piccirilli Brothers' block-long marble workshop in the Bronx. The Piccirillis managed the foremost marble workshop in the United States, and French was more than confident in their abilities. His patronage and reliance on their skills and techniques was of mutual benefit. To have them carve the statue in pieces so that it could fit through the entranceway of the Memorial was a forgone conclusion. Using a device called a pointing machine, taking careful measurements between the model and the stone, skilled craftsmen chipped away at the Georgia marble. The twenty-eight pieces were shipped by rail to Washington in November 1919, where over several months, pulled up by block and tackle and hoists, they were assembled like a giant jigsaw puzzle inside Bacon's temple. Once the sculpture was installed, the sixty-nine-year-old sculptor climbed up on his Lincoln and methodically did the fine finishing work, his lithe frame in contrast to the monumental Lincoln. When finished, the sculpture weighed 340,000 pounds. Writing to a friend in May 1920, French proudly said, "The Lincoln statue with its pedestal, is an accomplished fact . . . as nearly perfect technically as I can make it."

I like it because it works so well in the space. Even though it is massive in size, I can still connect with Lincoln the man and understand why he was able to guide the nation through its worst crisis. Somehow the depth of Lincoln's magnanimity, humanity, resolve, and compassion—his most human qualities—are magnified, as they should be in French's figure. There is great comfort here in observing Lincoln both the gentle man and the unwavering president.

When the Lincoln Memorial was dedicated there was no discussion of slavery. In 1922, it was more important for aging veterans of the Blue and the Gray to be reconciled than for the nation to deal with the difficult issue of race. The only time the word *slavery* is mentioned is in the memorial's text of the Second Inaugural Address. Royal Cortissoz's inscription, etched in stone above Lincoln's head, makes it quite clear why this memorial was created: "In this temple as in the hearts of the people for whom he saved the Union the Memory of Abraham Lincoln is enshrined forever." Justifying his sentiment, Cortissoz wrote Bacon, "The Memorial must make common ground for the meeting of the north and south. By emphasizing his saving the union you appeal to both sections. By saying nothing about slavery you avoid rubbing old sores."

Those alive at the time of dedication had no inkling that the Memorial's meaning would shift and evolve over time. Slavery is addressed more directly in the least successful elements of the

Memorial, one of Jules Guerin's two sixty-foot-long by twelve-foot-high painted murals, *Emancipation of a Race* above the Gettysburg Address, complete with idealized allegorical figures of African Americans proves a muted reference at best. *Reunion*, above the Second Inaugural Address, deals thematically with the Memorial's original intent. On the numerous occasions I have visited the Memorial no one seems to take notice of the murals. Though they have been recently restored, they still fail to receive the attention of visitors.

Nothing has changed this evening.

With a sigh Steve adds to the moment. "Yeah, but they should have dealt with slavery. But I do like it. French accomplished what he set out to do. It does portray Lincoln in a positive light. And I think Lincoln would have liked it. It is simple. His gaze is protecting Washington."

The mild-mannered, genial, gentlemanly French would be pleased by Steve's reaction. Writing shortly before the Memorial was dedicated, French confided in a friend, "What I wanted to convey was the mental and physical strength of the great President and his confidence in his ability to carry the thing through to a successful finish. If any of this 'gets over,' I think it is probably as much due to the whole pose of the figure and particularly to the action of the hands as to the expression of the face."

"The right side of his face does look softer," Alyce quips. "And I guess that makes sense, given that it is his right hand that is open."

The hands are a very important part of this composition. French wanted people to understand Lincoln's duality as he managed the Civil War. To achieve this, he used Leonard Volk's casts and made several of his own hands to get the physiognomy right. French's hands were huge, and using them for fifty years to model clay served to shape them well. You can see both sets of casts at Chesterwood. Lincoln's right hand is open, demonstrating his compassion, flexibility, and willingness to reconcile the shattered nation as gently as possible. His left hand, though, is clenched, depicting his resolve and firmness when it came to the preservation of the Union.

Depending on which National Park Service ranger you listen to during the short programs inside the Memorial, a visitor might hear any number of "tales" regarding Lincoln's hands. One story is that his hands are signing the Alpha and Omega, reflecting his Christlike persona, particularly since both met violent deaths on Good Friday and both are considered saviors. The other popular story is that Lincoln is signing the letters A and L, for "Abraham Lincoln." For years I had a good-natured running debate with our high school's American Sign Language teacher. She insisted that Lincoln was signing his name. Whenever I taught my Lincoln unit, students we shared in common would report to each of us. I would pass Meg in the halls, and she would chide me, "Jim, you have the Lincoln Memorial all wrong."

There is nothing in French's papers that provides evidence to support this argument. However, in 1889 his portrait sculpture of the founder of American Sign Language, Thomas Gallaudet, was dedicated on the campus of Gallaudet College in Washington. The sculpture depicts Gallaudet signing the letter A with his first pupil, Alice Cogswell. Lincoln, interestingly, signed the school's institutional charter.

The year 1939 proved to be good for the Lincoln Memorial for reasons other than Marian Anderson's concert. Director Frank Capra rolled into Washington and appropriated the Memorial to tell his vision of America—bold, optimistic, and idealistic—in his now-classic film *Mr. Smith Goes to Washington*, starring James Stewart. Once the filming began, Capra "never left the set, never took phone calls, never heard or saw anything unless it pertained to the scene we were shooting. I was a tuning fork that vibrated only to the wave length of *Mr. Smith*."[3] On October 16, 1939, a day the city hailed as "Mr. Smith" Day, four thousand Washingtonians jockeyed for tickets to enjoy the premier, which Capra believed would "out-Hollywood Hollywood."[4] The venue: DAR Constitution Hall.

Only one scene is needed to demonstrate the power of Lincoln and the Lincoln Memorial. Capra lifted the scenes from his own epiphany there.

Drumbeats of war quickened in Europe as the Nazis marched into Austria and Czechoslovakia. Japanese aggression continued in China and the Far East. And Capra was in Washington fishing for ideas for a new film that would lift American spirits. A chance visit to the White House gave him an opportunity to quickly catch a glimpse of President Franklin Roosevelt. Capra was quietly ushered into the Oval Office during a press conference. There he huddled behind three rows of reporters, watching Roosevelt at his desk fielding questions about the problems the world and the United States faced. A euphoric state of patriotism overwhelmed him as he hailed a cab outside 1600 Pennsylvania Avenue. He asked the driver to take him to the Lincoln Memorial. Years later, Capra would recall, "And there in the most majestic shrine we have in America, sat the colossal marble figure of our greatest statesman . . . his eyes daily filling the hearts of thousands of Americans with the deep, deep compassion that seemed to well out from his own great soul; eyes that seemed to say: 'I have seen it all. It is good.'"

Prophetically, Capra witnessed a scene he would recapture on film. Dozens of tourists were milling around, but two caught Capra's keen eye as he stood before the text of the Gettysburg Address. "I heard a voice of a child," he wrote, "reciting the words. There next to me, an eight-year-old boy was holding the hand of a very old man—whose body and sight were failing—and reading him Lincoln's inspirational words in a voice as clear and innocent as a bell. And the old man smiled to himself, nodded proudly after each sentence. I looked up at the marble face of Lincoln. . . . I was sure he smiled."

Crossing the chamber to the opposite wall, the little boy then read to the old man the Second Inaugural Address. "Never had Lincoln's impassioned, moral, indictment of slavery sounded so eloquent," Capra reminisced, "so moving, so powerful as when that young boy read it to his grandfather. That scene must go into our film," he thought. "We must make the film if only to hear a boy read Lincoln to his grandpa." Capra left the Lincoln Memorial with a growing conviction that what the American people needed in his film was a "ringing statement of America's democratic ideals."[5]

I share this scene with all my students. However, Capra left seven critical seconds from this scene out of his autobiography. As the little boy reads the Gettysburg Address to his grandfather, an equally aged African American man enters the chamber reverentially, taking off his hat, and deferentially stands apart from the other players in the scene. As the words "a new birth of freedom" are read, the film lovingly captures the face of the old man in an angelic glow. The scene, given the tenor of the times regarding African Americans and the public space, speaks for itself. But only five minutes earlier in the film, African American railroad porters at Washington's Union Station stereotypically depict comic buffoonery in the mambo genre prevalent in motion pictures of this generation. Even Capra could not avoid racial ambiguity.

At least one unidentified Southerner did demur. "And another thing," this Texan wrote, "If they don't stop showing me that statue of Lincoln with some guy standing before it vowing to right all the wrongs, I'm going to scream. I love my country, and am willing to admit as much as any southerner that Lincoln was a great man, but there is such a thing as over-doing the thing."

Not only is the segment of Capra's a stroke of cinematic genius, but it is also a masterful use of Lincoln memory and iconography, dripping with American civil religion, that singular American phenomenon that takes any story and converts it into something powerful and mythic with providentially sacred overtones.

"This is a church," LauraBeth says. "It's a temple. It even says it in the words above Lincoln—"In this temple.""

"The words do say it all," joins Alyce.

"The two speeches included here certainly convey that theme," I add.

William Howard Taft, Chairman of the Lincoln Memorial Commission, at the Memorial's dedication articulated a religious and spiritual message. "Here is a shrine," Taft said, his voice carried over the cleverly concealed public address system, "at which all can worship, here an altar upon which the supreme sacrifice was made in the cause of liberty, here a sacred religious refuge in which those who love country and love God can find inspiration and repose."

Nowhere is American civil religion more eloquently enshrined than at the Lincoln Memorial. Lincoln is the high priest of that religion. His writings in the latter half of the Civil War reflect a kind of "secular holiness." The Declaration of Independence remained for Lincoln the singular piece of American Scripture to be upheld by not only the people but the states as well—hence secession was illegal and an abomination for which Lincoln would not stand. His letters and speeches are replete with references to the Declaration. Standing in front of Independence Hall in Philadelphia in February 1861, during his railroad journey to his first inauguration, Lincoln expressed his feelings. "I have never," he said, "had a feeling politically that did not spring from the sentiments embodied in the Declaration of Independence."[6] The Gettysburg Address and the Second Inaugural invoke God as a being who oversees the universe, in the former intoning that "this nation, under God, shall have a new birth of freedom" and in the latter, "with firmness in the right, as God gives us to see the right," creating what he earlier called "the last best hope of earth." American history has been rooted in this sentiment. Our civic holidays—Thanksgiving, President's Day, Memorial Day, Veterans Day, and the Fourth of July—are our holy days of obligation. At least they used to be. Now they are opportunities for Wal-Mart and K-Mart to cash in on the other American deity: money.

In some respects, American civil religion is a kind of patriotism that coexists with traditional faiths. Robert Bellah explains it as "an understanding of the American experience in light of the ultimate and universal reality. . . . At its best [it] is a genuine apprehension of universal and transcendent religious reality as seen in or, once could almost say, as revealed through the experience of the American people. American civil religion has its own prophets and its own martyrs, its own sacred events and sacred places, its own solemn rituals and symbols. It is concerned that America be a society as perfectly in accord with the will of God as men can make it, and a light to all the nations."[7]

Abraham Lincoln's life and words are at the crux of this experience. In some ways, he has grown in mythic shape and stature because civil religion relies on folkways, myths, and traditions.

The chamber is getting darker as the sunlight fades, but the crowds inside and coming up the stairs seems to be swelling. My colleagues need to leave, but since I have my car parked nearby I decided to stay with Lincoln a bit longer.

Looking at Lincoln, I think about how the United States is replete with historic sites where people can have a dialogue about race in American history. Plenty of Southern plantations are historic house museums open to the public. Colonial Williamsburg has done an outstanding job integrating the difficulties of racial history into their public programs and interpretation, as have George Washington's home, Mount Vernon, and Thomas Jefferson's Monticello.

At the Lincoln Memorial, memories about race collide in a different way. Bill Gwaltney, a National Park Service ranger and native of Washington, witnessed average tourists become openly emotional visiting one of several stops in a city full of monuments to famous Americans. He asked one visitor, "Sir, have you enjoyed your visit to the nation's capital so far?" The visitor replied, "It's been great. I just wish the white people had one, too." The tourist was clearly uncomfortable at Washington's large African American population. On another occasion, Gwaltney and a white ranger were standing together in the chamber when a tourist asked them each the exact same questions over a period of a few minutes. When she was finished with the questions and satisfied with the answers, she said, "Thank you. I just wanted to have it in black and white."

But all is not serious, Gwaltney assured me. One day a woman casually asked him, "What time does the statue stand up?" After a pause, he proceeded to give a brief overview and history of the Memorial. She stopped him and said, "I know he stands up. I've been here before. He stands up and gives a speech." Gently, Gwaltney asked her if she had ever been to Disneyworld in Orlando, Florida. She had. Then she realized that she had confused the Lincoln Memorial with Disney's Lincoln in the Hall of Presidents Show.

I find a spot at the top of the staircase and lean back against one of the thirty-six Doric columns—each one representing a state in the Union at the time of Lincoln's assassination—that support the roof. The columns tower at a height of forty-four feet and consist of eleven separate drums stacked and cemented together. Each state's name is carved into the marble frieze above the columns. The names of the states admitted to the Union after the Civil War are carved into the exterior attic wall. Beneath the name of each state, in Roman numerals, is the year in which each state was admitted into the Union. Decorative medallions of paired wreaths of Southern pine tree boughs with cones intertwine with Northern laurel branches on the carved entablature between the names of each state, a symbolism in stone demonstrating the unification of both regions.[8] Alaska and Hawaii have a respective commemorative plaque in the Memorial's plaza. Carved eagles, connected by strands of decorative garlands, complete the arrangements on the entablature. Bacon, using the Parthenon in Athens as a prototype, cleverly rotated the building so that the entrance off the Mall would be on the long axis as opposed to the narrower façade, giving the structure its seminal rectangular shape and providing for an appropriate ending to the Mall's western terminal axis. Nestling against one of the twenty smooth-textured flutes of the Colorado Yule marble column feels good.

I have a clear view across the Reflecting Pool and can easily see the pillars of the new World War II Memorial. The Washington Monument cuts brilliantly into the sky, and the dome of the Capitol glistens.

Hundreds of people are converging on the Memorial. Some, like me, are seated looking out over the Mall. Teenagers belonging to school groups from across the country, each group wearing a different-colored T-shirt, make for a rainbow spectacle as they race up the steps. Other people walk up more reverentially in the relaxed, yet festive air. Many of them carry cameras. Inside an obligatory photo opportunity commences as numerous folk pose for a snapshot with Mr. Lincoln. Laughter abounds.

Watching the throng of people, I recall Langston Hughes's poem "Lincoln Monument: Washington." His verse registers in my mind in the mild evening air:

> Let's go see Old Abe
> Sitting in the marble and the moonlight,
> Sitting lonely in the marble and the moonlight,
> Quiet for ten thousand centuries, Old Abe.
> Quiet for a million, million years.
>
> Quiet
>
> And yet a voice forever
> Against the timeless walls
> Of time
> Old Abe.

But what would Old Abe think of the hypocrisy of the dedication of the Memorial in 1922? Would he have understood the ambiguity of much of the day? With Washington being a segregated city, African American dignitaries and the black press were relegated to a separate seating area across the road from the Memorial.

Many African Americans indignantly walked out in protest. A Washington newspaper reported that their ire was further inflamed when the "language of the ill-tempered Marine who herded the 'niggers' into their seats caused well-bred colored people as much indignation as the segregated seating itself." An explanation offered by former president and Supreme Court justice William H. Taft, chair of the Lincoln Memorial Commission, that the "arrangement had no official sanction," did nothing to placate those offended.[9] But aged Union veterans of the Grand Army of the Republic, black and white, sat together side by side, a useful yet quiet racial device. Not too far away sat gray-clad veterans of the Confederacy, the fusion of Union and Confederate warriors cementing the theme of reunion that had become central to the American experience after the end of Reconstruction.

Robert R. Moten, president of Tuskegee Institute, sat on the platform with the other speakers, including President Warren G. Harding, Taft, the poet Edwin Markham, the sculptor, the architect, and Lincoln's sole surviving son, seventy-nine-year-old Robert Lincoln. Initially Moten planned to use his speaking time to challenge the white-brotherhood sentiment of the day. The text of his speech reads,

> My fellow citizens, in the great name which we honor here today, I say unto you that his memorial which we erect in token of our veneration is but a hollow mockery, a symbol of hypocrisy, unless we together can make real in our national life, in every state and in every section, the things for which he died. This is a fair and godly land. Much right have we, both black and white, to be proud of our achievements at home and our increasing service in all the world. In like manner, there is abundant cause for rejoicing that sectional rancors and racial antagonisms are softening more and more into mutual understanding and increasing sectional and inter-racial cooperation. But unless here at home we are willing to grant to the least and humblest citizen the full enjoyment of every constitutional privilege, our boast is but a mockery.[10]

The Lincoln Memorial Commission would have none of this. Moten's speech was reworked, and any reference to discrimination against African Americans was dropped.

Those in the crowd and listening on the radio heard Moten instead close his speech with these words:

> Twelve million black Americans share in rejoicing at this hour. As yet, no other name so warms the heart or stirs the depth of their gratitude as that of Abraham Lincoln. To him above all others we owe the privilege of sharing as fellow-citizens in the consecration of this spot and the dedication of this shrine. In the name of Lincoln twelve million black Americans pledge to the nation their continued loyalty and their unreserved cooperation in every effort to realize to realize in deeds, the lofty principles established by his martyrdom. With malice toward

none, with charity for all we dedicate ourselves and our posterity, with *you* and *yours*, to finish the work he so nobly began, to make America an example for all the world of equal justice and equal opportunity for all.[11]

A token appearance had made at best for a palliative bromide.

Taft spoke about the history of the Memorial, recounted how the Memorial had come to be, and described its features. For Taft, the fifty-seven-year wait for a memorial to the "nation's savior and greatest leader" since Lincoln's death was well worth it, for "it permitted a generation instinct with the growing and deepening perception of the real Lincoln to develop an art adequate to the expression of his greatness. . . . The ideal of these great American artists has found expression in the memorial as you see it. It is a magnificent gem set in a lovely valley between the hills, commanding them by its isolation and its entrancing beauty, an emblem of the purity of Greek art in the simple Doric, the culmination of the highest art of which America is capable." In keeping with the tenor of the times and the theme of the Memorial, Taft concluded, "Seen in all is grandeur from Arlington where lie the nation's honored dead, who fell in the conflict, Union and Confederate alike, it marks the restoration of the brotherly love of the two sections in this memorial of one who is as dear to the hearts of the South as to those of the North." President Harding, accepting the Memorial for the American people, saying perhaps more than he knew, added, "This Memorial is less for Abraham Lincoln than those of us today and for those who follow after."

The seven-foot chain-link fence that prevents visitor access around the sides and back of the Memorial gives me another reason to pause. Ironic, pathetic, and sad, its presence reminds me of what life is like in a post–9/11 world. America's greatest public space to democracy and freedom, its central figure, are enslaved to prevailing conventions. Visitors are limited to a particular space, the steps and the chamber. Lincoln is once again presiding over a fortified city, a place less aesthetic and friendly than it once was. Ugliness has scarred majestic beauty, reinforced by trash in the form of discarded bottles, dead grass, weeds, broken cinderblocks, and sandbags that litter the spaces directly behind the fences. The memorial is also showing its age.

Camera flashes illuminate the chamber as it gets darker. At 8:00 p.m. the statue magically is bathed in a celestial glow. Lighting is critical to the success of a sculpture, and the Lincoln Memorial is no exception. French and Bacon had their struggles. Neither sculptor nor architect took into consideration the adverse affect of natural lighting into the chamber, particularly from sunlight reflected off the water of the Reflecting Pool, which was not filled when the full-scale plaster model head was tested. Other factors played a role, too, particularly the completed approaches to the memorial and the cleared staircase. Before the dedication, French wrote to the secretary of the Lincoln Memorial Commission: "I have been talking with Mr. Bacon about the possibility of lighting the statue artificially by some arrangements of electric lights. While the present lighting of the statue is tolerably good at some times of the day, it at no time brings out the expression of the face as it ought to. The ideal lighting for most sculpture is from above at an angle of forty-five degrees, more or less. I had hoped that the light from the sky-light would be sufficient to overcome some degree the light that comes in at the opening in front, but it fails to do this even in the afternoon when no sunlight enters the building."

A composite photograph French made demonstrated the difference in positive and negative lighting. Without the use of counterbalancing artificial light, Lincoln's face looked washed out, as if someone was holding a flashlight, shining it up into the face. By the time of the Memorial Day dedication the lighting issue had yet to be resolved. Frustrated with the lighting as late as 1924, French wrote to Charles Moore, head of the Commission of Fine Arts: "What would you think of the idea of lighting the interior of the Lincoln Memorial at night? It seems to me it would be a popular move. The Memorial would have added interest as seen from a distance, and I think it would be visited by a great many people in the evening."

Tonight, as on other nights, French's prediction is a reality. Congress finally authorized funding for the interior lights in September 1926, much to the sculptor's delight.

Sitting here, I wonder if all these people fully understand or even appreciate how this memorial came to exist. Like the weekend, do they think it has always been here? Would it ever occur to them that at one time the place on which they are standing was a gigantic construction site? Giant block and tackles and hoists of varying sizes covered this end of West Potomac Park. Workers in hard hats clambered for years over the grounds and the structure that rose here from 1915 to 1922. There's a story in this, too: a very American story indeed, complete with all manner of the American penchant for bombast, controversy, and the proverbial stirring of the pot of collective memory. The story of the Lincoln Memorial is about not only the man it honors but also the men who raised the memorial. And like the men, the story tells us something about the time. Memorials are erected with motivations conscious and unconscious. Those who planned for a national memorial to Lincoln at the turn of the last century were influenced by the prevailing sentiments of the age.

African Americans never really figured into the equation. Jim Crow, in its heyday of segregated public facilities in the America of the 1920s, still ruled the Southern way of life and had crept into the capital, where blacks found life increasingly marginalized even in the federal workplace.[12] In 1915, when construction on the monument began, President Woodrow Wilson screened D. W. Griffith's film *The Birth of a Nation* at the White House. This classic motion picture was an apology to the South, glorified the role of the Ku Klux Klan, and demeaned African Americans. That same year, seventy-nine blacks were lynched in the United States.[13] The selection of Robert Moten as representative of the black race to speak at the dedication makes perfect sense; a disciple and devotee of the accommodationist Booker T. Washington, he was a safe choice.

The work left over from the era of Reconstruction and the subsequent denial to African Americans of their rights remains unfinished. So, then, does the Memorial. That is its most significant measure of instruction. Of all the Lincoln statues and monuments I have visited, the Lincoln Memorial is the most "living" of them. Certainly a dialogue about race as I have had with numerous people at Lincoln statues can occur, but that dialogue resonates much more deeply at the western terminus of the National Mall. And I wonder, is Lincoln's work really over? Will it ever be over?

The genesis of the Lincoln Memorial can be found with the report issued by the Senate Park Commission in 1902. Republican Senator James McMillan of Michigan charged the Commission with the task of studying the park system in Washington and making appropriate recommendations for its improvement. The commissioners included architects Daniel H. Burnham and Charles F. McKim, landscape architect Frederick Law Olmstead Jr., and sculptor Augustus Saint-Gaudens. The blustery chairman, Burnham, had been chief planner of the Chicago 1893 Columbian Exposition, the catalyst of the "City Beautiful" movement, which would transform the artistic features and the layout of many American cities. All the commissioners had played a major role in shaping the Columbian Exposition, a self-indulgent celebration of American art, science, and ingenuity tied to the first voyage of Christopher Columbus. Their plans for the future of Washington would be a litmus test for the movement. Saint-Gaudens and McKim had collaborated on public monuments honoring Union Civil War heroes, notably Colonel Robert Gould Shaw in Boston and General William T. Sherman in New York City.

The commission presented its conclusions in January 1902, of which the centerpiece would be an extension of the Mall west from the Washington Monument to the banks of the Potomac River. In doing so, it honored the groundwork laid by Washington's initial designer, Pierre L'Enfant, by completing his vision of a "grand avenue" in the heart of the nation's capital. Central to this new plan was a "ceremonial core" linking the Capitol with the Potomac. The Lincoln Memorial was to rise on an artificial knoll on reclaimed land west of the Washington Monument.

Political nitpicking and turf squabbles ensued between 1902 and 1911. In 1909, the centennial of Lincoln's birth, Congress established the bipartisan, seven-member Lincoln Memorial Commission, headed by Taft, who was also at the time president of the United States. Several Southern Democrats were selected to sit on the commission to provide regional balance. The commission considered other sites in and around Washington, including an alternative proposal, backed by lobbyists of the automobile industry, that called for the building of a Lincoln Highway from Washington to Gettysburg, adorned with sculptures of Civil War heroes. Inside the Republican Party, who controlled Lincoln's memory was also at stake as urban progressives vied for his mantle with the more traditional Midwestern bloc.

Adding frustration to the mix was the widow of sculptor Augustus Saint-Gaudens, Augusta, who in a lively lobbying effort waged a battle to have a duplicate cast of her husband's 1887 *Standing Lincoln* installed in the memorial. She confronted Bacon, who rose to the challenge, later recalling,

I told her there were several reasons; the first being that Saint-Gaudens modeled the Chicago Lincoln to be executed in bronze, whereas I wished to have the statue for the Memorial executed in marble. Moreover the Chicago Lincoln was executed to be seen from a particular point of view, and if a replica of it was used for the Lincoln Memorial, it would have to be enlarged which would necessarily make the point of view . . . at a greater distance from the statue itself.

I also stated that I wished to have the statue for the Lincoln Memorial a seated one instead of a standing one. I further stated that if the Saint-Gaudens' Lincoln was enlarged certain of the proportions would undoubtedly have to be changed, to which Mrs. Saint-Gaudens replied, that it was easy enough to get this done by living sculptors. In answer to this, I stated that it would be an outage to modify this important work of Saint-Gaudens, and that I believed that if he knew of it, he would turn in his grave.

After holding a quasi-competition between architect John Russell Pope and Henry Bacon, the commission selected the little-known but highly regarded Bacon. Two years later, upon Bacon's request, the commission appointed French to be the sculptor. This put French in an awkward position, for he was chairman of the Commission of Fine Arts, one of the several governing bodies that oversaw monument and memorial construction in the nation's capital. To ease matters and support his architect friend, French resigned his chairmanship and took up his sculptural tools to begin work.

Ground was broken on Lincoln's birthday, February 12, 1914. On the same date in 1915 the cornerstone was laid. Construction continued unabated from 1917 from 1922. Pylons were driven, concrete poured, and a huge subaltern foundation was laid forty-four to sixty-five feet below the original grade to bedrock; when completed, the Memorial weighed 38,000 tons. Work slowed but never stopped during World War I, and a labor strike also added to the delay. Calling it "magnificent and compelling in its purity of line and simplicity" the *New York Times* gushed with praise the day after the dedication. Even a onetime formidable opponent, the irascible and powerful Speaker of the House of Representatives, "Uncle" Joe Cannon, was won over. He once vehemently articulated his opposition to the chosen site, saying, "So long as I live I'll never let a memorial to Abraham Lincoln be erected in that God damned swamp." Visiting the site as the Memorial grew, Bacon recalled, Cannon concluded, "I guess you boys are all right."

A mile to the east at the base of Capital Hill sits a majestic equestrian tribute to General Ulysses S. Grant, dedicated a few months after Lincoln's tribute. Here we have the symbolic union of the nation's preeminent founder, George Washington, and the two men most credited with saving the Republic that Washington had helped create.

Crossing over the Memorial Bridge, erected in 1932, the visitor reaches Arlington National Cemetery, another piece of hallowed ground filled with the dead of those who fought for the Union so strongly defended by Lincoln. Long after the planners and commissioners passed away, history continued to march on. The Mall, keeping pace with the times, changed as well. In addition to the Korean War Memorial, the Vietnam War Memorial, and the Franklin Delano Roosevelt Memorial, in 2004 the National World War II Memorial was dedicated along 17th Street. It, too, was rife with acrimony, controversy, and consternation.

We owe more than artistic merit to Bacon and French, both eventempered individuals who were skillful diplomats in navigating their way through a colossal federal building project, for which the government appropriated $2 million and which exceeded that by $900,000 more. Together they never lost focus of their charge, and they worked well together, in keeping with the harmonious spirit of the memorial they made.

The crowd swells, and Lincoln greets it. School groups compete for space inside the central chamber. The quiet, meditative atmosphere dissolves. A couple walks from behind one of the columns. The young woman asks her boyfriend, "Can you get my picture with that obelisk thing behind me?" So much for cultural literacy, I think.

"Hey!" shouts a father to his son, "no sliding down the banisters." The ten-year-old boy neither listens to his father nor pays attention to the sign that makes the same request. Chattering away on cell phones, people outside prattle on about who knows what. A family talks about the movie *Forrest Gump* and where actor Tom Hanks might have stood during the filming of the anti–Vietnam War rally scene filmed at the Memorial. Not more than two minutes later, a German couple recounts the same scene. I long to hear someone ask where Jimmy Stewart stood, but Mr. Smith is nowhere to be found. All of this is a curious mix of kitsch and reverence, rolled into one and somehow typically American.

Commercial motor coaches and tour buses from everywhere across the United States continue to fill the parking area adjacent to the Korean War Memorial. It appears that Lincoln will continue to have much company tonight, recalling those days during the Civil War where he had endless lines of office seekers descending upon the White House for government work. Some things never change. The evening has been a living embodiment of Jimmy Stewart's line to Jean Arthur in *Mr. Smith Goes to Washington*, "There he is, just looking straight at you as you come up those steps. Just sitting there like he was waiting for somebody to come along."

A full moon slides behind wispy low clouds over the Reflecting Pool as I gaze down at the new Martin Luther King Jr. "I Have a Dream" speech inscription tastefully carved in the granite. Placement of this memorial inscription was not without controversy. Some argued that it would destroy the artist and architect's original attempt and be an impediment to the traffic flow up the steps. Some argued that a plaque should be placed somewhere off to the side parallel to where King and others spoke. In the end, the Commission of Fine Arts agreed with King's widow, Coretta Scott King, that to do King and the March on Washington justice, the inscription needed to be located in the exact historic spot from which he spoke. One must look out over the Mall from where King stood in order to see those four famous words. The addition affirms the ever-evolving meaning of the Lincoln Memorial.

Looking back at Lincoln seated up there, I wonder if most Americans' collective memory about King stops with his August 28, 1963, speech. The march wasn't even King's brainchild, but that of the aging head of the Brotherhood of Sleeping Car Porters, A. Phillip Randolph. On the cover of the September 6, 1963, issue of *Life Magazine* was a photograph, not of King, but of Randolph and march organizer Bayard Rustin standing beneath French's statue. In an ironic twist of fate, civil rights leader John Lewis would have his prepared remarks censored like those of Robert Moten forty-one years earlier. It was not the white power structure this time but march leaders who were afraid that his rhetoric was too radical and would threaten the support of the Kennedy administration. In deference to a personal request by Randolph, Lewis sat at the feet of Lincoln, editing and toning down his speech.

King, like Lincoln, has been sanitized in our collective memory. Both men grew in their last years of life. Most Americans since that fateful August day would be unfamiliar and uncomfortable with the King who became more radical and moved far beyond the words he delivered here on these steps in Lincoln's shadow. He, like Lincoln was gunned down. King will soon have his memorial on the Mall near the Franklin D. Roosevelt Memorial, adjacent to the Tidal Basin. A. Philip Randolph has his memorial in Washington, too. Ed Dwight's portrait sculpture guards the terminal exits at Union Station beside a Ben and Jerry's and a Starbucks.

The work of both Lincoln and King and the nation they loved remains unresolved, and we must, as Lincoln urged in his Second Inaugural, "strive on to finish the work we are in." Moten had intended to deliver the following words:

> So long as any group within the nation is denied an equal opportunity for life, liberty, and the pursuit of happiness, that task is still unfinished. So long as any group is denied the fullest privilege of a citizen to share both the making and the execution of the law which shapes its destiny—so long as any group does not enjoy every right and every privilege that belongs to every American citizen without regard to race, creed, or color, that task for which the immortal Lincoln gave the last full measure of devotion—that task is still unfinished. What nobler thing can the nation do than hear about this shrine to dedicate itself by its own determined will to fulfill to the last letter the lofty task imposed upon it by the sacred dead?

Pausing on the lowest plaza, I look back up at Lincoln and think of Moten's words. Framed nicely by the soft light inside the chamber and the bright light outside, illuminating the exterior walls and the attic, Lincoln appears comfortable, if a bit wary. There is reassurance in that comfort—and a challenge in that wariness.

While laboring on his statue in Massachusetts, Daniel Chester French remarked, "I have lived with Lincoln so long that I feel as if he were a personal friend." I know just how he feels.

AFTERWORD

ONE OF MY EARLIEST childhood memories took place on the steps of the Lincoln Memorial. As a three-year-old, I lived in nearby Silver Spring, Maryland. One summer night in the early 1960s, my family went to hear the United States Marine Corps Band on the banks of the Potomac, just behind the Memorial. After the performance we visited Lincoln. I remember looking at the big marble man. Carried down the steps on my dad's shoulder, I looked back and waved at the statue, saying, "Bye-bye, Lincoln." It is fitting that my path as an adult crossed with so many monumental Lincolns. I never really stopped looking back.

Somewhere during our brief time living in the Maryland suburbs my parents purchased for me a tiny metal portrait bust of Lincoln, only a couple of inches tall. In the intervening years it has crisscrossed the country with my moves. A bit worn for the wear, this Lincoln now sits on my desk in my home office adjacent to a larger Lincoln bust sculpted by Robert Berks. I draw inspiration from both.

My good friend, biographer James McGrath Morris, half-kidding, accuses me of engaging in the craft of hero worship. He may be right, but I'm fine with it.

Richard White, that great scholar of the frontier, once told me that Americans prefer celebration to history. Admittedly, we do celebrate a kind of preferred memory, always couching events as if a happy ending were preordained. In the case of Lincoln, there are plenty of happy myths. But, those aside, there is a reality upon which the many monuments devoted to him are based. His principles and ambition remind us of the values that we hold in common. With that knowledge, we may better understand the direction in which we ought to be headed.

In the meanwhile, events can make us wonder about what direction we're headed in. Shortly before this book went into production, the tragic shootings on the campus of Virginia Tech University took place on April 16, 2007. Leslie Sherman, one of the high-school students whom you met in chapter 1, lost her life in a senseless act of violence while in her French classroom in Norris Hall. Like Lincoln, Leslie was a visionary, and understood that change for the better just does not happen. She fully immersed herself in life helping those in need, spending time in New Orleans after Hurricane Katrina working on a project for Habitat for Humanity, expressing concern for the least among us, and in college taking a job in a dormitory dining hall washing pots and pans, because John Lewis, the civil-rights activist and former leader of the Student Nonviolent Coordinating Committee put himself through college in such a fashion.

In the course of writing and researching this book, I came to recognize that Abraham Lincoln should be remembered for how he lived, and not how he died. His legacy is one of compassion coupled with a keen intellect. So it was with Leslie. As I grew to love her I recognized her place in my teaching as one of those rare students who inspired me among the thousands I have been fortunate to teach. I had been looking forward to sharing this book with her on publication, and some of the proceeds from sales will now go to support the Leslie Sherman Memorial Scholarship Fund at West Springfield High School.

On the wardrobe of Room 255, in the corner of the Social Studies Hall of that school, hangs a poster provided to schools from the Abraham Lincoln Bicentennial Commission. Adjacent to the wardrobe is the classroom door, with a window. The 1865 image of Lincoln reflects in the window when my door is closed. Standing in the back of my room, I often catch a glimpse of Lincoln in the poster's reflection of the window. From such a vantage point, he seems to be peering into my room, checking up on my teaching. I take comfort in that.

APPENDIX 1
Other Lincoln Memorials of Note

As I traveled to study *the Lincoln sculptures discussed in the preceding pages, I visited many other statues of Lincoln that are not included here but are worth noting for varying reasons. Here are fourteen of them, given here in order of their creation. Like the seven sculptors addressed in the text, their creators were all born in the nineteenth century.*

Lincoln (1871) by Randolph Rogers (1825–1892), Philadelphia

An early composition in the genre of the Great Emancipator, Rogers's sculpture depicts Lincoln seated at the top of a massive two-tiered pedestal adorned with eagles, fascias, laurel wreaths, and crossed swords. On the lower portion of the pedestal, beneath the eagles on each of the four sides are panels with inscriptions, one reading, "To Abraham Lincoln—From A Grateful People," while the other three include excerpts from the Emancipation Proclamation and the Gettysburg Address. Lincoln holds a quill pen in his right hand, while in his other hand and draped across his left knee is the Emancipation Proclamation. Funds for the sculpture were raised by the Lincoln Monument Association of Philadelphia.

The Lincoln Tomb (1874) by Larkin G. Mead (1835–1910), Springfield, Illinois

Abraham Lincoln's tomb in Springfield's Oak Ridge Cemetery has had a long and checkered career, having been dedicated in 1874 and then disassembled and reassembled at the turn of the last century and again in 1930–31 to repair structural weaknesses and external deterioration. In 1901, Lincoln's remains were disinterred and looked upon for the last time by thirty-six lucky Springfield residents who had won a lottery to peek inside a small hole cut into the lid of the coffin and thus certify that the body in the casket was indeed Abraham Lincoln's. Among the thirty-six was thirteen-year-old Fleetwood Lindley, whose father encouraged him to skip school on this day and bike over to the cemetery to be a part of the historic moment. A quarter of a century earlier, Vermonter Larkin G. Mead secured the $200,000 commission for what at the time was the largest memorial project in the country, funded by the National Lincoln Monument Association, a group consisting of primarily residents of Springfield. Union war veterans raised additional funds for the tomb. The design of the thirty-four-year-old Mead was selected from thirty-seven competitive submissions by thirty-one different sculptors. His ten-foot figure of Abraham Lincoln, *The Emancipator*, stands at the base of the granite twenty-eight-foot-tall memorial obelisk, elevated above a walkaround terrace surrounded by four additional elevated pedestals twelve feet above it. On the terrace reside heroic military groupings, also sculpted by Mead, representing the infantry, cavalry, artillery, and navy. A chain of shields, each bearing the name of thirty-seven states in the United States during the Civil War, links all of them. The military groupings were installed in 1877, 1882, and 1883. The statue of Lincoln stands seven feet higher than the military groupings. Directly beneath Lincoln on a bronze plaque is featured the nation's coat of arms, a representation of the Constitution, which physically symbolizes Lincoln's stand on the Union. President Ulysses S. Grant, among other local and state dignitaries, was one of the dedication speakers. Directly beneath the statue is a gift from citizens of Rome sent to the United States in 1865, called the Servius Tullius stone, purported to be from an ancient Roman wall erected 2,500 years ago by an emperor who freed Roman plebeians and granted them citizenship. Lincoln's tomb is constructed of brick and Quincy granite, quarried in Massachusetts. On the exterior, only the granite shows. The four sides, each which is fifteen feet high, measure 72.5 feet apiece. Protruding on the north and south axis of the square are two semicircular projections, each with a radius of twelve feet, making the north–south axis 119.5 feet. The total height of the tomb is

117 feet. On either side of the projections are sets of staircases providing access to the terrace. Visitors enter through the south portal to gain access to the burial chamber, located on the north side, where Lincoln lies ten feet below grade, encased in thirty-square feet of reinforced concrete. Nine flags surround the red cenotaph, including ones that represent the ancestral states of the Lincoln family: Massachusetts, New Jersey, Pennsylvania, Virginia, Kentucky, Indiana, and Illinois. In the middle stand the colors of the United States, and the presidential flag is to the right. The cenotaph is simply inscribed, "Abraham Lincoln, 1809–1865." Above it, etched in gold lettering in French black marble, are the words that Lincoln's secretary of war, Edwin Stanton, is said to have uttered upon Lincoln's death, "Now He Belongs To The Ages." Along the interior walls are four bronze tablets, one a brief biography of Lincoln's life, the others Lincoln's Springfield Farewell Address, the Gettysburg Address, and an excerpt from his Second Inaugural. Lincoln's wife Mary and three of his four sons, Edward Baker, William Wallace, and Thomas, are buried in the chamber as well. Two memorial hallways that include bronze reductions of Lincoln statues by Saint-Gaudens, French, Crunelle, Weinman, and Taft lead visitors to and from the burial vault. The figure of Lincoln stands erect with his right arm and hand slightly raised, while his left hand holds a scrolled Emancipation Proclamation. Though it was praised at its unveiling, compared to other monuments discussed here it is a mediocre work at best. Taft, always the qualifier said, "Lincoln stands well on its feet and has dignity and seriousness, but the figure is commonplace. The bronze image which so inconsistently extends to us the scroll inscribed 'Proclamation,' may be the very earthly counterfeit of the great Commoner. It may have all his attributes but it gives us no thrill. The essence of greatness is not in it."

LINCOLN (1909) BY ADOLPH A. WEINMAN (1870–1952), HODGENVILLE, KENTUCKY

Adolph A. Weinman immigrated to the United States from Germany and worked as an assistant for both Augustus Saint-Gaudens and Daniel Chester French. His two important sculptures of Lincoln are in Kentucky. Located a few miles from Lincoln Birthplace National Historic Site, in Court House Square in downtown Hodgenville, the six-foot seated figure rests on a twelve-foot pedestal. Lincoln is seated in a wingback chair, his right arm resting on the arm, his hand grasping the end. His left arm is more relaxed, the elbow bent at a 45-degree angle resting on his thigh. In his left hand he holds several sheets of paper. Unveiled on Memorial Day 1909 the Ladies Lincoln League of Hodgenville oversaw the installation as part of a city beautification project. Among the ten thousand people on hand for the dedication was Robert Lincoln, who, reported the *Courier Journal* of Louisville, told Weinman, "That is a noble work." A duplicate cast was made the same year for the campus of the University of Wisconsin–Madison. In 1911, Weinman's standing figure of Lincoln was unveiled in the Rotunda of the state capitol in Frankfort.

LINCOLN (1910) BY JOHN ROGERS (1829–1904), MANCHESTER, NEW HAMPSHIRE

John Rogers is best known for his mass-produced plaster-cast parlor pieces, the most popular called *The Council of War* and depicting Lincoln, Secretary of War Edwin Stanton, and General Ulysses S. Grant discussing war plans. This figure of Lincoln dominates the courtyard of Manchester Central High School. Here the seated Lincoln is the war president, his right arm draped over the back of a chair and holding in his hand a compass. Rolled out across his lap and crossed knees and cascading down the side of his chair is a battlefield map. Cast in bronze for a 1910 dedication, in the wake of the Lincoln Centennial, Rogers's work was originally an 1895 plaster cast that he presented to the city and was situated in the public library. Funds were raised by Manchester's Lincoln Memorial Association at the urging of local Civil War veterans.

LINCOLN OF THE FAREWELL ADDRESS (1918) BY ANDREW O'CONNOR (1874–1941), SPRINGFIELD, ILLINOIS

On the grounds of the Illinois state capitol is Andrew O'Connor's interpretation of Lincoln bidding farewell to the people of Springfield as he boarded the train in February 1861 to take him to his first inaugural in Washington. The beardless, excessively gaunt Lincoln conflicts with history, for by the time he left for Washington he had grown his trademark beard. On the plinth behind the statue are inscribed the words of his farewell address, but they are today obscured by the hedge that has grown behind the architectural framework of the statue, dedicated while doughboys fought in the trenches of World War I. Poet Vachel Lindsay recited the poem he wrote for the occasion, "Abraham Lincoln Walks at Midnight in Springfield, Illinois," an ode to a brooding spirit of Lincoln as he reckons with the carnage of war. The keynote address was delivered by Lincoln biographer Lord Charnwood, invoking Lincoln's memory within the context of the Anglo-American struggle in Europe.

LINCOLN THE LAWYER (1927) BY LORADO TAFT (1860–1931), URBANA, ILLINOIS

Chicago sculptor and art historian Lorado Taft's tribute to *Lincoln the Lawyer* recalls Lincoln's work on the Eighth Circuit Court as a prairie attorney. Standing before the bar, on which his hands rest gently, Taft's Lincoln is a dignified figure of quiet yet firm grace, his head held high. His shoulders are erect as his chest extends upward in confidence. Taft was deliberate in his pose, preferring to portray a good-natured Lincoln who was fond of telling tales and swapping stories with his fellow litigators as they crossed the plains. The sculpture was funded through the estate of Judge J. O. Cunningham, an attorney friend of Lincoln's who traveled the circuit with him. Located in Carle Park, across from Urbana High School, the two times larger than life statue is frequently dressed up by locals during the year to reflect different holiday celebrations.

LINCOLN THE DEBATER (1929) BY LEONARD CRUNELLE (1872–1944), FREEPORT, ILLINOIS

French-born Leonard Crunelle was a student of Lorado Taft. On the seventy-first anniversary of the famed Lincoln-Douglas Debate, held in Freeport, his tribute to *Lincoln the Debater* was unveiled in Taylor Park. Though not located on the site of the debate held on August 27, 1858, Crunelle's Lincoln depicts the aspiring senatorial candidate as he might have looked during that particular time, complete with his long coat tugged at by the breeze, wrinkled and creased vest, and pants buckled in at the ankles. Crunelle intended to portray Lincoln as at this time when he was "the active and successful lawyer, eager, keen, shrewd, watchful of his opponents to win his case or baffle his opponent," as the monument dedication records. On his face "is a serious look as if impressed with the great issues of the hour. It is intended to portray Lincoln as he was at that time, the logician and debater, but a very human and natural being, sprung from the same stock as the people and neighbors all about him." Lincoln's arms are behind his back; in his hands he holds rolled paper, what some locals like to argue is a copy of or a metaphor for the "Freeport Doctrine," the trick Lincoln employed during the Freeport debate to trip Douglas up into saying that residents of a territory could get around the Dred Scott decision by electing officials who refused to uphold the law. Though Douglas did in fact agree with Lincoln's point, thereby undermining his argument, there was no such actual document. The statue was a gift to Freeport from local businessman, entrepreneur, and vanilla industry magnate William T. Rawleigh.

Captain Lincoln (1930) by Leonard Crunelle (1872–1944), Dixon, Illinois

On the site of Fort Dixon, a log compound erected in 1830 during the Black Hawk War, stands the only statue of Lincoln wearing a military uniform. Dedicated for the centennial of the town, *Captain Lincoln* commemorates Lincoln's six months in service to the state militia during the war to suppress an Indian uprising led by Chief Black Hawk of the Sauk and Fox tribes. Lincoln stands erect, though not quite at attention, and over his right arm hangs a coat with his hand resting on the belt that holds in place the sword and scabbard that are held against his hip by his left hand. Lincoln, elected captain by fellow residents of New Salem, claimed that this was the one election in his life that gave him the most satisfaction. During the Black Hawk War Lincoln saw no combat and claimed that at best he killed a few mosquitoes. Among those who served at Fort Dixon was Lt. Jefferson Davis of the U.S. Army, though no records exist that document any encounter between the two principal political adversaries of the Civil War.

LINCOLN (1932) BY CHARLES KECK (1875–1951), WABASH, INDIANA

Like other assistants of Augustus Saint-Gaudens, Charles Keck, too, produced a Lincoln statue of merit. In the genre of the "man of sorrows" Keck's 1932 tribute to Lincoln sits on a boulder in kind of a kindred spirit with that of Fraser's in Jersey City, New Jersey. This brooding Lincoln rests on the grounds of the Victorian Palladian terraced Wabash County Court House. Lincoln leans forward with his right arm upon his right knee while his right leg is extended slightly forward, with his boot slightly beyond the bronze plinth that buffers the statue from the granite base, providing a slight sense of forward motion. Wearing his familiar long coat, which drapes, in part over the side of the boulder, Lincoln's left arm rests on his left thigh, just above the knee with his leg drawn back toward the rock. On the pedestal are inscribed the words from the second inaugural, "With Malice Toward None. With Charity For All." Bullard argues that Keck captured Lincoln "in an hour of repose." The sculpture was a gift from Alexander New, a native of Wabash who was born in 1861. Like Lincoln, he came from humble stock and made it good as a lawyer, studying and first practicing in Kansas City and then moving to New York City where he amassed a considerable fortune. Lincoln was New's hero and inspiration. In an effort to honor his parents and the community where he had been raised New sought to have a suitable statue of Lincoln erected. New contacted Keck, visited him at his studio, and brought to the meeting his friend Frederick H. Meserve, the famous collector and student of Lincoln photographs. After studying two designs, one seated and one standing, New settled on the seated figure of Lincoln on the rock, which Meserve called, "an inspiration." New died a year before the sculpture was unveiled, but not before his ashes were returned to his hometown where they were interned in the local Jewish cemetery. At the dedication on May 30, 1932, remarks made by James E. Jaynes, former pastor of Fort Wayne's First Christian Church, echoed the patron's sentiment saying, "Facing the sunrise, it is a prophecy and a promise so long as the people do not lose their dreams and their ideals. It will tell in silence the story of America as a place of opportunity. It will tell what such a life as Lincoln means." A replica was unveiled seven years later in Hingham, Massachusetts, the New England town where the Lincoln family traced its English roots in America. Keck would also sculpt *Lincoln and the Boy* (1949), depicting a fatherly Lincoln holding near him an African American youth. His sculpture is located on the grounds of the Abraham Lincoln Public Housing Project in Harlem.

LINCOLN (1935) BY HENRY HERING (1874–1973), INDIANAPOLIS

Another student of Saint-Gaudens, Henry Hering, sculpted a lovely, dignified Lincoln statue that sits on a red granite pedestal in University Park in Indianapolis. This seated figure of Lincoln reflects the statesman motif. Lincoln sits in a shawl-covered, fringed chair of state with his right arm extended above and out beyond the chair's arm, fingers spread, as if he were gesturing to make a point. Behind the chair's left, Lincoln's stovepipe hat rests on the ground. Hering explained his design this way: "After reading the life of Lincoln over and over again and the story of the troublesome times he went through, it occurred to me that he was getting little support, and it is at this period that I decided to depict him in an attitude of assuring the public that if they will only be calm and patient he will pull them through." Civil War veteran Henry C. Long, an Indianapolis lumber merchant, willed $10,000 upon his death in 1901 for a statue of Lincoln to be raised in his city. The effort to raise a statue languished for over three decades due to all manner of political and legal squabbles. Hering was chosen because of several successful public monuments he had sculpted for the city, including, most notably, "Pro Patria," which at the time was the largest bronze casting in the United States. It graces the steps to Memorial Hall, the city's tribute to its World War I veterans.

LINCOLN—THE DREAMS OF YOUTH (1935) BY PERCY BRYANT BAKER (1881–1971), BUFFALO, NEW YORK

British-born sculptor Percy Bryant Baker, best known for *Pioneer Woman* (1930) in Ponca City, Oklahoma, created for Buffalo's Delaware Park an idyllic image of Lincoln as a young man setting down his ax and picking up a book, thereby replacing manual labor with intellectual pursuits. Seated on a log, with a dreamy look on his face,

Lincoln is dressed in a linsey-woolsey shirt, breeches, and boots. He holds in his right hand a book, his fingers placed between the leaves. His hand rests relaxed on his bent right knee, while his left foot is bent and pressed against the log. "I wanted," Baker said, "to express the vision that later proved him to be above all else a great philosopher, statesman, and humanitarian." Inscribed on the granite pedestal is James Russell Lowell's reflection of Lincoln's life, "For Him Her Old World Moulds Aside She Threw, And Choosing Sweet Clay From The Breast Of The Unexhausted West, With Stuff Untainted Shaped A Hero New." The sculpture was given to the city at the bequest of Julia Spitzmiller, who left $25,000 for a memorial to be raised in Lincoln's memory.

Lincoln Trail Monument (1938) by Nellie V. Walker (1874–1973), Lawrence, Illinois

Spanning the Wabash River between the city of Vincennes, Indiana, and Lawrence County, Illinois, is the Lincoln Memorial Bridge. Just over the bridge on the Illinois side of the river, alongside the highway, is a small park, home to Nellie V. Walker's *Lincoln Trail Monument*, also called *Lincoln Led by the "Spirit of Destiny."* This monument, on a six-foot granite foundation, combines a twenty-six-foot-long and ten-foot-high bas-relief limestone panel of those in the Lincoln family party who crossed the Wabash River in 1830 in this vicinity, with a bronze sculpture-in-the-round of a twenty-one-year-old Abraham Lincoln in the foreground. The group of six, led by Lincoln's father Thomas, follows behind and includes a Conestoga wagon pulled by a team of oxen. Above the group and toward the forward area of the panel floats a female angelic figure, "Destiny," somewhat reminiscent of the flowing-gown angel above the figures in Augustus Saint-Gaudens's heroic tribute to Robert Gould Shaw and the 54th Massachusetts Volunteer Infantry, her right arm extended pointing the way. She looks back at Lincoln. Period postcards of the memorial explain the figure as the spirit of Lincoln's dead mother, Nancy Hanks. Lincoln holds in his right hand a long stick, perhaps a goad used as a cattle prod, and a coonskin cap in his other hand. Around his neck, draped and tied, is a long scarf. Walker, an assistant of Lorado Taft, received the commission from the Illinois Daughters of the American Revolution.

THE RESOLUTE LINCOLN (1954) BY AVARD T. FAIRBANKS (1897–1987), PETERSBURG (NEW SALEM), ILLINOIS

Avard T. Fairbanks ranks as one of the most prodigious Lincoln sculptors of all time, sculpting nine major works of him. His first heroic statue, *The Frontiersman*, was unveiled on Lincoln's birthday, February 12, 1944, on the campus of the Ewa Plantation Elementary School in Hawaii. *The Resolute Lincoln* follows a similar design, depicting Lincoln as a young adult, once more in the genre of giving up manual labor to pursue a more purpose-driven life. In his right arm and hand he holds a large tome, intended to be one of four volumes of William Blackstone's *Commentaries on the Laws of England*, which Lincoln was fond of using as he taught himself law. His left hand is in a position of laying the ax down. The figure's attitude suggests a stepping forward motion, symbolizing Lincoln's beginning a new career as an attorney. The commission and funding came from the Society of the Sons of Utah Pioneers, a Mormon organization. Fairbanks, himself a Mormon, sculpted a number of memorials to the church's legacy. *The Resolute Lincoln* was dedicated on June 12, 1954, on the entrance plaza to New Salem Historic Site, the accurately restored village on the site of the town in which Lincoln settled in 1831.

LINCOLN, THE PRAIRIE YEARS (1964) BY ANNA HYATT HUNTINGTON (1876–1973), PETERSBURG (NEW SALEM), ILLINOIS

Located just outside the entrance to Lincoln's New Salem Historic Park along Illinois Route 97 sits one of the rare Lincoln equestrian statues, this one by noted animal sculptor Anna Hyatt Huntington. The larger-than-life figure depicts a young Lincoln absorbed in reading a book as he rides a horse. The statue was originally designed to grace the entrance to the Illinois Pavilion at the 1964–65 New York World's Fair. Huntington was a highly skilled and reputable sculptor of equestrian figures that include a mounted figure of Joan of Arc

(1915) erected on New York's Riverside Drive and a figure of Cuban patriot Jose Martí (1965) as he was mortally wounded while riding at the southern entrance of Central Park. The horse on which Lincoln rides walks at a slow pace with its head down. Lincoln holds the book in his right hand held close to him, while his left arm is extended over the horse's neck holding the reins. The horse is a stronger work of art than the figure of Lincoln.

APPENDIX 2
State-by-State Breakdown of Lincoln Sculptures

The chart below approximates by state the number of Lincoln statues located in the United States. This list was compiled using the Smithsonian Institution's Inventory of American Sculpture database. I am also indebted to David Wiegers, who has worked prodigiously to photograph every Lincoln statue in the country.

State	Count	State	Count
California	10	North Dakota	1
Colorado	1	New Hampshire	2
Connecticut	4	New Jersey	4
District of Columbia	8	New York	12
Hawaii	1	Ohio	8
Idaho	1	Oklahoma	2
Illinois	42	Oregon	3
Indiana	6	Pennsylvania	13
Iowa	11	Rhode Island	1
Kansas	3	South Dakota	2
Kentucky	7	Tennessee	2
Massachusetts	9	Virginia	1
Michigan	7	Vermont	1
Mississippi	1	Washington	2
Missouri	7	West Virginia	1
Minnesota	3	Wisconsin	9
Nebraska	5	Wyoming	1

NOTES

Chapter 1: Charlotte's Seed

1. Mills, *Their Last Battle*, xxvii.
2. Ball, *My Threescore Years and Ten*, 168–69.
3. *Ballou's Pictorial Drawing Room Companion*, 333.
4. Ball, *My Threescore Years and Ten*, 249, 252.
5. Ibid., 252–53.
6. Cited in Guelzo, *Lincoln's Emancipation Proclamation*, 232.
7. Quarles, *Lincoln and the Negro*, 7.
8. Taft, *History of Sculpture in America*, 146–47.
9. Reinhart, *Abraham Lincoln on Screen*, 258.
10. Savage, *Standing Soldiers, Kneeling Slaves*, 115, 120.
11. Parrish, "The Western Sanitary Commission," 33.
12. Cited in Savage, *Standing Soldiers, Kneeling Slaves*, 233.
13. Quarles, *Lincoln and the Negro*, 4.
14. Ibid.
15. Ibid.
16. Murray, *Emancipation and the Freed in American Sculpture*, 198–99.
17. Savage, *Standing Soldiers, Kneeling Slaves*, 105.
18. Ibid., 105–106.
19. Ibid.
20. Ball, *My Threescore Years and Ten*, 281–82.
21. Savage, *Standing Soldiers, Kneeling Slaves*, 98–99.
22. Ibid., 93.
23. Ibid.
24. Elliot, *The Story of Archer Alexander*, 88.
25. Craven, *Sculpture in America*, 226.
26. Borrit, *Lincoln and the Economics of the American Dream*, 1.
27. Craven, *Sculpture in America*, 226.
28. Medford, "Beckoning Them to the Dream of Promise of Freedom," 49.
29. Bennett, *Forced Into Glory*, 66.
30. Arnold, *Lincoln and the Overthrow of Slavery*, 301.
31. CW, 1:75.
32. CW, 7:281.

33. CW, 7:304.
34. CW, 3:145–46.
35. Oakes, *The Radical and the Republican*, 128–29.
36. Guelzo, National Archives lecture, March 23, 2005.
37. Foner, "Shedding Lincoln's Mantle."
38. Inaugural Ceremonies of the Freedmen's Memorial Monument to Abraham Lincoln, Frederick Douglass Papers.
39. Douglass, "Oration at Dedication of Freedman's Monument," Frederick Douglass Papers.
40. Oakes, *The Radical and the Republican*, 242.
41. Cited in Quarles, *Lincoln and the Negro*, 10–11.
42. Bryant, *Complete Poems of William Cullen Bryant*, 316.

CHAPTER 2: PAUL MANSHIP'S *LINCOLN THE HOOSIER YOUTH*

1. Sandburg, *Abraham Lincoln: The Prairie Years*, 14.
2. Wilson, Rufus Rockwell, *Intimate Memories of Lincoln*, 480.
3. Robert Lincoln to George Payson, June 25, 1881.
4. CW, 4:62.
5. Bullard, *Lincoln in Marble and Bronze*, 293.
6. Manship and Herndon in Meade, *Heroic Statues in Bronze of Abraham Lincoln*, 21.
7. Bullard, *Lincoln in Marble and Bronze*, 293.
8. Durman, *He Belongs to the Ages*, 236.
9. Sandburg, *Abraham Lincoln: The Prairie Years*, 15.
10. Goodwin, *Team of Rivals*, 102.
11. CW, 1:8.
12. Cited in Epstein, *Lincoln and Whitman*, 133.
13. Hutchinson, "Lincoln and Liberty."
14. CW, 1:378.
15. Ibid.

CHAPTER 3: A DIFFERENT KIND OF CIVIL WAR

1. Greenway, *1845–1945: All Souls at the Cross Roads*, 98.
2. Ibid.
3. Ibid.
4. Bullard, *Lincoln in Marble and Bronze*, 228.
5. Duncan, *My Life*, 100, 216–18.
6. Ege, *The Power of the Impossible*, 151–53.

7. Moffatt, *Errant Bronzes*, 132–59.
8. AL quoted in W. M. Dickson, "Abraham Lincoln in Cincinnati," 62.
9. Ibid, 35.
10. Ibid, 40–43.
11. Ibid, 47.
12. Cited in Moffatt, *Errant Bronzes*, 50.
13. Moffatt, *Errant Bronzes*, 50–51.
14. Ibid, 75.
15. Volk, "The Lincoln Life-Mask And How It Was Made," 228.
16. Greenway, *1845–1945*, 98.
17. Moffatt, *Errant Bronzes*, 80.
18. Greenway, *1845–1945*, 98.
19. Moffatt, *Errant Bronzes*, 82.
20. Ibid., 90.
21. Ibid.
22. Ibid., 92.
23. Ibid., 92–93.
24. Ibid., 97.
25. *Outlook*, December 27, 1916.
26. Moffatt, *Errant Bronzes*, 99.
27. Ibid.
28. Ibid.
29. Ibid.
30. Ibid., 100–101.
31. Ruckstull, "A Standard of Art Measurement."
32. Bullard, *Lincoln in Marble and Bronze*, 239.
33. Moffatt, *Errant Bronzes*, 91.
34. "Barnard's Lincoln."
35. Ibid.
36. Ibid.
37. "A Mistake in Bronze," June 1917.
38. Moffatt, *Errant Bronzes*, 133.
39. *Art World*, November 1917.
40. "Barnard's Lincoln Once More."
41. Angle, "Robert Todd Lincoln and the Barnard Statue."
42. "The People's Lincoln."
43. "Those Who Love Lincoln."
44. "Barnard's Lincoln."
45. "Some Robert Todd Lincoln Letters on the 'dreadful statue' by George Grey Barnard."
46. Angle, "Robert Todd Lincoln and the Barnard Statue"
47. RTL to CTW, October 19, 1917.

48. House 65th Congress, 1st session, 1917.

49. Page, *Abraham Lincoln in New Hampshire*, 109–10.

50. Moffatt, *Errant Bronzes*, 165.

51. Ibid.

52. Ibid., 166.

53. "Barnard's Lincoln as a Noted Painter Sees It," October 28, 1917.

54. Moffatt, *Errant Bronzes*, 159.

55. Ibid., 173.

56. CW, 6:63–65.

57. "The Statue," September 16, 1919.

58. Greenway, *1845–1945*, 98.

59. Russell, *My Diary North and South*, 44–45.

60. Kaplan, *Walt Whitman*, 25.

61. Holzer, "Abraham Lincoln, American Hero," www.wethepeople.gov/heroes/holzerlecture.html.

62. Holzer, *Lincoln Seen and Heard*, 107.

63. CW, 8:356.

Chapter 4: Contemplative Statesmanship

1. Gilder, "The Farragut Monument."

2. Bullard, *Lincoln in Marble and Bronze*, 79.

3. Saint-Gaudens, *Reminiscences*, 1:312.

4. Stevens, "Story of a Statue," 5.

5. Gilder, *Letters of Richard Watson Gilder*, 149.

6. Taft, *History of American Sculpture*, 29.

7. Wilkinson, *Uncommon Clay*, 162.

8. Bullard, *Lincoln in Marble and Bronze*, 75.

9. Robert Todd Lincoln Papers, Reel 41, Abraham Lincoln Presidential Library.

10. *Chicago Tribune*, October 23, 1887.

11. Van Rensselaer, "Saint-Gaudens's Lincoln," 37–39.

12. Nicolay, "Lincoln's Personal Appearance," 933.

13. Cortissoz, *Augustus Saint-Gaudens*, 45.

14. Cited in Savage, *Standing Soldiers, Kneeling Slaves*, 124–25.

15. Cited in Epstein, *Lincoln and Whitman*, 25.

16. Quoted at the Saint-Gaudens National Historic Site, Cornish, N.H.

17. Taft, "American Sculpture and Sculptors."

18. Addams, *Twenty Years at Hull-House*, 27.

19. Fraser, "Essay on Saint-Gaudens."

20. *Reminiscences*, 1:51.
21. Ibid., 166.
22. "Saint-Gaudens's Lincoln."
23. Bloch, *Feudal Society*, 55.
24. Farber, *Lincoln's Constitution*, 9.
25. Bullard, *Lincoln in Marble and Bronze*, 9.
26. Lane and Wall, *Letters of Franklin K. Lane*, 368–69.

CHAPTER 5: LINCOLN OF GETHSEMANE

1. Oldroyd, *Words of Lincoln*, xii.
2. Borglum to Frank E. Elwell, November 4, 1909, Gutzon Borglum Papers, LOC.
3. Frankfurter, *Felix Frankfurter Reminiscences*, 55.
4. Dean, *Living Granite*, 29.
5. Borglum, "The Beauty of Lincoln."
6. Fite, *Mount Rushmore*, 105.
7. Bullard, *Lincoln in Marble and Bronze*, 209.
8. Sandburg, *Lincoln: The War Years*, 328–29.
9. Borglum, Lincoln Monument Dedication Program, May 30, 1911, Borglum File, LOC.
10. Borglum to J. Munnerlyn, March 11, 1914, Gutzon Borglum Papers, LOC.
11. Borglum, "The Beauty of Lincoln," 220.
12. Theodore Roosevelt Dedication Speech, Manuscript Collection, Newark Public Library.
13. Bullard, *Lincoln in Marble and Bronze*, 214.
14. Borglum to Theodore Roosevelt, June 1, 1911, Gutzon Borglum Papers, LOC.
15. Stoddard to Gutzon Borglum, June 8, 1911, Gutzon Borglum Papers, LOC.
16. Borglum to J. R. Milliken, March 13, 1915, Gutzon Borglum Papers, LOC.
17. Lincoln to Clinton Conkling, November 24, 1917, Robert Todd Lincoln Papers.
18. Randall, *Lincoln's Sons*, 155.
19. Donald, *Lincoln*, 569.
20. CW, 4:385–86.
21. Perret, *Lincoln's War*, 348.

Chapter 6: Lincoln the Mystic

1. CW, 4:234.
2. Goff, *Robert Todd Lincoln: A Man in His Own Right*, 70–71.
3. *James Earle Fraser*, 7.
4. Taft, *History of American Sculpture*, 556.
5. *James Earle Fraser*, 30.
6. Bullard, *Lincoln in Marble and Bronze*, 284.
7. "Statue Back at Lincoln High," *Jersey Journal*, February 5, 2004.
8. Bullard, *Lincoln in Marble and Bronze*, 284.
9. Ibid.
10. Ibid., 287.

Chapter 7: A Lincoln for the Masses

1. John Steinbeck to Lyndon Johnson, May 28, 1966, LBJ Library.
2. Interview with Mrs. Oscar L. Chapman, November 6, 1989, recorded by Scott A. Sandage.
3. Capra, *The Name Above the Title*, 273.
4. Ibid., 280.
5. Ibid., 260.
6. CW 4:240.
7. Bellah, "Civil Religion in America," 49.
8. Thomas, *The Lincoln Memorial and American Life*, 110.
9. Green, *The Secret City*, 199.
10. Fairclough, "Civil Rights and the Lincoln Memorial," 411.
11. Ibid., 412.
12. Thomas, *The Lincoln Memorial and American Life*, 128.
13. Ibid.

BIBLIOGRAPHY

Manuscript Collections

John Gutzon Borglum Papers (Library of Congress)
Daniel Chester French Papers (Library of Congress)
Frederick Douglass Papers (Library of Congress)
James Earle Fraser Papers (National Cowboy and Western Heritage Museum)
Harriet Hosmer Papers (Schlesinger Library)
Robert Todd Lincoln Papers (Abraham Lincoln Presidential Library)
Augustus Saint-Gaudens Papers (Dartmouth College Library)

Newspapers

Anglo American (Washington, D.C.)
Baltimore Sun
Boston Evening Telegraph
Chicago Tribune
Cincinnati Enquirer
Cincinnati Times Star
Daily Evening Bulletin (Washington, D.C.)
Evening Post (Washington, D.C.)
Jersey Journal (Jersey City, New Jersey)
London *Times*
Los Angeles Times
Manchester Guardian
New York Times
Newark Daily Advertiser
Newark Evening Call
Newark Evening News
Newark Morning Star
News Sentinel (Fort Wayne, Indiana)

Philadelphia Evening Telegraph
Washington Evening Star

ARTICLES

Angle, Paul M. "Robert Todd Lincoln and the Barnard Statue." *Chicago History*, Summer 1966.

"Ball the Sculptor." *Ballou's Pictorial Drawing Room Companion*, May 26, 1855.

"Barnard's Lincoln." *Literary Digest* (January 16, 1917): 18–19.

"Barnard's Lincoln As a Noted Painter Sees It." *New York Times*, October 28, 1917.

Bartlett, Truman Howe. "The Physiognomy of Lincoln." *McClure's Magazine* (August 1907): 391–407.

Bellah, Robert N. "Civil Religion in America." *Daedalus* 134, no. 4 (Fall 2005): 40–55.

Borglum, John Gutzon. "The Beauty of Lincoln." *Everybody's Magazine* (February 1910): 217–20.

Dickson, W. M. "Abraham Lincoln in Cincinnati." *Harpers New Monthly Magazine* 69, June 1884.

"Doing Lincoln Justice." *Literary Digest*, February 1917.

Fairclough, Adam. "Civil Rights and the Lincoln Memorial: The Censored Speeches of Robert R. Moton (1922) and John Lewis (1963)." *Journal of Negro History* (Fall 1997): 408–16.

Foner, Eric. "Shedding Lincoln's Mantle." *The Nation*, July 27, 2000.

Gilder, Richard Watson. "The Farragut Monument." *Scribner's Monthly* 22, no. 2 (June 1881): 16–67.

———. "Lincoln the Leader." *Century Illustrated Magazine*, February 1909, 479–507.

Hickey, James T. "Lincolniana: Some Robert Todd Lincoln Letters on the 'dreadful statue' by George Grey Barnard." *Journal of the Illinois State Historical Society* 73 (Summer 1980): 132–39.

Hodges, Leigh. "A New Tradition in American Art." *North American* (Philadelphia), November 25, 1917.

Medford, Edna Greene. "Beckoning Them to the Dream of Promise of Freedom: African Americans and Lincoln's Promise of Emancipation." In *The Lincoln Forum: Abraham Lincoln, Gettysburg, and the Civil War*, ed. John Y. Simon et al., 45–64. Mason City, Iowa: Savas Publishing, 1999.

"Mr. Barnard's Lincoln." *Outlook*, January 16, 1918.

"Mr. Barnard's 'Lincoln' Once More—Some Public Comments." *Art World* 3, no. 1 (October 1917): 7.

Nicolay, John G. "Lincoln's Personal Appearance." *Century Magazine*, October 1891, 933.

"The People's Lincoln." *Touchstone* 2, no. 1 (October 1917): 63.

"Robert Todd Lincoln and the Barnard Statue." *Chicago History* 7, no. 12 (Summer 1966): 353–59.

Roberts, Mary Fanton. "Lincoln As His Friends and Admirers Knew Him During His Lifetime." *Touchstone* 2, no. 2 (November 1917): 194.

Ruckstull, Frederick Wellington. "A Calamity in Bronze," *The Art World* 3, no. 2 (November 1917): 99.

———. "The Effect of Caricature of the Lincoln Controversy." *The Art World* 3, no. 3 (December 1917): 194.

———. "How to Give Europe a Worthy Lincoln Monument." *The Art World* 3, no. 4 (January 1918): 277.

———. "A Mistake in Bronze." *The Art World* 2, no. 3 (June 1917): 211.

———. "A Standard of Art Measurement," part 1. *The Art World* 1, no. 1 (October 1916): 323.

Sandage, Scott A. "A Marble House Divided: The Civil Rights Movement and the Politics of Memory, 1939–1963." *Journal of American History* (June 1993): 135–67.

Stevens, Frank E. "The Story of a Statue." *Journal of the Illinois State Historical Society* 24, no. 1 (April 1931): 3–8.

Taft, Lorado. "American Sculpture and Sculptors." *The Chatauquan* 22, no. 4 (January 1896).

Texley, Carolyn. "The Making of Lincoln: Sculptor Avard Fairbanks and The Lincoln Museum." *Lincoln Lore* 1870 (Fall 2002): 4–9.

"Those Who Love Lincoln: A Word for Barnard's Statue by Ida Tarbell." *Touchstone* 2, no. 3 (December 1917): 225.

Van Rensselaer, Mariana Griswold. "Saint-Gaudens's Lincoln." *Century Monthly Illustrated Magazine*, November 1887, 37–39.

Volk, Douglas. "Making the Life Mask of Abraham Lincoln." *Rare Lincolniana* 81 (1865): 16–24.

Volk, Leonard. "The Lincoln Life-Mask and How It Was Made." *Century Magazine* 23, no. 2 (December 23, 1881): 223–28.

Watson, Richard Gilder. "On the Life-Mask of Abraham Lincoln." *Century Magazine* 33, no. 1 (1886).

Books

Addams, Jane. *Twenty Years at Hull-House*. New York: Macmillan, 1910.

Arnold, Isaac, *Lincoln and the Overthrow of Slavery*. Chicago: Clarke and Company, 1866.

Ball, Thomas. *My Threescore Years and Ten: An Autobiography*. 1891. New York: Garland, 1977.

Bassler, Roy P., et al., eds. *The Collected Works of Abraham Lincoln*, 9 vols. New Brunswick, N.J.: Rutgers University Press, 1953–55.

Bennett, Lerone. *Forced Into Glory: Abraham Lincoln's White Dream*. Chicago: Johnson, 2001.

Bloch, Marc. *Feudal Society: The Growth of Ties of Dependence*. Chicago: University of Chicago Press, 1988.

Borritt, Gabor. *Abraham Lincoln and the Economics of the American Dream*. Urbana: University of Illinois Press, 1994.

Bullard, F. Lauriston. *Lincoln in Marble and Bronze*. New Brunswick, N.J.: Rutgers University Press, 1952.

Capra, Frank. *The Name Above the Title: An Autobiography*. New York: Macmillan, 1971.

The Complete Poems of Carl Sandburg. San Diego: Harcourt, 1970.

Cortissoz, Royal. *Augustus Saint-Gaudens*. New York: Houghton Mifflin, 1907.

Craven, Wayne. *The Sculptures at Gettysburg*. Conshohocken, Pa.: Eastern Acorn Press, 1982.

———. *Sculpture in America*. Newark: University of Delaware Press, 1984.

Cuomo, Mario M. *Why Lincoln Matters*. Orlando: Harcourt, 2004.

Dean, Robert J. *Living Granite: The Story of Borglum and the Mount Rushmore Memorial*. New York: Viking, 1949.

Donald, David Herbert. *Lincoln*. New York: Simon & Schuster, 1995.

Duncan, Isadora. *My Life*. New York: Boni and Liveright, 1927.

Durman, Donald, C. *He Belongs to the Ages: The Statues of Abraham Lincoln*. Ann Arbor, Mich.: Edwards Brothers, 1951.

Ege, Arvia MacKaye. *The Power of the Impossible: The Life Story of Percy and Marion MacKaye*. Falmouth, Mass.: Kennebec River Press, 1992.

Eliot, William G. *The Story of Archer Alexander: From Slavery to Freedom*. Westport, Conn.: Negro Universities Press, 1970.

Epstein, Daniel Mark. *Lincoln and Whitman: Parallel Lives in Civil War Washington*. New York: Random House, 2004.

Farber, Daniel. *Lincoln's Constitution*. Chicago: University of Chicago Press, 2003.

Fite, Gilbert C. *Mount Rushmore*. Norman: University of Oklahoma Press, 1952.

Forney, J. W. *Anecdotes of Public Men*. New York: Harper and Brothers, 1881.

Frankfurter, Felix. *Felix Frankfurter Reminiscences: Recorded in Talks With Dr. Harlan B. Phillips*. New York: Reynal, 1960.

Gilder, Rosamond, ed. *The Letters of Richard Watson Gilder*. New York: Houghton Mifflin, 1921.

Goff, John S. *Robert Todd Lincoln: A Man in His Own Right*. Norman: University of Oklahoma Press, 1969.

Goodwin, Doris Kearns. *Team of Rivals: The Political Genius of Abraham Lincoln*. New York: Simon & Schuster, 2005.

Green, Constance McLaughlin. *The Secret City: A History of Race Relations in the Nation's Capital*. Princeton, N.J.: Princeton University Press, 1967.

Greenway, Cornelius. *1845–1945: All Souls at the Cross Roads*. Brooklyn, N.Y.: All Souls Universalist Church, 1945.

Guelzo, Allen C. *Lincoln's Emancipation Proclamation: The End of Slavery in America*. New York: Simon & Schuster, 2004.

Holzer, Harold. *Lincoln at Cooper Union: The Speech That Made Abraham Lincoln President*. New York: Simon & Schuster, 2004.

———. *Lincoln Seen and Heard*. Lawrence: University Press of Kansas, 2000.

James Earle Fraser: American Sculptor, A Retrospective Exhibition of Bronzes from Works of 1913 to 1953, June 2nd to July 3rd, 1969. New York: Kennedy Galleries, 1969.

Kaplan, Justin. *Walt Whitman: A Life*. Boston: Houghton Mifflin, 1984.

Lane, Anne Wintermute, and Louise Herrick Wall, eds. *Letters of Franklin K. Lane*. Boston: Houghton Mifflin, 1922.

Marvel, William. *Andersonville: The Last Depot*. Chapel Hill: University of North Carolina Press, 1994.

Mead, Franklin B. *Heroic Statues in Bronze of Abraham Lincoln*. Fort Wayne, Ind.: Lincoln National Life Foundation, 1932.

Mills, Nicolaus. *Their Last Battle: The Fight for the National World War II Memorial*. New York: Basic Books, 2004.

Moffatt, Frederick C. *Errant Bronzes: George Grey Barnard's Statues of Abraham Lincoln*. Newark: University of Delaware Press, 1998.

Murray, Freeman Henry Morris. *Emancipation and the Freed in American Sculpture*. Washington, D.C.: Murray Brothers, 1916.

Oakes, James. *The Radical and the Republican: Frederick Douglass, Abraham Lincoln, and the Triumph of Antislavery Politics*. New York: Norton, 2007.

Oldroyd, Osborn H., ed. *Words of Lincoln*. Washington, D.C.: privately printed, 1895.

Page, Elwin L. *Abraham Lincoln in New Hampshire*. Boston: Houghton Mifflin, 1929.

Perret, Geoffrey. *Lincoln's War*. New York: Random House, 2004.

Quarles, Benjamin. *Lincoln and the Negro*. New York: Oxford University Press, 1962.

Rampersad, Arnold, and David Roessel, ed. *The Collected Works of Langston Hughes*. New York: Knopf, 1998.

Randall, Ruth Painter. *Lincoln's Sons*. Boston: Little Brown, 1955.

Rinehardt, Mark. *Abraham Lincoln on the Screen*. Jefferson, N.C.: McFarland and Company, 1980.

Russell, William Howard. *My Diary North and South*. New York: Knopf, 1988.

Saint-Gaudens, Augustus. *The Reminiscences of Augustus Saint-Gaudens*. Ed. Homer Saint-Gaudens. New York: Century Company, 1913.

Sandburg, Carl. *Abraham Lincoln: The Prairie Years*. New York: Harcourt Brace, 1925.

———. *Abraham Lincoln: The War Years*. New York: Harcourt Brace, 1939.

Savage, Kirk. *Standing Soldiers, Kneeling Slaves: Race, War, and Monuments in Nineteenth Century America.* Princeton, N.J.: Princeton University Press, 1997.

Starr, H. W., and J. R. Hendrickson, eds. *The Complete Poems of Thomas Gray.* London: Oxford University Press, 1966.

Sturgis, Henry C., ed. *The Poetical Works of William Cullen Bryant.* New York: Appleton and Company, 1913.

Taft, Lorado. *A History of American Sculpture.* New York: Macmillan, 1924.

Thomas, Christopher A. *The Lincoln Memorial and American Life.* Princeton, N.J.: Princeton University Press, 2002.

Wilkinson, Burke. *Uncommon Clay: The Life and Works of Augustus Saint-Gaudens.* San Diego: Harcourt Brace, 1985.

Wilson, Rufus Rockwell. *Intimate Memories of Lincoln.* Elmira, N.Y.: Primavera Press, 1945.

INDEX